It's another Quality Book from CGP

This book is for anyone doing GCSE Modern World History.

Whatever subject you're doing, it's the same old story — there are lots of facts and you've just got to learn them. GCSE Modern World History is no different.

Happily, this CGP book gives you all that important information as clearly and concisely as possible.

There's even a section to help you score full marks for your spelling, punctuation and grammar.

What CGP is all about

Our sole aim here at CGP is to produce the highest quality books — carefully written, immaculately presented, and dangerously close to being funny.

Then we work our socks off to get them out to you — at the cheapest possible prices.

Contents

Part One: International Relations

Section 1 — The Causes of the First World War

The Great Powers in Europe 1900 1
Tension Builds — 1900-1914 2
Trouble in the Balkans 3
The Outbreak of War 4
Revision Summary 5

Section 2 — The Peace Settlement

The Peace Settlement 6
The Versailles Treaty 7
Reactions to the Treaty 8
The Other Treaties 9
Revision Summary 10

Section 3 — The League of Nations

The League of Nations 11
Problems with the League of Nations 12
More International Agreements 13
The Effects of the Great Depression 14
The Manchurian Crisis 15
The Invasion of Abyssinia 16
The Failure of the League of Nations 17
Revision Summary 18

Section 4 — Causes of the Second World War

The Rise of the Dictators 19
Hitler's Foreign Policy 20
The Rhineland and Austria 21
Czechoslovakia and Munich 1938 22
Poland and the Outbreak of War 23
Revision Summary 24

Section 5 — The Origins of the Cold War

Planning the Post-War Future 25
Increasing Tensions 26
US Influence and the Berlin Blockade 27
The Hungarian Rising and the Berlin Wall 28
The Prague Spring and the Arms Race 29
The Cold War in Asia 30
The Cuban Missile Crisis 31
Vietnam and the USA 32
Revision Summary 33

Section 6 — The End of the Cold War & the Post Cold War World

Détente and the Afghanistan War 34
The New Cold War 35
The Soviet Withdrawal 36
The End of the Soviet Union 37
The USA after the Cold War 38
The UN 39
Revision Summary 40

Section 7 — Current World Issues

Terrorism 41
The Iraq War 43
Revision Summary 45

We've included the most popular options for GCSE Modern World History — you'll need to check with your teacher which topics you should revise for your exams.

Part Two: Depth Studies

Section 8 — The First World War

The Schlieffen Plan 46
Stalemate in the West 47
Life in the Trenches 48
The Eastern Front 49
The Gallipoli Campaign 50
The War at Sea 51
The End of the Fighting 52
Revision Summary 53

Section 9 — Germany Between the Wars

The Weimar Republic 54
Years of Unrest 1919-1923 55
Stresemann and Recovery 56
The Roots of the Nazi Party 57
The Rise of the Nazis 58
Hitler Comes to Power 60
Nazi Methods of Control 61
German Growth Under the Nazis 62
Young People and Women 63
Opposition to the Nazis 64
Persecution 65
Impacts of the Second World War 67
Revision Summary 68

Section 10 — The USA 1919-1941

The USA's Reaction to World War One 69
Growth of Isolationism 70
Prosperity in the 1920s 71
Poverty in the 1920s 72
Intolerance in the 1920s 73
Prohibition and Organised Crime 74
Social Developments 75
The Wall Street Crash 76
Consequences of the Wall Street Crash 77
Election of Roosevelt (FDR) 78
The New Deal 79
The TVA and the Second New Deal 80
Opposition to the New Deal 81
How Successful was the New Deal? 82
Revision Summary 83

Section 11 — Russia 1905-1941

Russia Under the Tsars 84
Countdown to Revolution 85
The Bolsheviks 86
The Provisional Government 87
The Bolsheviks Seize Power 88
1918 — Ending the German War 89
The Civil War 1918-1921 90
War Communism and Mutiny 91
The New Economic Policy 92
The Struggle for Power 93
The Terror and the Purges 94
Stalin the Dictator 95
The Five-Year Plans 96
Collectivisation 97
The Results of Collectivisation 98
Life in the Soviet Union 99
Revision Summary 100

Section 12 — The USA 1945-1975

The Impact of the Cold War 101
McCarthyism and the Red Scare 102
The Vietnam War 103
The Vietcong 104
Fighting the Vietcong 105
TV and Media Coverage 106
Anti-War Protests 107
Trying to End the War 108
Peace and Defeat 109
Civil Rights for African Americans 110
Civil Rights of Hispanic Americans 114
Civil Rights of Native Americans 115
Women's Rights 116
Student Protest and Youth Culture 117
Revision Summary 118

Section 13 — Changes in British Society 1890-1928

The Need for Reform 119
Conservatives, Liberals and Labour 120
Laws to Help Children and Old People 121
Laws Protecting Working People 122
Effects of the Liberal Reforms 124
Women's Rights in the 1890s 125
The Campaign for the Vote 1900-1914 126
The Start of World War One 127
Trench Warfare 128
New Weapons 129
The Western Front 130
The War at Home 131
Food Shortages 132
Attitudes to the War in Britain 133
The End of the War 134
Women and the Vote 1914-1928 135
Build-up to the General Strike 1918-1926 136
The General Strike 1926 137
Effects of the General Strike 138
Revision Summary 139

Exam Advice

How to Study History 140
Handling Sources 141
Exam Essay Skills 142
Spelling, Punctuation and Grammar 143
Index 147

Published by CGP

Editors:
Heather Gregson
Katherine Reed
Sabrina Robinson

Contributors:
David Barnes
Rene Cochlin
Robert Gibson
John O'Malley
John Pritchard

With thanks to Anthony Muller, Glenn Rogers and Hayley Thompson for the proofreading.
Coordinated by Paddy Gannon.

ISBN: 978 1 84762 282 2

Clipart from Corel®
Printed by Elanders Ltd, Newcastle upon Tyne.

Based on the classic CGP style created by Richard Parsons.

The Great Powers in Europe 1900

To really get to grips with why the war started, you'll need to know about the background to it.

There were Five main Rival Nations in Europe

1) **BRITAIN** ruled an empire of over one quarter of the world's people, and owned rich industries. Britain was an island, so it had a strong navy to protect itself and its colonies from invasion. During the 19th century, Britain had followed a policy of 'splendid isolation' — it didn't get involved in European politics.

2) **FRANCE** also had an overseas empire. The French were bitter about losing Alsace and Lorraine to Germany in the Franco-Prussian War in 1871.

3) **RUSSIA** was poor, but the biggest country in Europe. It was ruled by Tsar Nicholas II. It had no lands overseas, but wanted land in Europe and Asia with access to the sea.

4) **AUSTRIA-HUNGARY** was a central European empire, made up of 10 different nationalities — many of whom wanted independence. It was ruled by the Emperor Franz Joseph I.

5) **GERMANY** had a small empire ruled by Kaiser Wilhelm II. The Kaiser was jealous of Britain's superior sea power and rich colonies. He wanted to increase German influence and wealth abroad. The Kaiser described Germany's small empire as its 'place in the sun', and was keen to expand it.

	Navy	Army
BRITAIN	185 warships	700 000 men
FRANCE	62 warships	1 000 000 men
RUSSIA	30 warships	1 200 000 men
AUSTRIA-HUNGARY	28 warships	800 000 men
GERMANY	100 warships	2 000 000 men

Approx. sizes of European Armies and Navies in 1914

Alliances were formed for Security

Countries often made agreements to help each other out.

1) 1879: Dual Alliance between Germany and Austria-Hungary.

2) 1882: Triple Alliance when Italy joined the Dual Alliance.

These alliances created a large group of allies in Central Europe — making both France and Russia nervous.

3) 1892: Franco-Russian Alliance against the Triple Alliance.

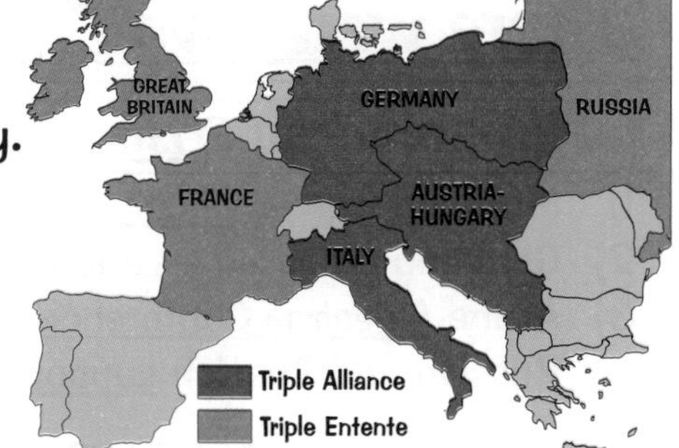

4) 1904: Entente Cordiale between Britain and France.

5) 1907: The Anglo-Russian Entente completes the Triple Entente between Russia, Britain and France.

Kaiser Wilhelm II

These ententes were not military agreements — but they ended up involving the military because of the tensions between the Triple Alliance and the Triple Entente.

Following the Franco-Russian Alliance, Germany had a fear of encirclement — it was worried about being attacked on two fronts at the same time. Russia was worried about Austria's intentions towards the Balkans. Meanwhile, Britain and Germany competed to build the best navy in the world...

International politics — a sneaky business...

Countries make alliances with nations who share their ideas. It's also a way of ganging up on enemies. Scribble a list of the main strengths of these countries and the alliances they formed.

Tension Builds — 1900-1914

Europe was drifting towards a major war — and Germany and Britain played a big part.

Germany and Britain began an Arms Race

1) The Kaiser wanted Germany to be a major world power, but he needed a bigger navy. Germany began to follow a policy known as 'Weltpolitik' — a more aggressive foreign policy aimed at increasing military strength and expanding Germany's empire.
2) Between 1900 and 1914 Germany attempted to double the size of its Navy.
3) Britain had a policy called the Two Power Standard — the Royal Navy always had to be as big as the next two strongest navies in Europe put together. It meant Britain would never be outnumbered at sea.
4) Britain responded to Germany's improvements in 1906 by building the first Dreadnought — a new and superior kind of battleship.
5) Germany built its own version in 1907-8 — but, by 1912, Britain had a new, bigger kind.
6) By 1914 Britain had 29 Dreadnoughts and Germany had 17.

The Major Powers made Plans for War

1) Faced with enemies on both its eastern and western borders, Germany came up with the Schlieffen Plan in 1905. The plan was that in a war, Germany could defeat France before Russia mobilised, and then fight Russia afterwards.
2) France prepared Plan 17 to recapture Alsace and Lorraine from Germany.
3) Britain created an Expeditionary Force of 150,000 men, ready to travel immediately to Europe in case of war. The Territorial Army was also set up.
4) Russia started to build up its army in 1909 in case of war.

There were Two Crises over Morocco

The Moroccan Crisis 1905-6

1) Morocco was an uncolonised African country, but France wanted to add it to its empire.
2) Germany objected — and demanded an international conference on Morocco's future.
3) At the Algeciras Conference in 1906, Germany was forced to back down by British, Italian, Russian and Spanish support for France taking control of Morocco's police and banks.

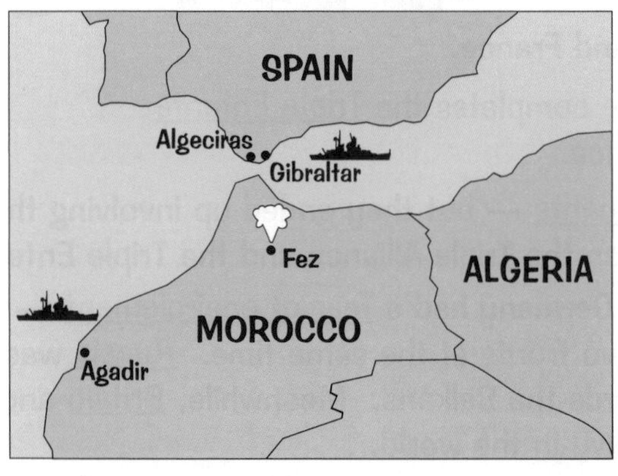

The Agadir Crisis 1911

1) The French sent troops to Fez to fight Moroccan rebels.
2) Germany accused France of trying to take complete control over Morocco.
3) Germany sent a warship called the Panther to Agadir, hoping to force France to give them the French Congo.
4) Britain was worried that Germany might build a naval base at Agadir, which would threaten key British sea routes — so Britain also sent warships.
5) Germany backed down and recognised French influence in Morocco. The Germans felt increasingly anti-British.

Countdown to conflict — only a matter of time...

There you go then, three major factors in the start of the First World War. As soon as the arms race began, it was clear a war was possible — Germany was trying to overtake British power.

Trouble in the Balkans

The Balkans were known as 'the powder keg of Europe' — a spark of trouble could mean chaos.

The Balkans were Controlled by the Turkish Empire

1) The Balkans were a very poor area of south-eastern Europe.
2) The Turkish Empire (also known as the Ottoman Empire) was very weak. It suffered from increasing corruption and the rise of nationalism among many of the countries it controlled. People called it 'the Sick Man of Europe'.

The Balkans 1912 (before the First Balkan War)

Other powers wanted Influence

1) **GERMANY** wanted to build a railway to the East through the Balkans.
2) **AUSTRIA-HUNGARY** wanted to stop Serbia from stirring up the Slavic people inside its own lands. The Slavs wanted independence and hoped Serbia (a Slavic country) would help them.
3) **RUSSIA** is also a Slavic country. It wanted sea access from the Black Sea to the Mediterranean, through straits controlled by the Turkish Empire.
4) **ITALY** wanted to control the other side of the Adriatic Sea. It took Tripoli in North Africa in 1911.

In 1908 Austria-Hungary annexed Bosnia & Herzegovina

1) Austria-Hungary had been given control of Bosnia by an 1878 treaty. They wanted to make it an official part of their empire. They cut a deal with Russia — who would support this 'annexation' if Austria-Hungary backed Russian hopes of getting access for its warships through the Turkish Straits.
2) Russia didn't get what it wanted, as other powers stood against it — but Austria-Hungary went ahead with the annexation. Russia protested, but Germany, Austria-Hungary's ally, backed them. Russia wasn't strong enough to intervene against them both. This left Russia feeling angry and humiliated.

Two Wars created more tensions

The First Balkan War

Greece, Bulgaria, Serbia and Montenegro formed the Balkan League and attacked the Turkish Empire in 1912. The Turks were beaten easily and were driven out of the Balkan area and forced to give up their lands.

The Second Balkan War

In 1913 the Balkan League quarrelled — Bulgaria went to war with Greece and Serbia. Turkey and Romania joined the Greek and Serbian side and Bulgaria was soon defeated — losing land to the four victors.

The Balkans after the Second Balkan War (note increased size of Serbia)

In both of these wars, the British tried to keep the peace, instead of supporting Russia, who were on Serbia's side. Germany saw this as a sign that the Triple Entente was weak.

There'll be more trouble in the Balkans...

Tension in the Balkans was a main cause of World War One. The Slav question is key here — Serbia wanted to unite the Slavs in the region and was angry about the annexation of Bosnia.

The Outbreak of War

Tension suddenly exploded into the First World War — and it began in the Balkans.

The Black Hand was a Serbian Nationalist Group

1) The Black Hand was started in Serbia with the aim of uniting all the Serbian peoples.
2) Austria-Hungary had many Serbian citizens and feared a rebellion in its lands, especially in Bosnia.

Franz Ferdinand's Assassination spelled trouble

Archduke Franz Ferdinand was the heir to the Austro-Hungarian throne. He went to Bosnia to try to strengthen the loyalty of the Bosnian people to Austria-Hungary.

Princip - The Serbian student who shot the heir to the Austro-Hungarian throne

Dimitrijevic - Leader of the Black Hand

The Archduke was killed by a Serb student called Princip in Sarajevo in June 1914. Princip was a Black Hand member — Austria was furious.

Events Moved Quickly towards War

The sequence of events is important. Also remember the Triple Alliance and the Triple Entente (see p.1) because they determined how the two sides shaped up for World War I.

23 JULY	Austria-Hungary blames the Serbian government for the assassination, demanding compensation and the right to send troops into Serbia.
28 JULY	Serbia refuses to let these troops in. Austria-Hungary declares war on Serbia and shells Belgrade.
29 JULY	Russia begins mobilising troops ready to help Serbia.
30 JULY	Germany demands that Russia stop mobilising.
1 AUGUST	Russia refuses. Germany declares war on Russia.
2 AUGUST	France begins mobilising to help Russia.
3 AUGUST	Germany declares war on France.
4 AUGUST	Germany sends troops through Belgium to attack France, following the Schlieffen Plan. Belgium is neutral, and Britain has agreed to protect Belgium. Britain orders Germany to withdraw. Germany refuses. Britain declares war on Germany.
6 AUGUST	Austria-Hungary declares war on Russia.

Now count the number of days in which all this happened — not much time for sensible thinking.

The First World War — everybody got sucked in...

I know, it's all a bit complicated. Make sure you know the sequence of events and how the alliance system meant Russia helped Serbia, so Germany helped Austria-Hungary, etc., etc...

Revision Summary

Time for the best part of every section — the page with those fab revision questions to see how much you remember. I know it's a bit boring, but it's something you've got to do. It'll help you learn everything in the section — which you'll be really grateful for when you're sat in the exam. When you've finished the questions, check the answers you weren't sure about. Then have another go...

1) Which of the Great Powers had the biggest empire in the world in 1900?
2) Which two bits of land had France lost to Germany in 1871?
3) Who ruled over Germany at the time?
4) Which of the major powers had (1) the largest navy? (2) the largest army?
5) List the key alliances between 1882 and 1907 which split the major powers into two opposing camps.
6) Name the type of battleship which figured strongly in the naval arms race.
7) What dispute was settled by the Algeciras Conference in 1906?
8) Write a paragraph on the Agadir Crisis of 1911.
9) What was the nickname given to the Turkish Empire to show its weakness?
10) Give the reasons why Germany, Austria-Hungary, Russia and Italy all wanted influence in the Balkans at this time.
11) What did Austria-Hungary do in the Balkans in 1908? Why was it potentially so serious?
12) Which Balkan states started the Balkan League? When?
13) What was the First Balkan War about? When did it happen?
14) What happened in the Second Balkan War? How did this leave Serbia?
15) Who were the Black Hand? What did they want to achieve?
16) Who was the heir to the Austro-Hungarian throne at the time? Where was he visiting in June 1914? What happened to him there?
17) What did Austria demand from Serbia after the assassination?
18) What did Russia do when Serbia asked for help?
19) What was Germany's reaction to Russia's action?
20) What did France do after Germany's declaration of war on Russia?
21) What was the name of the German plan to invade France through Belgium?
22) Why did Britain decide to declare war on Germany?
23) How many days passed between Austria-Hungary's demand to Serbia and Britain's declaration of war on Germany?
24) Write down at least four reasons for the outbreak of World War I. (Think about the whole section.)

The Peace Settlement

World War One lasted from 1914-1918. Fighting ended with the armistice on November 11th 1918. The winners (Britain, France and the USA) then had to agree a peace treaty with the losers.

There were Three Concerns to think about

1) Millions of people were dead or injured. Countries like Belgium and France were devastated — the main powers had spent too much money on the war.
2) Many people wanted Germany to take all the blame, especially in Britain and France — so Germany and their allies weren't allowed to take part in the talks.
3) Everyone wanted to make sure a war like this wouldn't happen again, but they couldn't agree on how to do this — the system of alliances had obviously failed.

The Big Three were France, Britain and the USA

1) All three countries had ideas about the settlement, and they often disagreed.
2) So a compromise was reached — only some of their ideas became part of the settlement.
3) The key fact to remember is that the French had suffered badly, and the British had also suffered — this meant they both wanted to punish the Germans. But people in the USA had suffered less — so they were less emotional and wanted to stay impartial.

Wilson suggested 14 Points

1) President Wilson had come up with the Fourteen Points in January 1918 when the Germans were asking for a truce.
2) Germany rejected them then, but when the fighting ended they changed their minds and wanted to base the peace settlement on them.
3) The Allies refused Wilson's Points because the Germans had rejected them before.
4) But the Fourteen Points were an important part of the peace process — especially point 14 which called for a League of Nations to settle disputes. This was going to become very important between the two world wars.

WILSON'S FOURTEEN POINTS JANUARY 1918

1. No secret treaties
2. Free access to the sea for all
3. Free trade between countries
4. Disarmament by all countries
5. Colonies to have a say in their own future
6. Russia to be free of German troops
7. Belgium to be independent
8. Alsace-Lorraine to go to France
9. New frontier between Austria & Italy
10. Self-determination for people of Eastern Europe
11. Serbia to have access to sea
12. Self-determination for people in Turkish Empire
13. Poland to be independent with access to the sea
14. League of Nations to settle disputes

The Fourteen Points — giving peace a chance...

Once the war was over you'd have thought the squabbling would stop, but instead the winners argued about what should happen next. Don't forget the reasons why Britain and France had different ideas from the USA. Then scribble a list of the Fourteen Points and get it learned.

The Versailles Treaty

Wilson's Fourteen Points would have been pretty good for the Germans — but things didn't work out that way. After a lot of negotiating, the reality was the Treaty of Versailles.

The Treaty of Versailles was signed in June 1919

1) This treaty (agreement) dealt with Germany, but the other defeated countries made separate treaties.
2) This map shows the key changes, so go around it carefully and make sure you know who got what.
3) Start by looking at the land Germany lost — especially Alsace and Lorraine (A), the large piece of land to the west of Germany.
4) The Rhineland (R) was demilitarised — Germany wasn't allowed to have troops there as it was close enough to invade France and Belgium from.
5) Look at the new countries set up, particularly the ones near Germany. Some contained many different nationalities within their borders. They were potentially unstable.

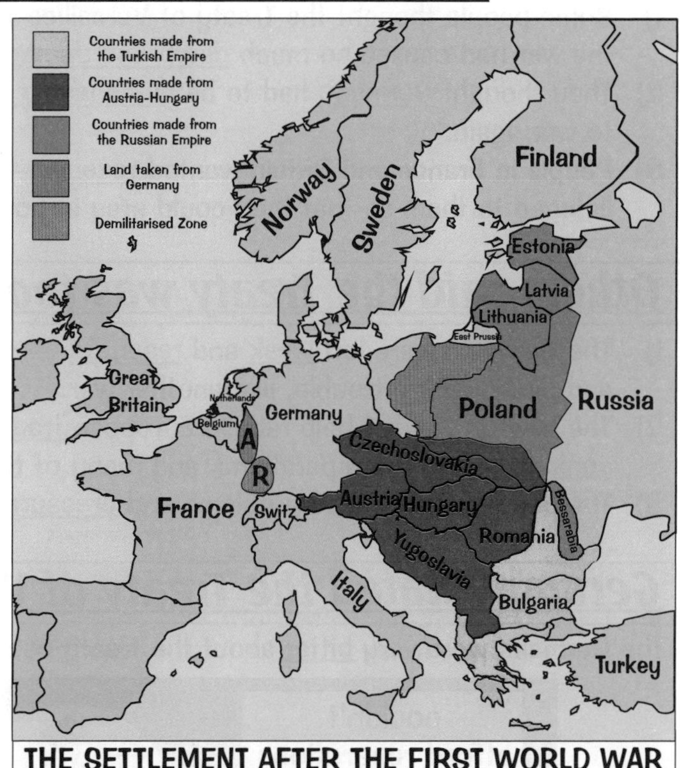

THE SETTLEMENT AFTER THE FIRST WORLD WAR

The Results of the Versailles Treaty were Severe

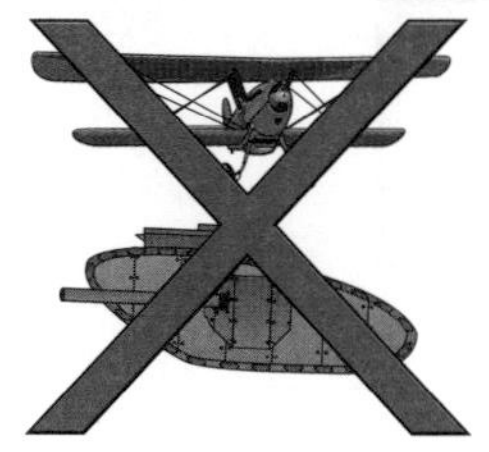

1) It wasn't just land that Germany lost. Article 231 of the treaty said Germany had to take the blame for the war — the War-Guilt Clause.
2) Germany's armed forces were reduced to 100 000 men, only volunteers, without armoured vehicles, aircraft or submarines, and only 6 warships.
3) Germany was forced to pay £6600 million in reparations — payments for the damage caused. The amount was decided in 1921 but was changed later. It would have taken Germany until the 1980s to pay.
4) Germany lost its empire — areas around the world that used to belong to Germany were now called mandates, and they were going to be run by...
5) ...the League of Nations, which was set up to keep world peace — you're going to have to learn a lot more about this organisation.

Versailles — no treats for the Germans...

This treaty was the key document in Europe for the next twenty years — and it was a major cause of the Second World War. The Germans were very unhappy with the results of the treaty, and it would cause major problems later...

Reactions to the Treaty

A lot of people didn't like the Treaty of Versailles — Lloyd George and Wilson thought it wouldn't work, and Clemenceau was criticised by many French people who thought it wasn't harsh enough.

Some people said the Treaty was Fair

1) Some people thought the Treaty of Versailles was fair because the war had caused so much death and damage.
2) They thought Germany had to be made weaker so it couldn't go to war again.
3) People in France and Britain wanted revenge — politicians listened to them so that they could stay in power.

Others said the Treaty was too Harsh

1) The Germans were left weak and resentful — this could lead to anger and cause future trouble, like another war.
2) The treaty wouldn't help rebuild European trade and wealth — Germany couldn't afford the reparations, and many of the new countries were poor.
3) The peacemakers faced problems and pressure from the people at home.

Germany Hated the Treaty of Versailles

The Germans were very bitter about the treaty because they...

Problems were Building up for the Future

1) Europe couldn't recover properly while countries like Germany remained poor.
2) Self-determination would be difficult in new countries like Poland and Czechoslovakia where many people from different nationalities had been thrown together as an artificial country.
3) German anger would lead to trouble in the future. The Germans called the treaty a 'Diktat' — they had no choice about accepting it.
4) Without Germany, Russia or USA in the League of Nations, it'd be hard to keep the peace.

After the Treaty — there may be trouble ahead...

I'm afraid we've got more treaties to come — but the key here is that you understand the main points and effects of the Treaty of Versailles. Scribble two lists — one for the reasons some people thought the treaty was too harsh, and the other with the reasons some people said it was fair. Remember — you need to be able to give both sides of the case.

The Other Treaties

Versailles was really only about Germany — other treaties dealt with the rest of the losers.

Four more treaties Caused Trouble

TREATY	DEALT WITH	MAIN POINTS
ST. GERMAIN 1919	AUSTRIA	Separated Austria from Hungary. Stopped Austria joining with Germany. Took land away, e.g. Bosnia. Made Austria limit its army. Created new countries (see p.7).
TRIANON 1920	HUNGARY	Took land away, e.g. Croatia. Made Hungary reduce its army. Created new countries (see p.7).
NEUILLY 1919	BULGARIA	Took away some land. Denied access to the sea. Made Bulgaria reduce its army.
SÈVRES 1920	TURKEY	Lost land — part of Turkey became new mandates, e.g. Syria. Turkey lost control of the Black Sea.

1) New countries like Czechoslovakia and Yugoslavia were formed out of Austria-Hungary.
2) Austria and Hungary's separation was important — and the fact that Austria wasn't allowed to join with Germany. Both Austria and Hungary suffered badly after the war.
3) The Turks hated Sèvres. Turkish nationalists like Mustafa Kemal resisted the treaty and forced some later changes — at the Treaty of Lausanne in 1923. This reduced the amount of territory to be lost by Turkey and scrapped all reparations.
4) The Arabs who fought alongside the Allies didn't gain as much as they'd hoped.

The Treaties had Similar Results

1) All the defeated countries lost land, and had to disarm.
2) They were all punished, following the pattern of Versailles.
3) Versailles, St. Germain and Trianon were the harshest treaties — Germany, Austria and Hungary lost valuable industrial land. Bulgaria wasn't so badly treated because it hadn't played such a big part in the war.
4) Countries which were created or increased because of the treaties — like Czechoslovakia, Yugoslavia and Poland — were now governing people of many different nationalities.
5) Czechoslovakia, for example, had Germans, Slovaks, Hungarians, Poles, Ukrainians, and over 6 million Czechs. Tricky one deciding what language to speak.

The treaty was a charmer — so disarming...

You'd be smart to get the names of the treaties and the countries involved all learned now. Learn the five key results of the treaties and the patterns that show how they all followed the example of Versailles. The new countries were artificial — and would cause big problems later.

Revision Summary

Time for some magnificent mind-bending questions yet again — just so you know how you're getting on. The important thing is to see what you know and to work out what you don't. Then go back over the section and have another go at these spiffing questions. Keep at it until you can get every single one of them right — I know it sounds much too hard, but you can do it... It's the only way to win yourself top marks when the exams come around.

1) On what date did the fighting end in the First World War?
2) Who were the 'big three' who led the talks at Versailles?
3) Which of the big three wanted Germany punished most?
4) Who came up with the Fourteen Points?
5) When was the Treaty of Versailles signed?
6) Which area of Germany was demilitarised?
7) What was Article 231 of the Versailles Treaty?
8) What size armed forces was Germany allowed?
9) How much was Germany expected to pay in damages? What were the payments called?
10) What were 'mandates'?
11) Give three reasons why the Treaty of Versailles could be seen as fair.
12) Give three reasons why the Treaty of Versailles could be seen as too harsh.
13) Explain why the Germans hated the Treaty of Versailles.
14) Name the other treaties which followed Versailles. Write briefly what each one did.
15) Name at least three nationalities living in the new Czechoslovakia.

The League of Nations

There were high hopes for the League of Nations. Lots of people admired its moral principles.

The League came from the Fourteen Points

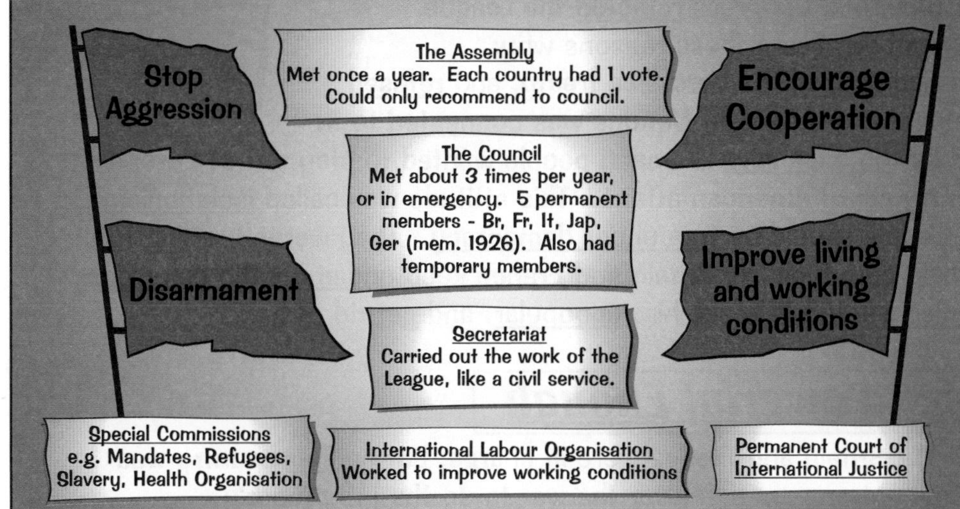

The flags show the four main aims of the League.

The rest of the diagram shows how the League was organised and which parts of the organisation were responsible for what.

The League was intended to Police the World

1) It began work in January 1920.
2) There were 42 members to start with, and around 60 by the 1930s.
3) All the members followed a Covenant (agreement) of 26 rules.
4) Every member country had a vote in the Assembly and the Council.
5) The League could warn countries in disputes, apply economic sanctions (block international trade with misbehaving countries), then send troops in.
6) The League tried to improve social conditions, working on health, slavery and refugees.
7) The Permanent International Court of Justice decided on border disputes between countries. Everyone hoped this would avoid another major war.

There were some early Successes

1) The League resolved several difficult situations over territorial claims — without fighting.
2) It solved the dispute in 1921 between Germany and Poland over Upper Silesia, the dispute between Sweden and Finland over the Aaland Islands in 1921, and the conflict when Greece invaded Bulgaria in 1925. These successes gave it a good reputation.
3) It also did a lot of good work to help refugees after the First World War.
4) It worked to combat the spread of serious diseases such as leprosy, malaria and plague — and inoculated against them.
5) It fought against slavery, and tried to create better working conditions for people all across the world.

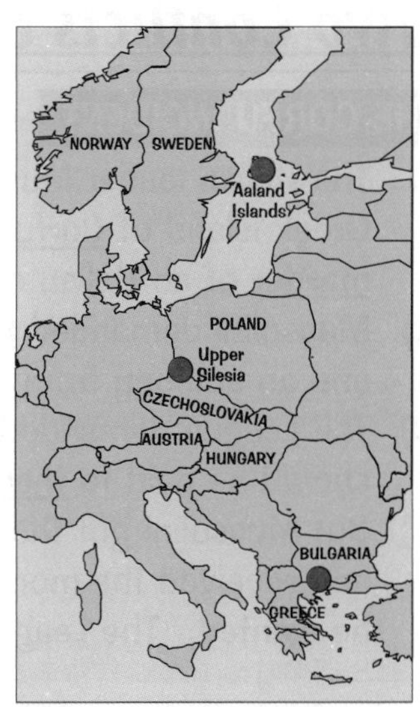

Policing the nations — in a league of its own...

The main thing you need to know here is how the League was supposed to work, its main aims, and some examples of its early successes.

Problems with the League of Nations

From the start, the League of Nations had real problems.

The USA Didn't Join the League

Wilson was very ill by this time, and Congress rejected the League.
The USA never became a member. Learn these reasons why:

1) The people of America hadn't liked the Versailles treaty, and refused to accept it. They thought the League of Nations was connected to it.
2) They believed it would be too expensive — many people wanted to stay out of Europe, and wanted only to worry about American affairs. This attitude was called isolationism.
3) Many thought that all people should be free under democracy. They weren't willing to be dragged into wars to help countries like Britain and France keep undemocratic colonies.
4) Wilson's political enemies wanted to make him unpopular, and get rid of him.

The League Wasn't Powerful Enough

1) Britain and France were in charge, but neither country was strong enough after the war to do the job properly.
2) Economic and military sanctions could only work if a powerful nation like the USA was applying them. Most countries were too busy rebuilding to be able to apply them.
3) Germany and communist Russia were not allowed to be members when the League was first formed.
4) The League had no army of its own, and most members didn't want to commit troops to war. Some countries like Italy were quite prepared to ignore the League.
5) The organisation was a disaster — in the Assembly and the Council everyone had to agree before anything could happen. The Court of Justice had no powers to make a country act.

Two Conflicts caused the League Problems in 1923

THE CORFU INCIDENT

1) The Italian leader Mussolini occupied the Greek island of Corfu in 1923 after the murder of an Italian diplomat.
2) Mussolini demanded financial compensation and an apology from Greece.
3) The League demanded that the money should be paid to them, not Italy.
4) But Mussolini got the decision overturned and received the money and the apology he wanted. The League looked weak.

FRENCH OCCUPATION OF THE RUHR

1) Germany failed to keep up with its reparation payments.
2) In retaliation, France invaded and occupied an industrial region of Germany called the Ruhr in 1923.
3) The League of Nations didn't intervene.
4) The United States helped resolve the situation with the Dawes Plan (see p.13).
5) France withdrew from the Ruhr in 1925.

Big problems — hardly the Premier League...

The League was doomed from the start, I'm afraid — but you need to be able to argue for the good and the bad sides of the League. The biggest problem it had was when the USA didn't join — even though the idea had come from the US President in the first place.

More International Agreements

Despite problems with the League of Nations, countries were learning to get on with each other.

Agreements were made in the 1920s

1) Between 1921 and 1929, the political situation seemed to be getting better as countries tried to cooperate.
2) There were loads of important agreements over arms reduction and economic aid.
3) Germany even accepted her new western borders.

There seemed to be a Chance of Lasting Peace

1) The Washington Conference showed that some countries were keen on disarmament.
2) The Geneva Protocol seemed to be strengthening the League of Nations.
3) The Dawes Plan and the Young Plan were helping Germany to recover — this would create increased trade and cooperation.
4) The Locarno Treaties suggested that Germany was at last prepared to accept the terms of the Versailles Treaty. The Germans joined the League of Nations in 1926.
5) The Kellogg-Briand Pact seemed to be a step towards lasting peace.

But all of these agreements had Problems

1) After the Washington Conference, nobody wanted to reduce arms further — the League had failed in its disarmament plans. Defeated countries were angry they had been forced to disarm.
2) The benefits of the Dawes and Young Plans were wiped out by the economic Depression (see p.14) which was soon to affect everybody.
3) Countries began to make agreements without the League of Nations because they didn't trust it to be effective — France made treaties with several countries because it didn't trust Germany. The Locarno Treaties had nothing to do with the League of Nations.
4) Germany agreed to its western borders at Locarno, but nothing was said about the East — which worried Czechoslovakia and Poland.
5) No one knew what'd happen if a country broke the Kellogg-Briand Pact.

Everybody agreed — to disagree...

The main point here is that everybody was willing to agree, but only up to a point. Sooner or later there was going to be a real crisis. Scribble a list of these agreements with their dates and what they tried to do, and what problems they had.

The Effects of the Great Depression

One of the things that really undermined the League of Nations was the Great Depression...

The American Stock Market Crashed in 1929

1) In the 1920s, the USA was the most prosperous country in the world, with high wages and mass production of goods. The 'Booming Twenties' saw billions of dollars loaned by the USA to help European countries recover from the effects of the First World War. American companies were selling lots of goods, so people borrowed money to buy shares in them.
2) But problems started to emerge. Many American producers overproduced — there was too much supply and not enough demand. There was competition from countries like Japan.
3) In 1929, the American stock market crashed — people realised some companies were doing badly and rushed to sell their shares.
4) Wall Street is the trade centre for the USA — by October 1929 the selling was frantic, and prices dropped because people no longer wanted to buy shares at high prices.
5) Businesses collapsed and thousands of people were ruined — by the end of the month they were selling shares for whatever they could get for them. This was the start of the Great Depression — a global economic downturn.

The Depression caused big problems in America

1) In 1929 the USA stopped lending money abroad and called in its loans.
2) By 1930 nearly 2000 banks collapsed as people rushed to withdraw savings.
3) Three years later there were over 12 million people unemployed in the USA.

The Depression Affected other Industrial Countries

1) Most industrial countries were affected — banks failed, industries struggled, and trade ground to a halt. The least affected country was the USSR, which had a communist system.
2) Within three years there were over 2.5 million people unemployed in Britain, and more than 30 million unemployed in the industrial countries of the West.
3) Germany, which had relied on American loans, was particularly badly affected, with banks failing, exports suffering and unemployment rising to over 6 million Germans by 1932.

The Depression made the League's work more Difficult

1) The Depression caused widespread poverty. People were more likely to support extreme right-wing leaders — hoping they'd provide strong government.
2) In 1933, the Nazis, led by Hitler, were elected in Germany. The Nazis wanted to defy the League of Nations by overturning the Treaty of Versailles.
3) The Depression meant that countries like Britain and France were less willing to help the League by getting involved in resolving international conflicts. They wanted to concentrate on dealing with domestic problems like unemployment.
4) The Depression was also a factor in some international conflicts, e.g. the Manchurian Crisis (see p.15).

The Wall Street crash — a depressing subject...

The Depression didn't just affect the world economy — it affected world politics too. Countries that had nearly recovered from World War One found themselves in dire straits again.

The Manchurian Crisis

On the other side of the world, Japan had suffered badly during the Depression.

The USA saw Japan as a Threat

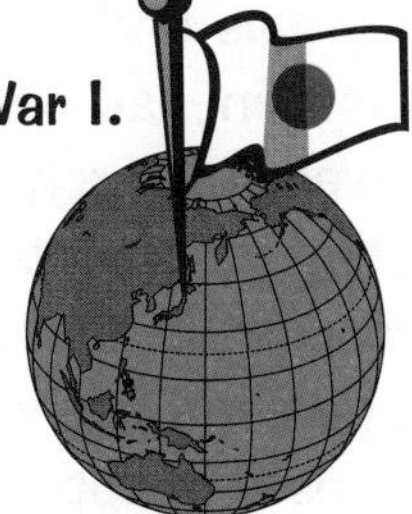

1) Japan had been at war with Russia in 1904.
2) Japanese industries had grown while Europe was busy fighting World War I.
3) The USA was worried about Japanese competition, and tried to limit its power and reduce the size of its navy.
4) When the Depression wrecked Japanese industries, the military leaders and business interests in Japan called for military expansion to strengthen the country.

Japanese Aggression led to the Manchurian Crisis

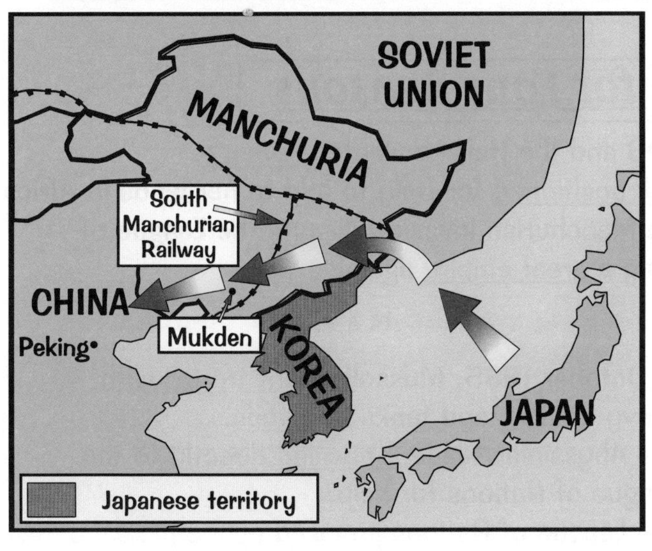

1) Japan had a large army and navy. Since 1905, it had controlled the territory of the South Manchurian Railway.
2) In September 1931, it used the excuse of a disturbance to take Mukden and send its troops to overrun the rest of Manchuria.
3) The Japanese pretended to give Manchuria independence. They put a weak leader called Puyi (who'd been the last emperor of China) on the throne so they could control him.
4) The League of Nations sent Lord Lytton to assess the situation. He produced a report, which said the Japanese had been wrong, but the League didn't do anything else — it failed to stop Japan and end the crisis.

This was the first major challenge for the League of Nations, and the whole world saw it fail to confront the Japanese aggression.

The League was Weakened

1) Japan refused to accept Lord Lytton's report and withdrew from the League in 1933.
2) In 1933 the Japanese invaded China's Jehol Province, which bordered Manchuria.
3) Dictators like Hitler and Mussolini saw the obvious weakness of the League.
4) Japan signed a treaty with Germany in 1936 and in 1937 started to invade China — again the League did nothing to stop it.

The League of Nations — a Drama out of a Crisis...

This is where things started to go seriously wrong for the League of Nations. Japan's suffering in the Depression made them look for ways to get stronger — by expanding and attacking other countries. The League's weakness meant it'd be a matter of time before someone else tried too.

The Invasion of Abyssinia

Next it was the Italians who tested the strength of the League of Nations.

Italy was ruled by Mussolini's Fascists

1) Italy was under the control of Benito Mussolini and his Fascist Party.
2) Mussolini had been made Prime Minister in 1922 after threatening to take power by marching on Rome. He used his new position to change the voting rules, and in the 1924 election the Fascists swept to power.
3) From 1925, he began to change Italy into a dictatorship.
4) Opposition political parties were banned. He used a harsh secret police against his opponents.

In the early 1930s, Mussolini was more on the side of France and Britain. He joined them at the Stresa Conference in 1935 to stand against a possible German invasion of Austria.

Mussolini Invaded Abyssinia for Four Reasons

1) Italy had been defeated by Abyssinia in 1896 and the Italians wanted revenge.
2) Abyssinia — now called Ethiopia — was well positioned for Italy to add to her lands in Africa.
3) Mussolini had seen Japan get away with the Manchurian invasion despite the League of Nations' threats. He dreamed of making Italy a great empire again.

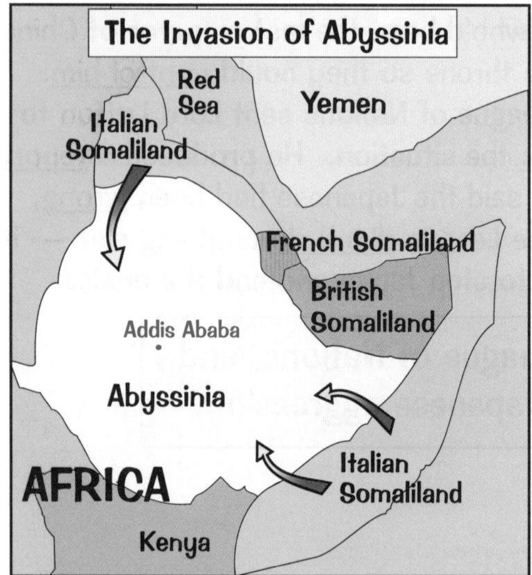

1) In October 1935, Mussolini sent troops with heavy artillery and tanks to invade.
2) The Abyssinian leader appealed directly to the League of Nations for help.
3) The League of Nations imposed economic sanctions, but delayed banning oil exports in case the USA didn't support them.
4) Britain and France didn't close the Suez Canal to Italian ships — so supplies got through despite the sanctions.
5) By May 1936 Italy had conquered all of Abyssinia.

The League of Nations appeared Ineffective

1) The League's reputation was in tatters. But Italy became more confident — and started making pacts with the fascist leader of Germany, Adolf Hitler.
2) Mussolini and Hitler agreed the Rome-Berlin Axis in 1936, and in 1937 Italy joined Japan and Germany in the Anti-Comintern Pact.
3) Italy also attacked Albania in 1938, and signed the Pact of Steel with Hitler in 1939.

Some world problems were out of its league...

Once again, the League was too weak and ineffective. Its failure to protect Abyssinia would have dire consequences. The new alliance between Mussolini's Italy and Hitler's Germany gave Germany the extra strength it needed to bounce back after the losses of Versailles.

The Failure of the League of Nations

It's important to see why the idea of the League of Nations didn't work.

The League Didn't Achieve its original Aims

The League set out to prevent aggression, to encourage cooperation, to work towards disarmament and to prevent a major war breaking out again. In the end, it failed on all these.

The League did have some success in improving the lives of ordinary people around the world — combating slavery and poor working conditions — but this wasn't its main purpose.

There are Arguments in Defence of the League...

It was always going to be tough...

1) Once the USA refused to join, Britain and France had a very difficult task — when they weren't that strong themselves. You can't enforce sanctions if nobody else wants to do it.
2) The Depression made the political situation tougher worldwide — it was nobody's fault.
3) No organisation could have stopped leaders like Mussolini or Hitler peacefully. Italy and Germany were members themselves, and could have worked harder for the League instead of against it. The same was true of Japan.
4) The League of Nations had to defend a settlement made after World War I which many of the nations themselves thought was unfair.

...and there are Arguments Against the League

It made some big mistakes...

1) The Manchurian crisis was the turning point — the League should have resisted Japan.
2) Too many members didn't keep to the rules. When they were attacked for it, they simply left the League, e.g. Germany and Japan in 1933, Italy in 1937.
3) Britain and France didn't lead strongly, and were often very slow to do things.
4) Members of the League who could have opposed aggression didn't want to risk a war.
5) Ambitious members like Hitler and Mussolini weren't dealt with strongly enough.
6) Instead of cooperation, it let the old system of secret alliances creep back.

For

- Early successes in preserving peace between minor powers
- Helped to rebuild Europe and aid refugees of the war
- Improved health and labour conditions around the world
- Kellogg-Briand Pact 1928
- Provided the groundwork for the United Nations

Against

- Rise of dictators
- Manchurian crisis 1931
- Failed to force countries to disarm
- Germany and Japan leave 1933
- Abyssinian crisis 1935
- Rome-Berlin Axis 1936
- German aggression
- Italy leaves 1937
- USSR expelled from League 1939
- Powerless to prevent World War II

For and against — now you be the judge...

Make sure you know the League's original aims and can give your own verdict on whether the League can be blamed for its problems, or if they were unavoidable.

Revision Summary

Here are a few more cracking questions for you to have a go at. Don't skim past this page — you need to make sure you've learnt everything in this section before you go any further...

1) List the four main aims of the League of Nations.
2) Which countries were permanent members of the Council?
3) Name three early successes which the League enjoyed.
4) Give four reasons why the USA would not accept membership of the League of Nations.
5) Why did Britain and France find it difficult to lead the League?
6) Which two important nations apart from USA were not members at the beginning?
7) Write brief notes to show the importance of the Corfu Incident in 1923.
8) Why did the French occupy the Ruhr in 1923?
9) Briefly explain the purpose of the following international agreements:
   a) the Dawes Plan
   b) the Kellogg-Briand Pact
   c) the Young Plan
10) Describe a weakness of the Locarno Treaties.
11) What event sparked off the global depression in 1929?
12) The Depression started in America. How did it affect other countries?
13) Why did the Depression make the work of the League of Nations more difficult?
14) Why did the USA see Japan as a threat?
15) Why did Japan invade Manchuria?
16) Why did the Manchurian crisis make the League of Nations look weak?
17) Who was the leader of the Fascist Party in Italy in the 1920s?
18) Give four reasons why Italy invaded Abyssinia in 1935.
19) Why did the Abyssinian crisis make the League of Nations appear weak?
20) Who signed the Pact of Steel?
21) Give four ways in which the League of Nations could be judged a success.
22) Give four ways in which the League of Nations could be judged a failure.

The Rise of the Dictators

Poor conditions in 1930s Europe saw the rise of dictators, and increasing international tension.

Problems and Fears aided the rise of Dictators

Dictatorship might seem a scary idea, but for some people it solved a lot of worrying issues.

1) **LOCARNO** had only settled the western borders of Germany. The borders on the East were vulnerable if Germany wanted to expand — people wanted strong leaders to protect them.
2) **DEPRESSION** still affected most countries, causing widespread unemployment and poverty. People welcomed strong governments who could put things right.
3) **DEMOCRACY** was often blamed for the bad conditions — democratic governments seemed unable to prevent them happening or to improve the situation.
4) **COMMUNISM** was seen as a threat to all of Europe after the Russian Revolution in 1917 — people looked to strong leaders to fight the threat of world revolution by the workers.
5) **ISOLATIONISM** continued — the USA stayed out of world affairs, and Britain and France weren't strong enough to oppose the large numbers of foreign dictators.
6) **FRANCE** was still suspicious of Germany and was building strong defences along the Maginot Line — many Germans felt they needed a strong leader against this French threat.
7) **DISARMAMENT FAILED** — most countries refused to disarm to the same level as Germany in 1932. Germany saw this as unfair and became determined to rebuild their armed forces.

Dictatorships popped up All Over Europe

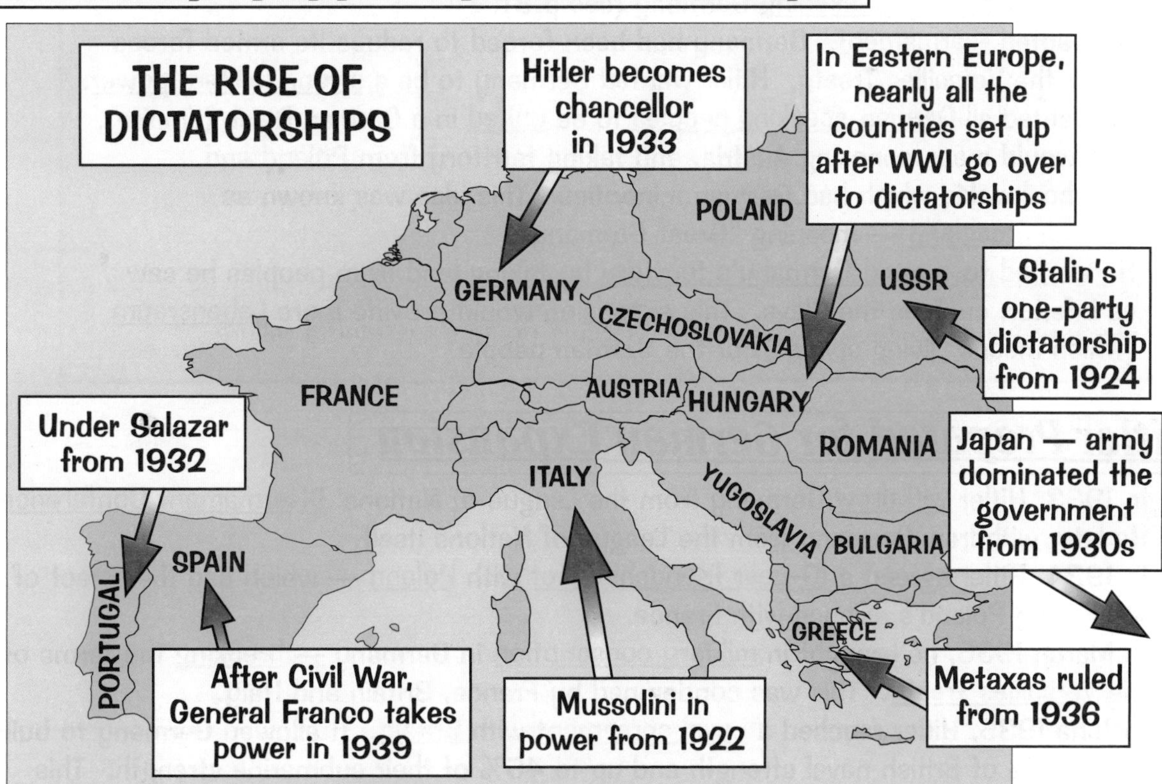

Dictatorship — simply irresistible...

This is really important stuff to learn. Europe was full of tension because of the economic crisis and the threat of war that still came from German anger over the Versailles Treaty. There was a power vacuum — people were afraid that no one was in control, so they turned to dictators.

Hitler's Foreign Policy

Hitler rose to power during a time of depression and international tensions in Europe — and his aggressive foreign policy just made things worse...

The atmosphere in Europe was Tense

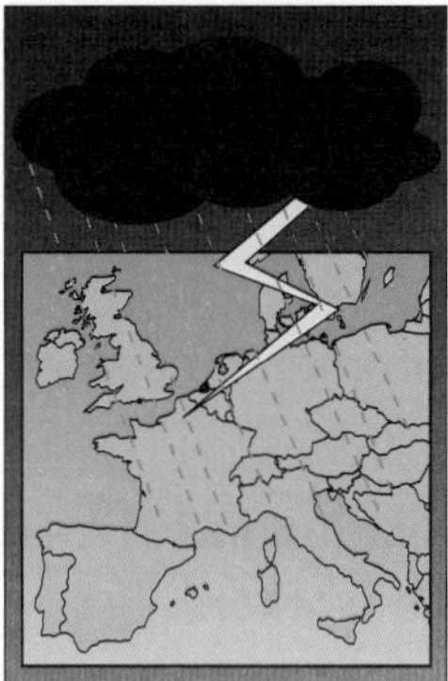

1) All the League of Nations' attempts at disarmament had failed.
2) Democracy had collapsed in much of Europe. Several countries were led by aggressive leaders who wanted to take over new territories, and weren't worried about defying the League of Nations.
3) Italy and Japan both invaded other countries' territory (see p.15-16) — and the League of Nations did virtually nothing to stop them.
4) Germany still resented its treatment after the First World War.
5) France had never stopped distrusting Germany.
6) Britain didn't want to get dragged into a war, whatever the reason.

German discontent helped Hitler rise to Power

1) During the Depression, extremist parties flourished (see p.14). There was widespread poverty and unemployment — people wanted strong leadership.
2) Adolf Hitler, the leader of the Nazi Party, got to power in Germany in 1933.
3) The main aims of Hitler's foreign policy were:

> 1) He wanted the Versailles Treaty to be overturned. Hitler hated the treaty which he saw as unfairly weakening Germany (see p.8).
> 2) He wanted rearmament. Germany had been forced to reduce its armed forces under the Versailles Treaty. Hitler wanted Germany to be a strong military power.
> 3) He wanted all German-speaking peoples to be united in a German Reich (empire). This would mean annexing Austria, and taking territory from Poland and Czechoslovakia which had German minorities. This idea was known as Grossdeutschland — meaning "Great Germany".
> 4) He wanted to expand Germany's territory by taking land from peoples he saw as inferior, such as the Slavs. This expansion would provide more Lebensraum (which means "living space") for the German people.

Hitler Prepared for German Expansion

1) In 1933, Hitler withdrew Germany from the League of Nations' Disarmament Conference. He later withdrew Germany from the League of Nations itself.
2) In 1934, Hitler agreed a 10-year friendship pact with Poland — which had the effect of weakening Poland's alliance with France.
3) In March 1935, he brought in military conscription in Germany — breaking the terms of the Versailles Treaty. This was condemned by France, Britain and Italy.
4) In June 1935, Hitler reached a naval agreement with Britain. It allowed Germany to build up to 35% of British naval strength and up to 45% of their submarine strength. This agreement implied that Germany had a right to rearm — breaking the Treaty of Versailles.

Hitler didn't lack ambition...

Hitler was an ambitious and ruthless leader. He wanted to make Germany a strong military power which could dominate Europe — and didn't care if he broke the rules to do it.

The Rhineland and Austria

Hitler's foreign policy became increasingly aggressive...

Hitler's first Territorial Success was in the Saar

1) The Saar was an industrialised region of Germany about 30 miles wide, bordering France.
2) Under the Treaty of Versailles, the Saar was put under the control of the League of Nations for 15 years from 1920. The plan was for the territory's status to be decided by popular vote in 1935.
3) In the January 1935 plebiscite (referendum), 90% of voters chose reunion with Germany — showing Hitler's popularity. The Saar was returned to Germany in March.

In March 1936 Hitler sent Troops into the Rhineland

1) The Rhineland was demilitarised by the Treaty of Versailles. Germany accepted this by signing the Locarno Treaties in 1925 (see p.13).
2) But the League of Nations was busy with Italy's invasion of Abyssinia. Hitler saw his chance.
3) Russia and France had recently made a treaty against German attacks. Hitler claimed that this threatened Germany, and that he should be allowed to put troops on Germany's borders.
4) Hitler reckoned Britain wouldn't get involved. But he was unsure how France would react.
5) The German forces had orders to pull out immediately if the French army moved in. But France was in the middle of an election campaign — so no one was willing to start a war with Germany. The League of Nations and Britain were angry but refused to take action.

Hitler was breaking part of the Treaty of Versailles — and no one tried to stop him.

Hitler then turned his attention to Austria

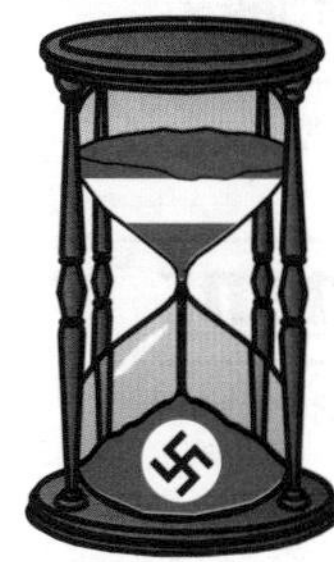

1) Hitler believed Germany and Austria belonged together. He wanted "Anschluss" (union).
2) In 1934, a Nazi revolt in Austria failed, after Mussolini moved Italian troops to the Austrian border, scaring Hitler off.
3) But by 1936, Hitler and Mussolini had become allies.
4) Hitler encouraged Austrian Nazis to stage demonstrations and protests. In February 1938, he demanded that an Austrian Nazi called Seyss-Inquart be made Minister of the Interior.
5) Instead, the Austrian Chancellor Schuschnigg called a plebiscite on whether Austria should remain independent. But Hitler couldn't be sure he'd get the result he wanted.
6) Hitler threatened to invade if Schuschnigg didn't resign. Schuschnigg couldn't take the risk — he and his cabinet resigned, except for Seyss-Inquart, who invited the German army into Austria to "restore order".

On 15th March 1938, Hitler entered Vienna to proclaim the Greater German Reich. Austria and Germany were united.

The late 1930s — storm clouds gathering...

Hitler was rapidly gaining power — after the humiliations of Versailles, Germany was on the up. Write a list of the main reasons why Hitler got away with sending troops into the Rhineland.

Czechoslovakia and Munich 1938

Czechoslovakia was afraid that Hitler, after taking over Austria, would try the same thing on them.

Hitler put Pressure on Czechoslovakia in 1938

1) Czechoslovakia's borders had been set at Versailles. The Sudetenland was a part of western Czechoslovakia which had a large population of Germans — about 3 million.
2) Britain, France and the USSR agreed to support the Czechs if Hitler invaded.
3) Hitler promised the British PM, Neville Chamberlain, that he wouldn't invade Czechoslovakia.
4) But soon Hitler claimed that the Czech government was discriminating against the Germans in the Sudetenland. The Nazis organised demonstrations in the Sudetenland demanding that the area should become part of Germany.
5) In May 1938, Hitler threatened to go to war. The Czech leader, Benes, was ready to fight.
6) But Chamberlain and the French PM Daladier then put pressure on the Czechs to give concessions to Hitler to avoid a war.

Chamberlain Negotiated with Hitler

1) In September 1938, Chamberlain flew twice to Germany, where he met Hitler to negotiate.
2) But Hitler changed his demands, and set a date of 1st October to "rescue" the Sudeten Germans. Chamberlain called this unreasonable, and the British Navy was mobilised for war.
3) Then on 29th September, Hitler invited Chamberlain, Daladier and Mussolini to a conference in Munich. Mussolini put forward a plan (really written by the German Foreign Office).
4) After discussions, the four leaders produced the Munich Agreement. This gave the Sudetenland to Germany but guaranteed the rest of Czechoslovakia would stay put. Chamberlain gave in to Hitler's demands because he believed Hitler would honour his promise.

The Munich Agreement was all about appeasement — giving aggressive countries like Germany and Italy what they wanted in order to avoid a major war.

Not Everyone was Happy with the Munich Agreement

1) It seemed like Chamberlain had prevented war. He claimed the agreement meant "peace for our time", and he flew back to Britain to a hero's welcome.
2) But Czechoslovakia and the USSR weren't invited to the Munich Conference. So the Czechs weren't even consulted on their own future.
3) And the USSR, who had big concerns about Hitler, were horrified at the agreement.

Appeasement may seem a bad idea now, but at the time, many people supported it.

1) No one in Britain wanted a war, and some people felt the Treaty of Versailles was unfair to Germany — so Hitler should be allowed to rebuild its power.
2) Many British politicians feared communism and the USSR much more than Hitler — they wanted Germany as a buffer between Britain and the USSR.
3) Britain's economy and armed forces were weak. Some historians say Chamberlain gave in to Hitler in order to buy time for rearming.

Appeasement — "Peace for our Time"...

Make sure you know what appeasement was — and scribble a list of the events of the Czech crisis.

Poland and the Outbreak of War

Most people were glad there wouldn't be a war — but in a poll soon after the Munich Agreement, over 90% of British people asked said they didn't trust Hitler.

In March 1939 Hitler took over the Rest of Czechoslovakia

1) After losing the Sudetenland, Czechoslovakia began to descend into anarchy. Slovakia began to demand independence.
2) Hitler persuaded the Czech president to allow German troops in to "restore order".
3) In May 1939, Germany signed the "Pact of Steel" with Italy. They promised to support each other if war was declared.
4) Britain and France did nothing — but it was clear that the appeasement policy had failed. Hitler had broken his promises and taken non-German lands.
5) Once the Nazis had taken the rest of Czechoslovakia, Britain abandoned appeasement and made an agreement with Poland to support it in case it was invaded.

The USSR made a Pact with Hitler

1) The USSR (Soviet Union) joined the League of Nations in 1934, and signed a treaty with France in 1935 against Hitler. The Soviet leader, Stalin, was suspicious of the Nazis.
2) But the USSR never trusted the French, and couldn't understand why nobody stood up to Hitler earlier. After Munich, Stalin decided to negotiate with Germany to protect the USSR.

3) The Nazi-Soviet Pact was signed in August 1939. The USSR and Germany agreed not to attack each other. They also secretly planned to carve up another country — Poland.
4) They agreed that if Germany invaded Poland, the USSR would get Latvia, Estonia, Finland and East Poland — but Hitler never really intended to let them keep those areas.

On 1st September 1939 Hitler invaded Poland. This was too much — Britain and France ordered him to leave. He ignored them and Britain declared war on Germany on 3rd September 1939.

The Road to the Second World War

These are the three key areas you need to cover in your revision of this topic:

1) Make sure you learn the final steps to war between 1936 and 1939 — the sequence of events is very important and you should practise the different names and spellings.
2) Be clear on the reasons why nobody stopped Hitler sooner — e.g. the weakness of the League of Nations, the policy of appeasement and the secret plotting of the USSR etc.
3) Remember the long-term causes of tension during the 1920s and 1930s — think about the problems caused by the Versailles Treaty and the League of Nations, and the consequences of the worldwide economic problems during the Depression (look back at Sections 2 and 3).

Twenty years on — Europe was at war again...

This is really important stuff. Remember — there were long-term causes as well as the short-term ones. Scribble a quick summary of the Nazi-Soviet pact. Then test your memory of Hitler's actions in the Rhineland, Austria, Sudetenland, Czechoslovakia and Poland.

Revision Summary

Yes, it's time for some more revision questions — just what you need to test your knowledge of this section. This is a really important section because it sits right in the thick of the action. All the problems after the First World War and then during the Depression suddenly came to a head. The key is to make sure you understand all of the different causes of the Second World War. Don't forget — it wasn't just one thing but a whole combination of long- and short-term causes. So start by working through these questions. Remember — you need to practise them till you know all the answers by heart.

1) List as many reasons as you can why several dictators came to power in Europe in the 1930s.
2) What was the name of the dictator who ruled in Italy?
3) Give four aims of Adolf Hitler's foreign policy in the 1930s.
4) Why did Hitler hate the Treaty of Versailles?
5) What conference did Hitler withdraw from in 1933?
6) When did Hitler bring in military conscription in Germany?
7) What was the result of the plebiscite (referendum) in the Saar in 1935?
8) Where did Germany send troops in 1936? Explain why nobody stopped them.
9) What was the name given to the joining of Germany and Austria? How did Hitler achieve it?
10) Name the area of Czechoslovakia that Hitler wanted in 1938.
11) What was agreed in the Munich Agreement in 1938?
12) What was appeasement? Give three reasons why it was a popular policy in Britain at the time.
13) What was the Pact of Steel?
14) Why did the Soviet Union make an agreement with Germany in 1939?
15) What happened after Hitler invaded Poland in September 1939?
16) Explain four causes of the Second World War.

Planning the Post-War Future

The Second World War lasted from 1939-1945. The main winners were Britain, the USSR and the USA. Two main summits were held between the Big Three allies during 1945 to decide on the future of Germany and Eastern Europe. These were the Yalta Conference and the Potsdam Conference.

There were Three Major Decisions at Yalta in 1945

The "big three" allied leaders — British Prime Minister Winston Churchill, US President Roosevelt and USSR leader Stalin — had already met at a conference in Tehran in 1943. They met again for the Yalta Conference in February 1945 — to plan what they wanted to happen after the war (although the conflict was still ongoing at this point).

1) Germany was to be split into four zones of occupation.
2) Free elections for new governments would be held in countries previously occupied in Eastern Europe.
3) The United Nations would replace the failed League of Nations.

Then the Situation Changed

1) Roosevelt died and was succeeded by Harry Truman, who was suspicious of the USSR.
2) In Britain, the Conservative PM Winston Churchill was replaced by Labour's Clement Attlee.
3) The USSR expanded westwards into Finland, Czechoslovakia, Romania and the Baltic states.

The allies were now suspicious of each other. Stalin wanted to control Eastern Europe so didn't want elections there — the USA and Britain suspected this. Truman and Attlee were new to their jobs — Stalin thought they'd be weak leaders so he could do whatever he wanted.

Agreements were Made at Potsdam in August 1945

Germany surrendered in May 1945. The allies made more decisions about post-war Europe:

1) The new boundaries of Poland were agreed.
2) The allies decided to divide Germany and Berlin between them.
3) They agreed to legal trials at Nuremberg of Nazi leaders for war crimes.

The USA and USSR had very Different Ideologies

Although the USA and USSR had been allies during the Second World War they had very different beliefs. The USSR was communist. The USA was capitalist. After the end of the Second World War, the two countries became rivals.

1) Economically, communism meant state control of industry and agriculture. The USA, by contrast, valued private enterprise — the 'American Dream' was that anyone could work their way to the top to be wealthy and successful.
2) Politically, communism meant a one-party state. The USA valued political freedom.
3) Communism aimed at world revolution, and so it was seen by Americans as a danger to their democracy. Likewise, the communists feared worldwide American influence.

Yalta learn this page — it's important...

Plenty for you to learn here — things changed fast after the war. Remember two of the Big Three changed leaders — you need to know what difference this made.

Increasing Tensions

After World War Two, the USA and USSR were the major world superpowers. Unfortunately, relations between them went rapidly downhill...

The USA and the USSR began an Arms Race

The USA and USSR became very competitive — each wanting to be the strongest, and feeling threatened by the other. There was an arms race to have the most powerful weapons.

1) Germany surrendered in May 1945, but the war against Japan continued. In August 1945, the USA dropped two atom bombs on Japan — destroying the cities of Hiroshima and Nagasaki. These bombs were incredibly powerful and thousands of civilians were killed. Japan surrendered immediately after this.
2) The USA had kept the atom bomb (A-bomb) secret from the USSR until just before it was used in Japan. For four years, the USA was the world's only nuclear power.
3) But in 1949, the USSR exploded their own A-bomb. The USA developed the even more powerful hydrogen bomb (H-bomb) in 1952. The USSR had followed with their own by 1955.

The USSR became Influential in Eastern Europe

1) At the end of the Second World War, the USSR's Red Army occupied Eastern Europe. Stalin had no intention of keeping the promise he made at Yalta to allow free elections in Poland.
2) Between 1945 and 1948, Stalin installed pro-Soviet "puppet" governments in Poland, Hungary, Romania, Bulgaria and Czechoslovakia. Free speech was suppressed.
3) Non-communist parties were banned, and even communist parties were controlled by the Cominform (Communist Information Bureau) to consist solely of Russian-style communists.
4) Comecon (the Council for Mutual Economic Assistance), set up in 1949, worked to nationalise the states' industries and collectivise agriculture.
5) For a while it seemed that Czechoslovakia might remain democratic. But when the Communist Party seemed likely to lose ground in the next election, it seized power in February 1948.
6) The exception to Soviet domination was Yugoslavia, which had freed itself from the Germans without the Red Army. Yugoslavia was communist but more open to the West. Its leader, Tito, argued with Stalin over political interference. Stalin cut off aid but didn't invade.

There was an 'Iron Curtain' between East and West

1) Increasing tensions between the USA and the USSR became known as the 'Cold War'.
2) It was called the Cold War because there wasn't any direct fighting — instead both sides tried to gain the upper hand with alliances and plans.
3) Both sides were afraid of another war because of the huge power of atomic weapons.
4) Countries in Western Europe tended to support the USA. Most countries in Eastern Europe were dominated by the USSR.
5) In a famous speech, Winston Churchill warned there was an Iron Curtain dividing Europe.

The Iron Curtain — it just wouldn't wash...

Nuclear weapons were capable of wiping out entire cities in one go — people thought it could be the end of humankind if a proper war broke out, which is why both sides were so cautious.

US Influence and the Berlin Blockade

If there was one thing the USA didn't want, it was for the whole world to go communist.

The USA was Worried about the Spread of Communism

President Truman was worried that other countries might also fall to communism. Truman tried to stop the spread of communism in two main ways:

1) The Marshall Plan

This promised American aid to European countries to help rebuild their economies — West Germany benefited massively. The USA was worried that if Western Europe remained weak it might be vulnerable to communism.

2) The Truman Doctrine

The USA would support any nation threatened by a communist takeover. For example, the USA gave $400 million of aid to Turkey and Greece to try to stop communism spreading. A civil war had started in Greece in 1946 between the pro-Western government and communists — Truman wanted to give the government all the help he could.

In 1948 the USSR and the West Disagreed over Berlin

1) There were four zones of occupied Berlin. The USA and Britain agreed to combine their zones into a zone called Bizonia in 1947.
2) The French agreed to combine their zone with them — the new western zone had a single government, and a new currency to help economic recovery.
3) The Soviet Union opposed these moves. Stalin wanted to keep Germany weak — so he decided to blockade Berlin.
4) Berlin was in Eastern Germany, which was controlled by the USSR — so Stalin ordered that all land communication between West Berlin and the outside world should be cut off.

West Berlin survived because of the Berlin Airlift. Between June 1948 and May 1949, the only way of obtaining supplies from the outside world was by air. By 1949, 8000 tons of supplies were being flown into West Berlin each day.

In 1949 Stalin Ended the Blockade

1) Two new states were formed — West Germany (German Federal Republic) and communist East Germany (German Democratic Republic).
2) In 1949 the Western Powers formed NATO (the North Atlantic Treaty Organisation) against the communist threat. The Eastern Bloc formed the Warsaw Pact in 1955 — a military treaty designed to counter NATO.

Two Germanies — and two German football teams...

Don't forget, the Cold War never led to any real fighting between the USA and USSR. Instead they seemed to be playing a giant game of chess. Make sure you know the two US policies intended to stop Europe turning communist, and the events that led to Germany being split up.

The Hungarian Rising and the Berlin Wall

Soviet policy softened a little after Stalin's death — but the problems were still far from over.

Stalin died in 1953

1) Stalin's death was a big turning point. He'd been the USSR's leader since the 1920s.
2) Soviet policy seemed to change under the new leader Khrushchev — he was critical of Stalin and his policies seemed less harsh. This became known as a "thaw" in the Cold War.
3) Khrushchev was in favour of peaceful coexistence between capitalist and communist states.
4) He made gestures of friendship to the USA — e.g. he met with US President Eisenhower at the Geneva Summit in 1955, and in 1959 he became the first leader of the USSR to visit the USA. He freed some prisoners and reduced censorship in the USSR. He also signed the Austrian State Treaty in 1955 along with the US, France and Britain (agreeing to withdraw occupying troops from Austria and allow it to become an independent state).

Hungary was treated Differently at first

1) After the war, the USSR helped put Rákosi, a brutal Stalinist, in charge of Hungary. His authoritarian regime became increasingly unpopular.
2) In October 1956, the people of Budapest protested against the government of Rákosi.
3) The secret police, who'd executed or imprisoned thousands of Hungarians, were hunted down.
4) Khrushchev allowed the liberal Nagy to become Hungarian Prime Minister.
5) Austria (which borders on Hungary) declared itself a neutral state in 1955. Nagy hoped that Hungary could also be a neutral state.

> In November 1956 Nagy announced that Hungary would withdraw from the Warsaw Pact and hold free elections — ending communism there.

Soviet Tanks Invaded Hungary

1) 20 000 Hungarians were killed or wounded. Nagy was arrested and later hanged.
2) Western countries condemned the USSR's actions, but the US couldn't come to Hungary's aid without risking a nuclear war. So they used the invasion as anti-USSR propaganda.
3) Kádár became Prime Minister and ensured loyalty towards the USSR.
4) The incident showed that despite the "thaw" in policy, Khrushchev could still be harsh.

The Berlin Wall was built in 1961

1) Between 1949 and 1961, more than 2½ million people left East Germany for the West through East Berlin. The communist government of East Germany was worried by this trend.
2) In 1958 Khrushchev tried to solve the problem by issuing the Berlin Ultimatum — a demand that the US, France and Britain remove their troops from West Berlin within six months. It was refused. In 1961 Khrushchev tried again. He gave another six-month ultimatum over West Berlin, but again this was refused.
3) So, on 13 August 1961, a 30-mile barrier was built across the city of Berlin overnight. The Berlin Wall was fortified with barbed wire and machine gun posts, and separated East Berlin from West Berlin.
4) Anyone who tried to escape East Berlin was shot. West Berliners were suddenly separated from relatives in the East — for the next 30 years.

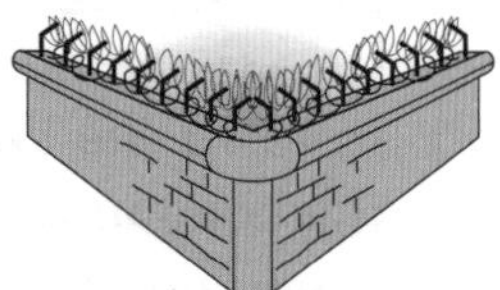

> In a famous speech in West Berlin on 26 June 1963, US President Kennedy declared his commitment to protect West Berlin, and his solidarity with its people. Kennedy said, "Ich bin ein Berliner" (I am a Berliner).

The Prague Spring and the Arms Race

The Cold War just got worse during the 1960s...

U-2 was an American Spy Plane

1) The U-2 spy plane was designed to fly so high it would usually be undetected.
2) It meant the USA could secretly get information about the USSR's weapons. It reassured President Eisenhower that the USSR didn't have as many missiles as they claimed.
3) The USSR shot down a U-2 in 1960. Eisenhower lied, denying it was a spy plane. But the USSR then produced the pilot (alive) and the plane wreckage as evidence.
4) The USA and USSR were supposed to be attending talks together in Paris a few days later. This summit fell apart because of the U-2 crisis. Khrushchev demanded an apology from the USA, but Eisenhower refused — so Khrushchev went home.

The Arms Race continued through the 50s and 60s

1) In 1957, the Soviets test-fired the first Intercontinental Ballistic Missile (ICBM), and also launched Sputnik 1, the world's first artificial satellite.
2) This new technology frightened the West as it was now clearly possible to launch a nuclear missile attack on the USA from the USSR.
3) But the USA soon made advances. The USA's Atlas ICBM was launched in 1957, and in 1960 the Polaris missile was the first submarine-launched ICBM.
4) The number of American ICBMs increased from 200 in 1961 to 1000 in 1967. Then the USSR began catching up again as American resources were diverted into the Vietnam War. Both sides now had enough bombs to destroy each other many times over.
5) As well as the arms race, there was a space race. The USSR got the first man in space — Yuri Gagarin in 1961. The US were the first to get men on the Moon in 1969.

Czechoslovakia Rebelled against Communism in 1968

1) Alexander Dubcek became Czechoslovakian leader in 1968 and made changes to the country:
   - Workers were given a greater say in the running of their factories.
   - Travel to the West was made available for all.
   - Living standards were to be raised.
   - Free elections were to be held.
   - Opposition parties would be permitted.

   This was called the 'Prague Spring'.

2) Dubcek was still a communist. He was careful to reassure the USSR that Czechoslovakia wouldn't leave the Warsaw Pact — unlike Hungary in 1956.
3) But the USSR was worried — it didn't want the Eastern Bloc to be weakened.
4) On 21st August 1968, 500 000 Soviet troops invaded Czechoslovakia and Dubcek was removed from office. Soviet control was restored. Many countries criticised the Soviets, but no action was taken. A UN draft resolution condemning the invasion was vetoed by the USSR.
5) Soviet leader Leonid Brezhnev (who had replaced Khrushchev in 1964) announced that in future the USSR would intervene in any country where socialism was under threat. This became known as the Brezhnev Doctrine.

Communism — the Bloc Party...

The superpowers were super-competitive. They kept trying to get one up on each other — who could have the biggest guns, bombs, spaceships... And neither wanted to lose face.

The Cold War in Asia

In 1949 the Communist State of China was set up by Mao Tse-tung — this meant that the USA was also worried by the communist threat in Asia.

In 1950 War broke out in Korea

Communist North Korea went to war with South Korea in order to reunite the country — this was seen as a direct challenge from communism to the West. The USA and the Western powers intervened on behalf of the United Nations to stop communism spreading.

The UN Aim was to Resist Communist North Korean Aggression

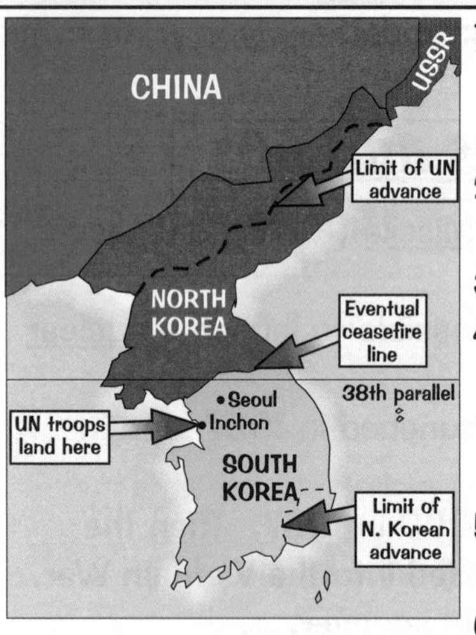

1) The UN ordered an immediate attack against the North Koreans. UN forces landed at Inchon and drove the North Koreans back over the 38th parallel by September 1950.
2) President Truman allowed General MacArthur (UN commander) to invade North Korea — most of the UN force were Americans.
3) This worried China, who feared a Western invasion.
4) In October 1950, China joined the North Koreans in an attack which drove the UN forces back, and captured Seoul (the capital of South Korea) by January 1951. A UN counteroffensive retook the city, and drove the North Koreans back to near the original border.
5) MacArthur wanted to attack China but Truman disagreed — after arguing with the President, MacArthur was sacked.
6) Truman looked for peace and a ceasefire was agreed in 1953.

A Communist Government came to power in North Vietnam

1) Indochina was a French colony that covered a large area of South-East Asia. In the 1940s and 1950s there was a revolt against the French — which turned into a long and bloody war. The resistance fighters were backed by communist China.
2) The Geneva Conference in 1954 was a meeting of international leaders to sort out problems in Asia — including this conflict.
3) Under the terms of the Geneva Accord, France withdrew from Indochina. Vietnam (formerly part of Indochina) was partitioned into communist North Vietnam and democratic South Vietnam. Laos and Cambodia were set up as independent states.

The USA tried to Protect South Vietnam from Communism

1) The Truman Doctrine meant America was willing to provide aid to South Vietnam to stop it falling to communism. President Eisenhower supported the choice of Diem as leader of South Vietnam. He was a corrupt and unpopular ruler — but he was anti-communist.
2) Under Eisenhower, and later Kennedy, the USA gave loads of money to South Vietnam. They also sent military 'advisers' — there were 12 000 American soldiers in Vietnam by 1962. The communist threat remained, and the US became more involved in countering it (see p.32).

The Asian Cold War — pretty hot really...

There you are, the main events of the Korean War — but you just need to learn the key points. The Korean War was a dangerous moment that could easily have become a World War — make sure you know the main reasons why the UN invaded and why China fought back.

The Cuban Missile Crisis

The USA wanted to keep all countries close to its shores friendly.

Cuba is Only 100 Miles from the USA

Fidel Castro

1) Since 1952, Cuba had been ruled by Batista, a ruthless and corrupt military dictator. Batista allowed American businessmen and the Mafia to make huge profits in a country where most people lived in poverty.
2) In 1953 Fidel Castro attempted to overthrow the government, but he was defeated and imprisoned. After his release in 1955, he fled Cuba.
3) In 1956 Castro returned and began a guerrilla war. By 1959, he had enough support to take Cuba's capital, Havana, and successfully overthrow the government.

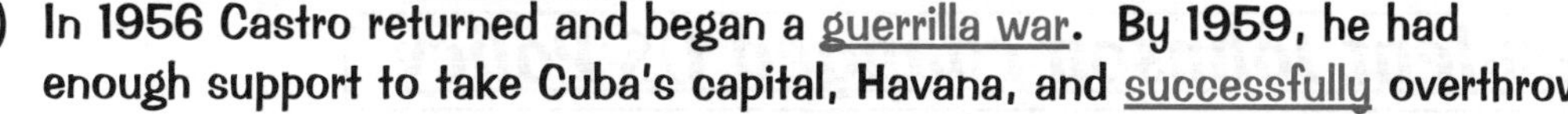

Castro wanted to Get Rid of American Influence

1) Castro made a big impact. He shut down the gambling casinos and the brothels. He also nationalised American-owned sugar mills.
2) The USA cut off diplomatic relations with Cuba.
3) Castro began to work with the USSR — he'd always been influenced by communism.
4) The USSR offered to buy Cuba's sugar instead of the USA.

Cuban Rebels in America plotted an Invasion

1) In 1961, President Kennedy authorised a CIA-trained invasion of Cuba by anti-Castro rebels.
2) In April 1961, the rebels landed in the Bay of Pigs, but the USA didn't give them air support as they had promised. The rebels were easily defeated — it was a bit of a fiasco.
3) This invasion meant Castro decided that Cuba needed Soviet military assistance.

Soviet Nuclear Missiles were shipped to Cuba

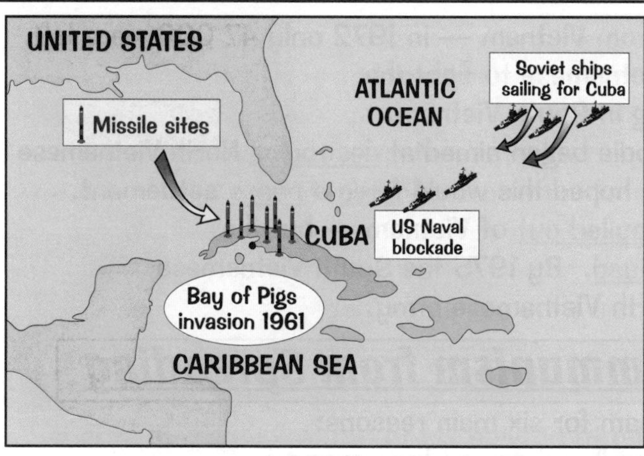

1) In 1962, the USA's U-2 spy planes detected Soviet missiles in Cuba. From Cuba these missiles could be used to attack US cities with very little warning.
2) President Kennedy ordered a naval blockade of Cuba. All Soviet ships were to be stopped and searched to prevent further missiles being transported to Cuba.
3) Kennedy demanded that Khrushchev withdraw his missiles and prepared to invade Cuba. The Soviet ships steamed on to Cuba.
4) The world was on the brink of nuclear war...

In the end, Khrushchev made a deal to remove the missiles from Cuba and ordered his ships to turn around. In exchange the US lifted the blockade, promised to not invade Cuba — and secretly agreed to remove their missiles from Turkey, which borders the USSR.

U-2 were spy planes — I always thought they were a rock band...

The 13 days of the Cuban missile crisis were the closest the world's been to nuclear war. There was a stalemate with nuclear weapons because if one side fired, so would the other and everyone would be destroyed. It was a no-win situation.

Vietnam and the USA

The USA was scared of countries turning communist — they didn't want to be outnumbered.

The Domino Theory of Communism

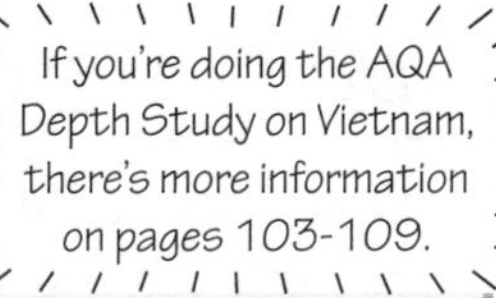

The domino theory says that when you knock over the first domino in a line the rest will fall down too. The USA thought this would happen if one country was knocked over by the communist threat — soon all the nearby countries would turn communist as well. So China, North Korea and North Vietnam could knock down the South Vietnamese domino.

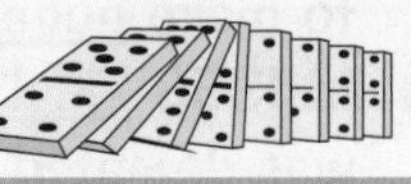

In 1963 President Johnson changed US Policy

The President was determined to keep South Vietnam free from communism:

1) He increased troop numbers from 23 000 in 1964 to 180 000 in 1965 and 500 000 in 1967.
2) He began a bombing campaign against communist North Vietnam.

The war became Unpopular in the USA

1) The Tet Offensive by the North Vietnamese in 1968 took the Americans by surprise.
2) The offensive was beaten but there were heavy casualties — about 14 000 US soldiers were killed in action in 1968.
3) The American public saw brutal images of the war on TV. They were also shocked by news of the 1968 My Lai massacre where civilians were murdered by US troops.
4) The war was very expensive, costing millions of taxpayers' dollars to support and finance.

President Nixon tried to Finish the war

1) American troops were gradually withdrawn from Vietnam — in 1972 only 47 000 were left.
2) Instead the US started training the South Vietnamese to fight the Vietcong — the communist guerrillas fighting in South Vietnam.
3) Heavy bombing of North Vietnam and Cambodia began aimed at destroying North Vietnamese supply lines — the Ho Chi Minh trail. It was hoped this would force a peace settlement.
4) In 1973 a ceasefire was agreed and the US pulled out of Vietnam — but the fighting between the North and South continued. By 1975 the South Vietnamese capital Saigon had been captured by the North Vietnamese army.

The US had Failed to stop Communism from Spreading

The Americans were effectively defeated in Vietnam for six main reasons:

1) The Vietcong treated the South Vietnamese well and gained their support.
2) American bombing killed many civilians and made North Vietnam more determined.
3) Vietcong guerrillas were very skilful soldiers. They didn't fight in open warfare, but used tactics like sudden raids and ambushes. They didn't wear uniforms and often operated in small groups.
4) American troops weren't used to fighting in the jungle.
5) The North Vietnamese had the support of China and the USSR.
6) American public opinion had turned against the war.

Vietnam — apocalypse then...

Phew, loads for you to learn here. Remember — the domino theory explains why the USA thought Vietnam was so important in the first place, so learn it right now.

Revision Summary

Yes, it's time for those awesome revision questions again — I know it's a pain but there's no way round it. It's the best way to test yourself on this stuff. So if you want to get the grades, you've really got to put the work in now. An important thing to remember here is that the USA and USSR were the only countries who were strong enough to interfere in world affairs after the Second World War — everybody else was too busy rebuilding their economies and industry. Make sure you can answer all of these lovely questions — and if you have problems go back over the section until you've got the lot sorted. So get going.

1) Name the two conferences held by the Big Three in 1945.
2) Which political leader was present at both of these conferences?
3) Was the USSR capitalist or communist?
4) Describe the difference between capitalism and communism.
5) Where and when did the USA use its atomic bombs?
6) When did the USA develop a hydrogen bomb?
7) Explain how the USSR developed a sphere of influence in Eastern Europe.
8) Which Eastern European country was communist but not under the USSR's influence?
9) What phrase did Winston Churchill use to describe the separation of Western Europe from Eastern Europe?
10) What was the Marshall Plan?
11) What was the Truman Doctrine?
12) Why did disagreements occur over the administration of Berlin in 1948?
13) What was the Berlin Blockade, and how did the Western powers deal with it?
14) Give the full official names of the two new states formed in Germany.
15) What does NATO stand for?
16) When did Stalin die?
17) Why was there a "thaw" in the Cold War when Khrushchev first came to power?
18) Why did Soviet tanks invade Hungary in 1956?
19) When was the Berlin Wall built?
20) What is a U-2?
21) Why did the U-2 crisis cause embarrassment for President Eisenhower?
22) Who got the first man in space — the USA or the USSR? What was his name?
23) What was the 'Prague Spring'?
24) Who became the leader of China in 1949?
25) Who was the UN commander during the Korean War?
26) What was decided about the future of Vietnam at the Geneva Conference in 1954?
27) Name the military dictator who was overthrown in Cuba in 1959.
28) How did Castro set about reducing American influence in Cuba?
29) Why did the world almost face a nuclear war in 1962?
30) Why did American public opinion turn against the war in Vietnam?
31) Give six reasons why the Americans failed to win the Vietnam War.

Détente and the Afghanistan War

After the Cuban Missile Crisis (see p.31), the USA and USSR made an effort to get on...

The USA and USSR wanted to Avoid a Crisis

The Cuban Missile Crisis of 1962 brought the world to the brink of nuclear war. Future misunderstandings between the Soviet Union and the USA had to be avoided.

1) A telephone hotline was set up between the Kremlin and the White House.
2) The Soviet Union and the USA signed a treaty in 1963 to stop further nuclear weapons testing.
3) Relations between the superpowers still weren't that friendly though. In 1963 the American president John F Kennedy gave a speech in West Berlin criticising communism.

Détente — a period of increasing US–Soviet Cooperation

1) The USSR couldn't afford to continue building up its nuclear arsenal.
2) The USA was trying to end the Vietnam War (see p.32) — an expensive and unpopular war against communists. The US hoped that improving relations with the USSR and China would isolate North Vietnam and force it to agree to a peace settlement.
3) From 1972, US President Nixon and the leader of the USSR, Brezhnev, began a series of talks aimed at improving relations. These were known as the Brezhnev-Nixon summits.
4) In 1972 the two superpowers agreed to limit their nuclear weapons when they signed the Strategic Arms Limitation Talks Agreement (SALT 1).
5) In 1975 the US, the USSR and other powers signed the Helsinki Agreement. This agreement officially recognised the European borders fixed at the end of the Second World War, including the division of Germany.
6) The Helsinki Agreement also included a commitment to human rights — for example, freedom of speech and travel. But since there was no enforcement procedure, these promises were not always kept by the communist countries.
7) China also wanted détente. Its relationship with the USSR had deteriorated, so China needed to gain the US as a powerful ally. It also feared a war, like the one in Vietnam, with the US.
8) In West Germany, the Chancellor, Willy Brandt, wanted better relations with the Eastern Bloc to improve trade and reduce military tensions.

Talks continued throughout the 1970s with a view to further limitations. President Carter signed a SALT 2 agreement in June 1979 at a US-USSR summit in Vienna — but the Senate had not yet ratified the treaty when the Soviet invasion of Afghanistan altered the political climate.

The USSR got bogged down in a war in Afghanistan

1) To prop up a pro-Soviet government besieged by rebels, the USSR invaded Afghanistan in December 1979. This decision turned out to be a disaster. The USSR got stuck with a seemingly unwinnable conflict in difficult mountainous terrain.
2) American distrust of the USSR increased. It worried the USSR had its sights on the oil-rich Persian Gulf (fairly close to Afghanistan). President Carter warned that the US would use force to prevent outside powers gaining control of the Gulf region. This warning became known as the Carter Doctrine.
3) The SALT 2 agreement was being debated by the Senate. Carter withdrew it from consideration, and called for an increase in the defence budget.
4) During the 1980s the US aided the Afghan resistance with military equipment.
5) Disagreement over Afghanistan led to a US boycott of the Moscow Olympics in 1980 — and in 1984 the Soviet team boycotted the LA Games.
6) The USSR finally gave up and began withdrawing their forces from Afghanistan in 1988.

The New Cold War

The Cold War had its last gasp in the 1980s... This was also known as the Second Cold War.

In 1980 the New Cold War began

The war in Afghanistan and the election of Ronald Reagan as US president in 1980 ended détente.

1) Ronald Reagan was a hardline anti-communist. He called the Soviet Union an "evil empire".
2) Reagan was keen to show off American technology and power through the development of new weapons — the start of another arms race.
3) The US developed and deployed medium-range Cruise and Pershing nuclear missiles which could be launched from almost anywhere.
4) The US also started to develop the Strategic Defense Initiative (SDI or Star Wars) for using laser weapons to shoot down Soviet missiles from space.

Ronald Reagan

Poland's People Rebelled in 1980

1) In the early 1970s Poland, under its communist leader, had achieved some rise in living standards. But in the late 1970s the economy suffered from foreign debt and shortages. In response the government raised prices.
2) In 1980 Lech Walesa led shipyard workers in the port of Gdansk in protest against the increase in food prices — with some success.
3) They set up their own independent trade union called 'Solidarity' and demanded the right to strike and to be consulted on all major decisions affecting their living and working conditions. Lech Walesa became the leader.
4) Solidarity became a broad-based anti-communist social movement which by the end of 1981 had 9 million members. Nothing like it had been seen before in the communist world. The movement was especially strong because of the support of the Catholic Church.
5) The Polish communist government was in a fix. It was scared to ban Solidarity — but neither could it meet demands for political reform, for fear of Soviet intervention.

The Military seized Control

In 1981 the Polish army leader General Jaruzelski, with Soviet support, seized control of the country and declared martial law. As a result:

1) Solidarity was completely banned.
2) Lech Walesa was arrested and imprisoned.
3) The price of basic foodstuffs was increased by 40%.

Lech Walesa

Solidarity lived on as an underground organisation. Lech Walesa became a symbol of resistance to Soviet oppression — he was awarded the Nobel Peace Prize in 1983. In 1988 further nationwide strikes again forced the government to negotiate with the union.

Solidarity — Rebels with a Cause...

There's plenty to learn here. The events in Poland are evidence of popular resistance to communism in Eastern Europe — which would eventually lead to the fall of the USSR.

The Soviet Withdrawal

Mikhail Gorbachev came to power in the USSR — and radically changed Soviet policies...

The Cold War created a Crisis in the USSR

1) The arms race with the USA was so expensive that Soviet living standards became worse as more money was spent on weapons.
2) Soviet farming was inefficient — there wasn't enough food and millions of tonnes of grain had to be imported from the USA.
3) The communist government was becoming more corrupt and was unable to give the Soviet people the same high living standards as people had in the West.
4) The war in Afghanistan was a disaster — it cost billions of dollars and 15 000 Soviet troops were killed.

Gorbachev introduced his 'New Thinking' Reforms

In 1985 Mikhail Gorbachev became General Secretary of the Communist Party. He was more open to the West than previous leaders. He introduced two major policies — Glasnost and Perestroika.

Glasnost meant New Freedom and Openness

The Soviet people won new rights:
1) Thousands of political prisoners were released, including the leading dissident, Andrei Sakharov.
2) People were told about the atrocities committed by Stalin's government.
3) Free speech was allowed.
4) Military conscription was soon to be abolished.

Perestroika meant Economic Restructuring

1) Gorbachev wanted to make the Soviet system of central planning of production more efficient.
2) However corruption in the Soviet economy was too great and he was unable to see through his plans.

These reforms were part of what is known as Gorbachev's 'New Thinking'. He didn't want to end communism, but he hoped that reform would help revive the USSR's struggling economy, which was falling further behind the US's and causing increasing discontent among the people.

Gorbachev changed Foreign Policy

Gorbachev's 'New Thinking' also covered foreign policy.
1) In 1987, a disarmament treaty was signed called the INF (Intermediate-Range Nuclear Forces Treaty). The USA and the USSR agreed to remove medium-range nuclear missiles from Europe within three years.
2) In 1988, Gorbachev announced the immediate reduction of the weapons stockpile and the number of troops in the Soviet armed forces.
3) Gorbachev tried to improve relations with the West. He met with the US President Reagan several times, for example at the Geneva Summit in 1985.
4) Gorbachev announced the complete withdrawal of Soviet troops from Afghanistan in 1988.

Gorbachev

In 1988, Gorbachev decided to abandon the Brezhnev Doctrine (see p.29). He told the United Nations that the countries of Eastern Europe now had a choice — the USSR wasn't going to control them any more.

It's feeling a bit less chilly in here...

By the late 1980s, the end of the Cold War was in sight — Mikhail Gorbachev was key to this.

The End of the Soviet Union

Communism toppled — and the Cold War was finally over...

Communism Fell all over Eastern Europe in 1989

1) Hungary opened its frontier with Austria in May.
2) Free elections were held in Poland in June. Solidarity won and a new non-communist government came to power.
3) Many East Germans crossed into Hungary, through Austria and into West Germany.
4) The Berlin Wall was torn down in November.
5) Anti-communist demonstrations took place in Czechoslovakia and the communist government collapsed in December.
6) In December a revolution began in Romania against the cruel and corrupt regime, and the dictator Nicolae Ceausescu was executed on Christmas Day.
7) The Warsaw Pact ended officially in 1991.

In 1990 Germany was reunified. Communist East Germany and democratic West Germany were one country again after 45 years. For many people this was a powerful symbol that the communist experiment was over.

Communism was Rejected in the USSR

The main nationalities within the Soviet Union demanded independence, especially the Baltic republics — Latvia, Lithuania, and Estonia. Gorbachev tried to prevent the rise of nationalism in the Baltic republics with military force, but gradually started to lose control.

An Anti-Communist Russian President was Elected in 1991

1) The newly elected President of Russia, Boris Yeltsin, was an opponent of Gorbachev, and became popular and powerful.
2) He demanded the end of communist domination and the break-up of the USSR. This led to a crisis in 1991.

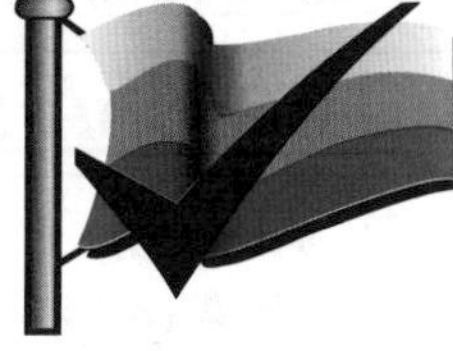

The Attempted Coup of 1991 Failed

1) The old communist leaders feared the reforms, so they decided to get rid of Gorbachev.
2) A military group tried to seize power by capturing Gorbachev, but Yeltsin rallied the Russian people to resist and the army supported him, and the coup failed.
3) Soon the individual Soviet republics became independent — the USSR didn't exist any more.
4) Now Gorbachev had no power and had to resign. Communism in Russia was dead.

The end of communism — when the reds got the blues...

Phew, there's even more stuff to learn here — but you've got to do it. Scribble a paragraph on why communism fell in Russia, and why 1991 was so important.

The USA after the Cold War

After the Cold War ended, the USA had to find a new focus for its foreign policy.

The USA was now the Sole Superpower

1) After the fall of the USSR, the USA was the only country with a military and economy strong enough to be able to take action across the globe — making it the world's only superpower.
2) The USA had the most powerful military in the world, even with post Cold War cuts in spending. Through the 1990s, the US's military expenditure made up more than a third of the world's military spending. No other country came close to spending as much as the US did.
3) The USA's economy was strong throughout most of the 1990s, remaining the biggest in the world while Russia struggled after the collapse of the USSR.
4) This gave the USA a lot of power to get involved in disputes around the world.

The USA saw itself as a Champion of Democracy

In the 1990s, the US tried to be a force for freedom and democracy in the world:

1) 1990-1991 — The USA supported UN demands for Iraq to withdraw from its invasion of Kuwait and led the UN coalition which successfully drove out Iraqi forces (see p.39).
2) 1992-4 — The USA led a UN force trying to bring peace and stability to Somalia, which was suffering from a chaotic civil war. But following the death of a number of US troops, President Bill Clinton pulled the US out.
3) 1994 — In Operation Uphold Democracy the US successfully intervened to restore the democratically elected president of Haiti after a coup.
4) 1994-1995 — After the break up of Yugoslavia, there was a violent civil war and genocide in Bosnia. The US led a NATO bombing campaign which lifted the Bosnian Serbs' siege of Sarajevo and helped to end the conflict.
5) 1999 — The USA led the NATO bombing of Serbia, in an attempt to end the conflict in Kosovo (see p.39). While this was a successful campaign — Serbia agreed to remove their troops from Kosovo — civilian casualties, including the deaths of three Chinese citizens, made the US intervention controversial.

Bill Clinton

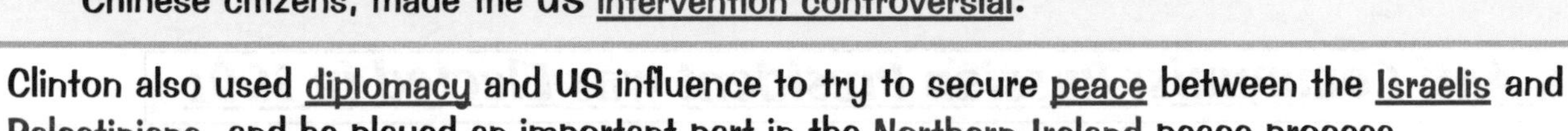

Clinton also used diplomacy and US influence to try to secure peace between the Israelis and Palestinians, and he played an important part in the Northern Ireland peace process.

The USA still wanted Friends in Europe

1) After the Cold War, Western Europe no longer needed protection from the USSR, so the USA reduced its military presence. US missiles were withdrawn from the UK in 1991.
2) The UK continued to be one of the USA's closest allies, supplying much of the support for the US-led interventions in Kuwait, Bosnia and Kosovo (see next page).
3) Other European countries, such as France, the Netherlands, Czechoslovakia, Hungary and Poland, all contributed to the US-led UN coalition in the Gulf War (see p.43).
4) The US was also willing to work more closely with former allies of the USSR. In 1999, three former Warsaw Pact members — the Czech Republic (which used to be part of Czechoslovakia), Poland and Hungary — joined NATO.
5) US involvement in Bosnia, Kosovo and Northern Ireland showed a US commitment to Europe.

There's no one left but US...

Somalia was a big turning point for the US in the 1990s — after the deaths of US troops in Somalia, Clinton avoided using American ground troops in overseas conflicts.

The UN

Even after the Cold War, the UN still had its hands full trying to resolve global conflicts...

The UN tried to get Iraqi Forces to leave Kuwait

George Bush

1) Saddam Hussein came to power in Iraq in 1979. He was a ruthless and brutal dictator, who had used chemical weapons against Iraq's Kurdish minority.
2) In 1990, Iraq invaded Kuwait, its southern neighbour. The UN demanded that Iraq withdraw, and introduced sanctions (a ban on people trading with Iraq).
3) When Iraq refused, the UN authorised the use of force to remove the Iraqi army from Kuwait.
4) In the Gulf War (1991), US President Bush (George W. Bush's father) was in charge of creating the coalition of international forces which drove Saddam Hussein's army out of Kuwait. See p.43 for more.

The UN used Tough Sanctions against Iraq

1) The UN kept its strict sanctions against Iraq after the Gulf War. They hoped the sanctions would force Iraq to give up its weapons of mass destruction (nuclear, biological and chemical weapons) and stop it from trying to get hold of or make more.
2) While these sanctions helped to cut the amount Iraq could spend on weapons, they hurt ordinary Iraqi people — shortages of food and medicine led to a big rise in the death rates of Iraqi children.
3) The UN tried to help the Iraqi people with the Oil-for-Food Programme — Iraq would be allowed to trade oil for food and medicines. This trade would be carefully monitored to make sure that oil exports weren't being used to buy weapons.
4) While it did help many Iraqis, the programme did face some accusations of corruption — it's believed that some profit was unlawfully made by UN and Iraqi officials.

The crisis in Kosovo was a Big Test for the UN

1) In the late 1980s, the government of Serbia took away much of the independence that Kosovo, a mainly ethnic-Albanian area of Serbia, had previously had.
2) The ethnic Albanians formed a group called the Kosovo Liberation Army (KLA) to fight for independence. The Serbians fought back fiercely, killing hundreds.
3) To stop the violence, NATO began a bombing campaign against Serbia in 1999. After two months, Serbia agreed to remove its troops from Kosovo and allowed KFOR, a NATO-led multinational force, to take control of the region.
4) A UN task force called UNMIK was sent to help get Kosovo back on its feet, helping with policing and reconstruction. But the process was very slow, and ethnic tensions remained, sometimes turning into violence. Local Serbs felt that they were being forced into leaving.
5) There were also reports that KFOR and UNMIK personnel, who were immune from local prosecution, got involved in crime and violence in Kosovo.

A mixed record on fixing the world, UN-surprisingly...

The UN was set up to promote peace and protect human rights. Although, it has helped many people, it isn't perfect. Make sure you learn the UN's failures as well as its successes.

Revision Summary

There's just time for the best bit — some mega-magnificent revision questions for you. You've really got to test yourself here, because there were loads of facts in a very small section. See how many you can answer first go, then look back over the areas you weren't so sure about. Just keep coming back to those questions — by the time you sit the exam you should know them backwards... Well, forwards will do. So get busy and get this lot sorted.

1) What does 'SALT' stand for?
2) Why didn't the USA go through with the SALT 2 agreement?
3) Why did the USSR invade Afghanistan in 1979?
4) Which country gave military equipment to the Afghans fighting the USSR?
5) What was President Ronald Reagan's attitude towards the USSR?
6) What was the Strategic Defense Initiative?
7) Who was the leader of the Solidarity movement in Poland?
8) Give the name of the Polish army leader who came to power in 1981.
9) When was Mikhail Gorbachev appointed General Secretary of the Soviet Union's Communist Party?
10) Explain what is meant by the terms Glasnost and Perestroika.
11) Why was Perestroika unsuccessful?
12) What was agreed in the INF treaty?
13) What doctrine did Gorbachev abandon in 1988?
14) What year was the Berlin Wall torn down?
15) What happened to Romanian dictator Nicolae Ceausescu in 1989?
16) What year was Germany reunified?
17) What was the name of the President of Russia elected in 1991?
18) Briefly describe the events of the attempted coup against Gorbachev in 1991.
19) What was Operation Uphold Democracy?
20) Which three countries joined NATO in 1999?
21) Why did the UN place sanctions on Iraq in 1990?
22) What was the Oil-for-Food Programme?
23) What was the name of the UN force sent to help rebuild Kosovo?

Terrorism

History didn't stop with the Cold War. This section is about current world issues that are rapidly finding their way into the history books — terrorism and the second Iraq War.

Terrorists use Fear to make a Political Point

1) Terrorism is the use of fear to achieve political goals. Terrorists use tactics such as bombing public places, taking hostages and hijacking aeroplanes.
2) It's usually condemned because it puts innocent civilians in danger.
3) Terrorists often claim that they use violence because they have no choice. They say it's the only way to get their voice heard — e.g. in a non-democratic state.
4) Sometimes a group is called "terrorists" by some people and "freedom fighters" by others. It all depends how sympathetic you are to what they're trying to achieve and on your views of their methods.
5) Terror networks are now international. Terrorist organisations trade with each other for weapons and training. Some terrorist groups receive money from governments who want to harm other countries without being held responsible.

The IRA wanted Ireland to be United

1) In 1921, Ireland was divided into Eire (the Catholic, southern part of the country) and Northern Ireland (the mainly Protestant northern area), which stayed part of the United Kingdom.
2) The Protestant majority living in the North discriminated against Catholics, for example in jobs and housing. In 1969 violence broke out in Northern Ireland over civil rights for Catholics.
3) The Provisional IRA (Irish Republican Army) wanted Northern Ireland to be united with Eire. They used terrorist tactics.
4) A long period of serious violence was known as the Troubles (1969-1998). Over 3000 people were killed and many more were injured on both sides of the conflict.
5) There were revenge killings between the IRA and its opponents — the "loyalist" UVF (Ulster Volunteer Force) and UDA (Ulster Defence Association).
6) The IRA wanted to wear down the British government so they would eventually decide that defending Northern Ireland wasn't worth the cost in lives and resources.

Key events during the 'Troubles'

- From 1971 the IRA began killing British soldiers, including 100 British soldiers in 1972.
- The IRA started bombing commercial targets, e.g. Belfast city centre in 1972.
- In 1973 the bombing spread to England. In 1974, there were pub bombings in Guildford and Birmingham. The Brighton hotel bombing in 1984 was an attempt to kill Margaret Thatcher.
- In 1997 the IRA agreed to a ceasefire.
- In 1998, the British and Irish governments, and most Northern Ireland political parties, including Sinn Fein (associated with the IRA), signed the Good Friday Agreement. It was a move towards power-sharing in Northern Ireland through new political bodies such as a Northern Ireland Assembly. It also included plans for the decommissioning of weapons by paramilitary groups, and a commitment to use only democratic and peaceful methods.

The Troubles were troubling times...

Terrorism and violence created a climate of fear in Northern Ireland during the 'Troubles'. In the end it was peaceful negotiation and the 'Good Friday Agreement' that helped to bring progress.

Terrorism

Some terrorists are willing to negotiate, but extreme organisations tend to rely on violence alone.

The PLO used both Terrorist Tactics and Diplomacy

1) Israel was created in 1948 as a homeland for Jewish people after World War 2. The region had historical and cultural significance for Jews. However, there was conflict between the Jewish settlers and Palestinian Arabs who lived in the region. 750 000 Palestinians became refugees.
2) The Palestine Liberation Organisation (PLO) was created in 1964 by Arab nationalists who wanted to win Palestine back from Israel. Yasser Arafat became the chairman of the PLO in 1969. He was a strong leader.

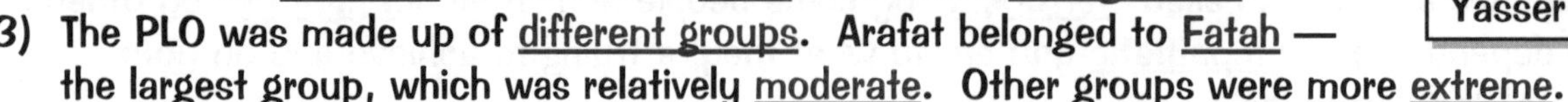

Yasser Arafat

3) The PLO was made up of different groups. Arafat belonged to Fatah — the largest group, which was relatively moderate. Other groups were more extreme.
4) The PLO used terrorist tactics, e.g. the 1978 Coastal Road Massacre killed 38 Israelis, including 13 Israeli children.
5) But it also wanted to be accepted as the representative of the Palestinian people.
6) Like the IRA, the PLO eventually reduced its demands. In 1988 it agreed to a two-state solution which would divide Palestine into separate Jewish and Arab states.
7) In the Oslo Accords (1993) the Israeli government recognised the PLO as the legitimate representative of the Palestinians. The PLO recognised that Israel had a right to exist in peace. Arafat became President of the new Palestinian Authority which controlled some of the territory previously occupied by Israel.

Al-Qaeda is an International terrorist organisation

1) Al-Qaeda is a global terrorist network with extreme Islamic views. Its members want to create a unified Muslim nation with strict religious laws and no Western influences.
2) Its founder was Osama bin Laden, a Saudi Arabian. During the 1990s, the Taliban regime in Afghanistan supported al-Qaeda and allowed them to build training camps for terrorists.
3) "Jihad" is the Islamic idea of a "spiritual struggle" but some terrorists use it to mean "holy war". In 1996 al-Qaeda announced a jihad to remove foreign troops from Islamic lands.
4) In 1998 bin Laden announced that it was the duty of every Muslim to kill Americans.

The Khobar Towers bombing in Saudi Arabia in 1996 was aimed at US servicemen (19 died). The East African US Embassy bombings in 1998 killed about 200 people, mostly locals.

Al-Qaeda attacked the World Trade Center in New York and the Pentagon in Washington on 11 September 2001. The attack destroyed the twin towers and killed around 3000 people. It was the worst terrorist attack in history. In response, the USA declared a "war on terror" and invaded Afghanistan. They destroyed many terrorist training camps but bin Laden wasn't captured.

Even though Osama bin Laden went into hiding, the attacks continued, e.g. the Bali nightclub bombings in 2002 and many suicide bombings in Iraq.

5) Bin Laden was eventually tracked down and killed in Pakistan by a US military raid in 2011.

Not all terrorist groups are willing to negotiate...

The IRA and PLO used violent tactics but eventually they were willing to negotiate in a peace process. Extreme terrorist groups like Al-Qaeda don't use diplomacy and won't compromise.

The Iraq War

The decision to invade Iraq in 2003 was extremely controversial...

The First Gulf War was in 1990-1991

1) Iraq is made up of different ethnic groups. It's mainly Arab, but there's a strong Kurdish minority (17%) in the North. The main religion is Islam, which in Iraq is divided into a Shi'ite majority and a Sunni minority.
2) Saddam Hussein came to power in 1979. His Ba'ath Party was socialist and secular (non-religious), but his rule favoured the Sunni minority.
3) The USA supported Iraq during its war with Iran in the 1980s.
4) But after Iraq invaded Kuwait in 1990 President Bush (George W. Bush's father) led international forces against Saddam Hussein in the First Gulf War (see p.39).

George W Bush wanted to Remove Saddam from Power

When George W Bush became US President in 2001, he wanted to invade Iraq. He claimed that Saddam had links to al-Qaeda and was developing weapons of mass destruction.

In October 2002 Congress passed the Iraq War Resolution. This made the invasion of Iraq legal because it hadn't met the conditions of the 1991 ceasefire. Congress accused Iraq of developing weapons of mass destruction (WMD), protecting terrorists and acts of brutality.

In November 2002 the UN Security Council passed Resolution 1441, giving Iraq a final chance to give up its weapons, but Iraq didn't comply. Some people argue that the case should have gone back to the UN because Resolution 1441 did not authorise the invasion.

In March 2003, the US invaded Iraq. British Prime Minister Tony Blair supported US policy and Britain became America's main ally in the war.

It turned out there weren't any WMD

After the invasion, it became clear that there was no evidence of WMD or links to al-Qaeda. This was embarrassing for the USA so they put forward other arguments for the invasion:
1) Getting rid of a dictator and establishing democracy could be seen as progress for Iraq.
2) The war was justified by Saddam's appalling human rights record.

Millions Demonstrated Against the War

There were anti-war protests involving millions of people in early 2003.

Some people didn't trust the USA's motives for war — they thought that the US wanted Iraq's oil supply and lied about the WMD.

Others felt uneasy about Western nations invading Iraq. Iraq had once been controlled by the British Empire — there were echoes of colonialism.

The idea of these Western, mainly Christian countries invading a Muslim country made some people feel uncomfortable.

The invasion of Iraq divided public opinion...

...some people thought the war was justified but others argued that it was illegal and wrong.

The Iraq War

The invasion was fairly quick and easy, but the conflict went on longer than anyone expected.

Saddam's regime Crumbled in just over a Month...

1) In March 2003, coalition forces led by the US invaded Iraq.
2) They captured the capital Baghdad on 9 April. The coalition had about 200 000 ground troops who were far better equipped than the Iraqis, and had total air superiority.
3) On 1 May President Bush announced US victory in Iraq.

...but the Conflict went on

Saddam Hussein

1) After Saddam's defeat, there was widespread looting and civil disorder. The coalition forces lacked the manpower to deal with the problem.
2) Many members of the defeated Iraqi Army became insurgents (resisting the invasion). They used weapons supplied by terrorists.
3) Saddam Hussein went into hiding but was captured in December 2003.
4) In 2004 resistance to the US coalition increased, helped by foreign fighters and al-Qaeda. Fighting included a 46-day battle for the city of Fallujah starting in November 2004. It was eventually won by US forces.

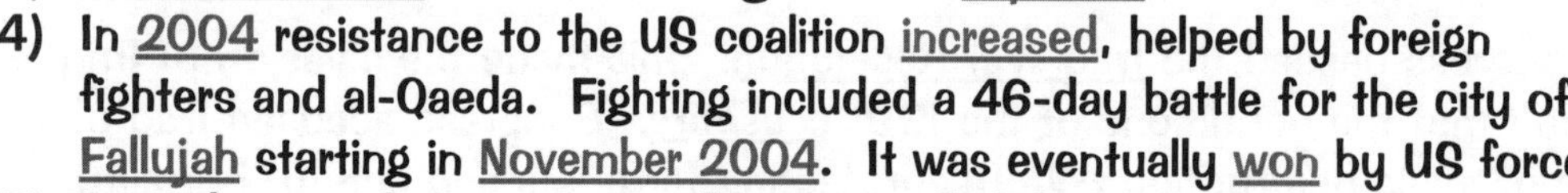

5) Over the next few years, 2 million Iraqis fled the country to escape the war. Some Iraqis were angry that the coalition couldn't protect civilians.
6) US soldiers were found guilty of abusing prisoners at Abu Ghraib prison in April 2004. This was a major blow to the moral justification for invading Iraq.

Achieving Democracy and Security was a Slow Process

Coalition forces tried to improve security but there was still some resistance.

2005
January – Iraqis elect a transitional government — many Sunnis refuse to vote
May – Sunni suicide bombers kill hundreds of Shias
October – a referendum approves the new Iraqi constitution
December – a national assembly is elected with Sunnis and Shias
2006
February – Sunnis bomb a Shia holy site, the al-Askari mosque
May – new Iraqi government takes office
November – violence increases, hundreds killed in Baghdad
December – Saddam Hussein is hanged for crimes against humanity
2007
President Bush sends 20 000 extra US troops to Iraq and David Petraeus becomes the new commander of coalition forces – security improves, violence decreases

The Iraq war — the conflict and the debate continue...

Coalition forces couldn't just invade Iraq and then abandon the Iraqi people — they had a responsibility to leave the country in a stable condition. People who oppose the war criticise the US for its lack of preparation for the aftermath of the invasion and the chaos which followed.

Revision Summary

I know, I know, that was quite a lot of information in a deceptively small section. How sneaky. Not to worry though, because here are some wonderful revision questions to test your knowledge and make sure you understand it all. There are a few facts and figures to remember but it's all really relevant to what's going on in the world today. It might even come in handy if you want to impress strangers at parties with your thoughts on current world events. Well, it's more interesting than talking about the weather and the price of onions anyway...

1) What do terrorists use to achieve their political goals?
2) Give three examples of terrorist tactics.
3) Which area of Ireland is mainly Catholic and which is mainly Protestant?
4) Which terrorist group wanted Northern Ireland to be united with Eire?
5) What were 'The Troubles'?
6) What is the name of the Northern Ireland peace process agreement signed in 1998?
7) What does PLO stand for?
8) Who was made leader of the PLO in 1969?
9) What was agreed at the Oslo Accords?
10) What is the main aim of al-Qaeda?
11) What is traditionally meant by 'jihad'? What do extremists sometimes use it to mean?
12) Name three terrorist attacks carried out by al-Qaeda.
13) What are the two main branches of Islam in Iraq?
14) What did the Iraq War Resolution do?
15) What was Resolution 1441?
16) Give three reasons why some people opposed the war in Iraq.
17) When did US coalition forces invade Iraq and what date did President Bush claim victory?
18) When was Saddam Hussein captured?
19) What crime happened at Abu Ghraib prison?
20) When did the new Iraqi government come into office?
21) When was Saddam Hussein hanged? What crime was he found guilty of?

The Schlieffen Plan

This section covers the main events of the First World War. If you're revising this topic, you also need to learn about the causes and outbreak of the war — which are covered in Section 1.

The Germans had to Fight France and Russia

1) France had been defeated by Germany in 1870-71 and wanted revenge. The French had a secret plan — Plan 17 — to take back lands they had lost in 1871 — Alsace and Lorraine.
2) France had made a treaty with Russia in 1894, so Germany expected a Russian attack from the East to help France.
3) Germany would therefore have to fight on two fronts at once. The answer was the Schlieffen Plan, thought up in 1905 (see p.2).

The SCHLIEFFEN PLAN aimed to attack and defeat France through Belgium before the Russians were ready, then turn back to fight the Russian Army.

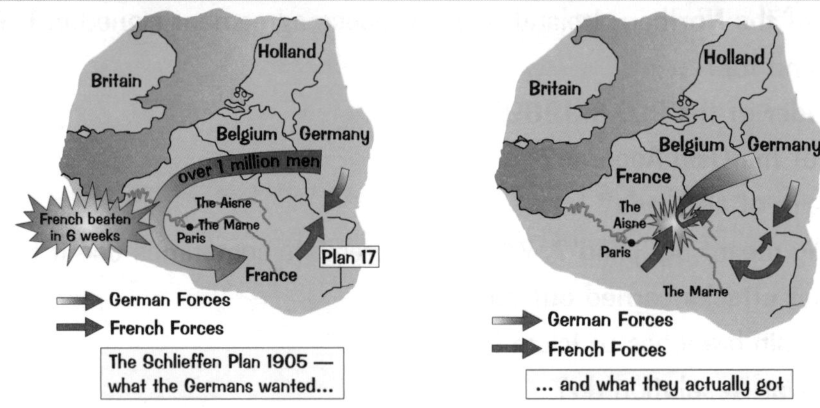

The Schlieffen Plan Didn't Work...

1) Belgium refused to let the German army through to attack France. So Germany had to use force, which delayed their advance.
2) Britain had signed a treaty with Belgium in 1839 to protect it as a neutral country. When Germany refused to withdraw from Belgium, Britain declared war.
3) Russia was ready for war quicker than the Germans had expected. Many valuable German troops had to march East to face them instead of pushing on into France.

A short period of Open Warfare followed

The early battles of the war in the West saw the two sides struggle for an advantage:

MONS — August 1914 — the British Expeditionary Force (BEF) — the first troops sent over from Britain — managed to slow down the German advance, but they didn't stop it. The German Kaiser called them a 'contemptible little army'.

MARNE — the Allied troops managed to save Paris, and forced the Germans to pull back to the river Aisne. The battle lasted five days.

YPRES — where both sides 'dashed to the sea' to stop the other side controlling the coastline. The Allied troops managed it, but with a terrible loss of life.

Neither side could push the other back, so they dug trenches to stop the enemy advancing further. By the end of 1914, the trench lines stretched all the way from the Belgian coast down to Switzerland and the two armies had reached a stalemate.

Get all these facts en-trenched in your brain...

Once the armies were stuck in the trenches, there was no hope of it being over by Christmas.

Stalemate in the West

The First World War began a new type of warfare — and it was shockingly horrible.

Changes in Warfare meant Stalemate in the Trenches

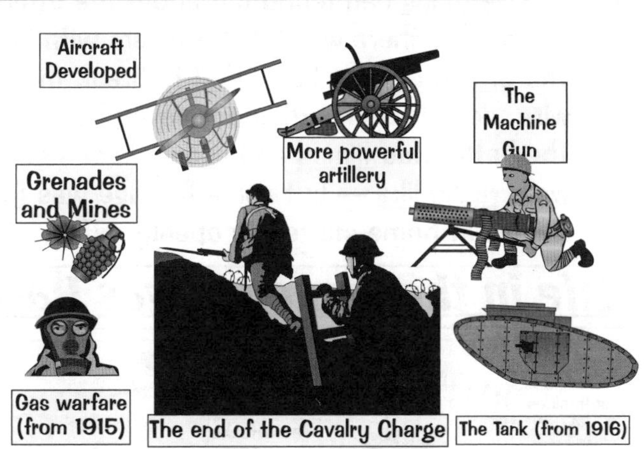

1) Nobody was used to trench warfare. It took a long time to work out how to break the stalemate.
2) No-one had commanded such huge armies before. They had to learn how.
3) It took time to train all the new soldiers. This was especially hard for the British who had had a small army before the war.
4) New weapons the armies had were better for defence than attack (see diagram).
5) Advancing troops couldn't hold on to the ground they won, and were pushed back.
6) Both sides were well supplied, and could always call up more arms and men.
7) 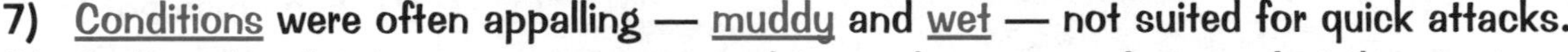Conditions were often appalling — muddy and wet — not suited for quick attacks.
8) 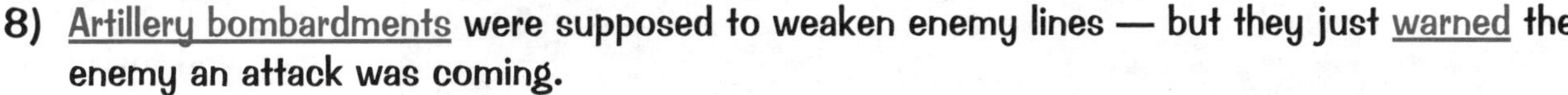Artillery bombardments were supposed to weaken enemy lines — but they just warned the enemy an attack was coming.

The Generals Kept Sending Troops 'Over the Top'

Both sides often tried to break the deadlock by sending thousands of men across No Man's Land. The result was huge slaughter of infantry. But some battles did affect the whole war:

1) At the 2nd battle of Ypres in 1915, the Germans first used poison gas against the Allied troops.
2) At Verdun in 1916, the French, under General Petain, held the Germans back from the city.
3) This victory for France boosted French morale — Verdun became a symbol of French freedom and demoralised the Germans, who were sure it would fall.
4) In order to relieve the pressure on Verdun, the British began a major attack at the Somme (July-November 1916). At this battle the British army used a new invention — the tank.

The Somme was a Major Battle and a Major Disaster

The Somme was one of the key battles of the war. The British commander was Sir Douglas Haig. After a massive artillery bombardment, the British soldiers were sent 'over the top' to charge the German trenches. They were under orders to advance slowly, not run. This gave the Germans time to get ready for the attack. The slow-moving British soldiers were an easy target. 57 000 Britons were killed or wounded on the first day alone. Later attacks were more successful, but the battle dragged on till November. Only about 12 km of land was gained in some places.

Trench Warfare — All quiet on the Western Front...

Phew, there's a lot for you to learn here. Have a go at covering the page and scribbling down everything you can remember about it. Then check what you missed, and do it again.

Life in the Trenches

The Somme made it clear that neither side would win a breakthrough in this new kind of war.

The Results of the Battle of the Somme

1) The Germans had found out about the offensive on the Somme before it happened, which meant that there was a big problem with keeping military secrets.
2) The British artillery had failed to break the enemy lines. It didn't even destroy their barbed wire, despite bombarding for several days.
3) The battle was filmed and shown back home. It gave people some idea of what the trenches were really like — but some footage was faked because the real battle was too horrific.
4) People at home started to openly criticise the generals and their tactics.

Life in the Trenches was Hard and Dangerous

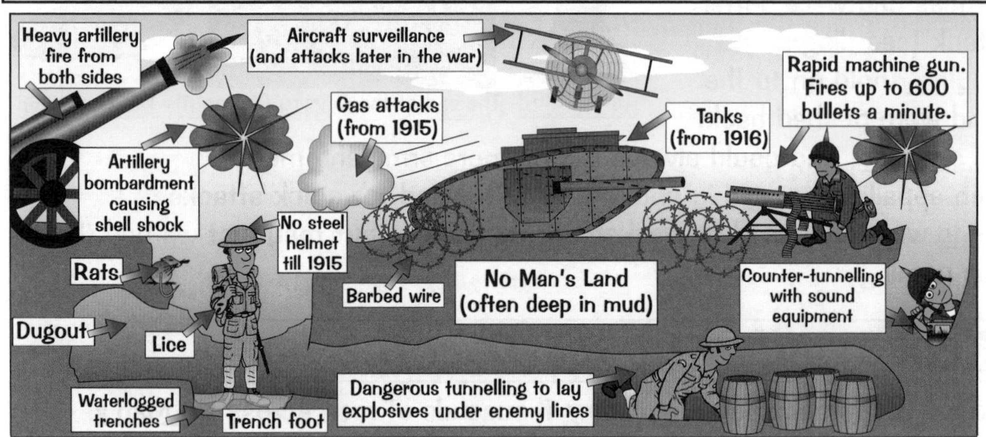

1) Life was almost as dangerous in the trenches as it was in No Man's Land.
2) Each man got paid one shilling (5p) a day, and their main rations were bully beef, jam and tea.

People Still Can't Agree whether the Tactics were Right

Many people nowadays still feel that the tactics used at the Somme and in other battles were wrong. Their picture of the First World War comes from TV, books and films — which often lay a lot of blame on Sir Douglas Haig, the "Butcher of the Somme". But in fact, it's much more complicated than that. Here are some of the main opinions on both sides.

Arguments supporting Haig's tactics

- Haig's main aim was to win the war, whatever the cost — not to save lives.
- If the British government at the time had thought there was a better strategy, they could have replaced Haig — but they didn't.
- Some of Germany's best troops were killed at the Somme — and couldn't be replaced.
- Haig couldn't wait for more tanks before the Somme — he had to relieve the pressure on Verdun, or the whole war might be lost.
- By 1918, Haig had learnt to adapt these attacking tactics so that they became more successful. In 1918 the British pushed the Germans back at the Battle of Amiens.

Arguments against Haig's tactics

- Hundreds of thousands of men were killed under Haig's command. He is quoted as saying, "The attacks are to be pressed, regardless of loss."
- Haig could have waited for more tanks at the Somme, which might have saved many lives.
- Once he saw the first day's slaughter at the Somme, he could have changed tactics.
- Haig could have learnt from his mistakes sooner. Instead he stuck to old-fashioned ideas about war that had already been shown to be disastrous — costing many lives.
- Some junior officers claimed that Haig didn't take account of bad weather conditions.

Trying to win the war — at a huge cost...

Opinions on the British tactics are a tricky business. You've really got to watch out for people just repeating modern ideas about Haig. Make sure you learn the main opinions on both sides.

The Eastern Front

There wasn't just a Western Front... This was a world war, and you've got to know about the Eastern Front as well.

The Russian Army was Supposed to be a Steamroller

1) The Allied plan was for Britain and France to hold the German army up in the West, while the Russian army advanced from the East. This would trap the Germans between their enemies.
2) At the start of the war, British newspapers talked confidently about the Russian steamroller crushing opposition as it advanced into Germany. It didn't happen.
3) On the other hand, the Russians did catch the Germans out — they were ready in just 10 days with 6 million men. The Germans had to send troops East before they'd defeated France — so the Schlieffen Plan had failed.

But the Russian Advance was a Failure

1) The Russian Army advanced into Germany, but they didn't have enough weapons. Many soldiers had to wait for someone to be killed so that they could get hold of a rifle.
2) The Russian plans were rushed because of the need to advance quickly. They weren't prepared for a long campaign.
3) The army was poorly organised. Many officers were inexperienced and discipline was poor.
4) 150 000 Russians were slaughtered in 1914 at the battles of Tannenberg and the Masurian Lakes by German troops under von Hindenberg and Ludendorff.
5) After this the Russians were driven back, and the Germans and Austro-Hungarians advanced.
6) A stalemate soon developed on the Eastern Front. The war was now like a chess match. The war effort put a great strain on Russia, as civilians went hungry so the troops could be supplied.

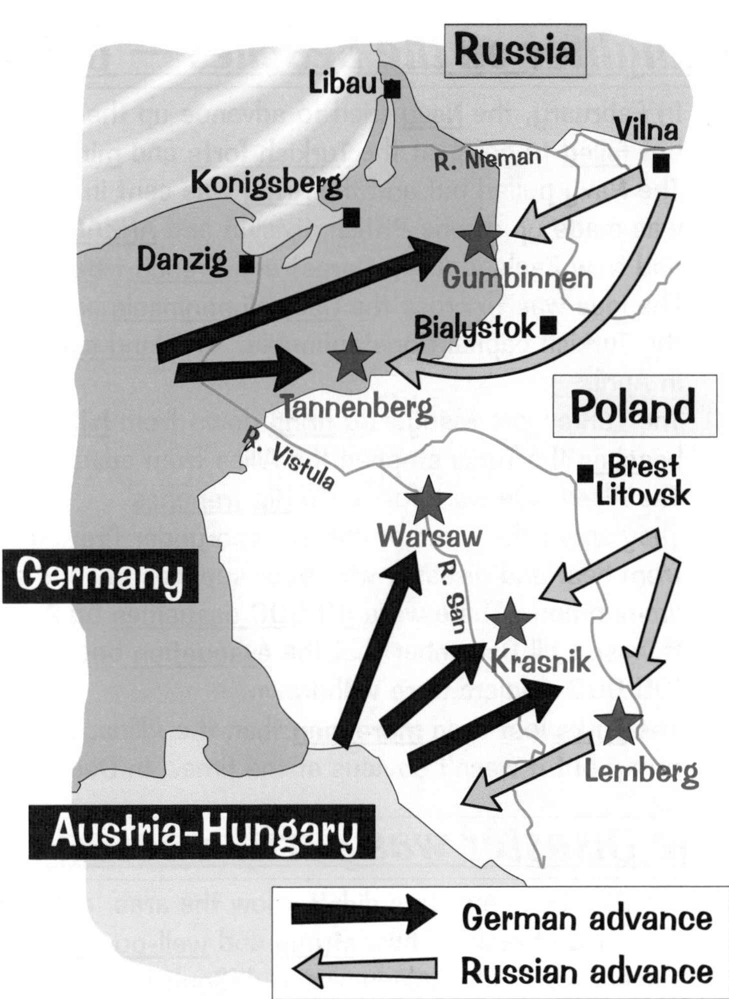

The Russian steamroller — it soon ran out of steam...

There you are then, just two key facts to learn here — what the Russians were supposed to do and what really happened. Remember — because the Russians were ready for war quickly the Schlieffen Plan failed. Scribble a list of reasons why the Russian advance was such a disaster.

The Gallipoli Campaign

The Ottoman Empire — which was centred on Turkey — was another enemy of the Allies.

The British Planned to Weaken Germany by Attacking Turkey

1) The Ottoman Empire had joined the war on the German side in November 1914. It attacked Russia in the hope of regaining a hold in the Balkans (see p.3).
2) Some leaders in Britain like Winston Churchill, the First Lord of the Admiralty, thought that Germany and Austria-Hungary could be weakened by attacking Turkey in the East.

The Plan was to Gain Control of the Dardanelles

1) Turkey controlled the Dardanelles — the narrow entrance to the Black Sea — and this was stopping Britain getting supplies through to Russia.
2) If Britain could land troops on the Gallipoli Peninsula they could take the Dardanelles, and then go on to take Constantinople, the capital of the Turkish empire.
3) Then other nearby countries like Greece and Romania might join in on Britain's side, and help the Allies to win the war, by attacking Germany from the East.

Slaughter on the Beaches — Gallipoli 1915

1) In February, the Navy tried to advance up the Dardanelles but failed to get past the Turkish forts and mines.
2) The Navy pulled out and the Army was sent in. The force was made up of one British division and ANZAC (Australian and New Zealand Army Corps) and French troops.
3) The idea was to cross the Gallipoli peninsula and capture the Turkish capital Constantinople. The land assault began in April.
4) The Turks were ready. By firing down from hills above the beaches the Turks stopped the Allies from advancing at all.
5) The Allied side were forced to dig trenches.
6) They spent the summer and autumn under fire, suffering from heat and disease, with poor supplies of food and ammunition. There were 40 000 casualties by August.
7) It wasn't till December that the evacuation began. 105 000 soldiers were withdrawn.

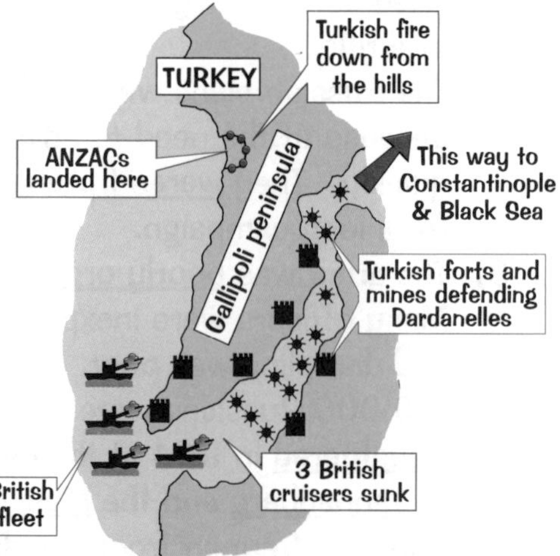

8) The Turks lost even more men than the Allies: 65 000 died. This seriously weakened their army, but it wasn't obvious at the time. In December 1915 it just looked like a complete mess.

The Disaster was partly caused by Bad Planning

1) The Allied commanders didn't know the area, and didn't have proper maps.
2) They hadn't realised how strong and well-positioned the Turkish forces would be.
3) The chosen landing place was in difficult terrain — a narrow beach backed by steep hills.

Over a third of the ANZACs sent to Gallipoli died. Churchill was removed from his post as First Lord of the Admiralty, and the Dardanelles remained under Turkish control.

It wasn't just the Western Front that had trench warfare...

Complicated stuff here and there's no way round it — you've got to learn what the Gallipoli campaign tried to achieve and why it went so horribly wrong.

The War at Sea

Blockades were more important than sea battles — stopping supplies getting to Germany.

The British Navy had Four Important Jobs

1) To protect trade ships so that the Allies could remain supplied.
2) To blockade ports, preventing the enemy being supplied.
3) To carry troops to wherever they were needed.
4) To protect British colonies overseas.

The U-Boat Changed the War at Sea

1) The U-Boat was a type of German submarine. It could attack ships without being detected.
2) From 1915, thousands of tons of merchant shipping was attacked and sunk, even though Germany only had around 20 U-Boats.
3) At first the Germans were careful not to attack ships from neutral countries or passenger liners. But the British realised this and began sending supplies on passenger liners too.
4) U-Boats started to attack non-military ships too — e.g. sinking the liner Lusitania in 1915.

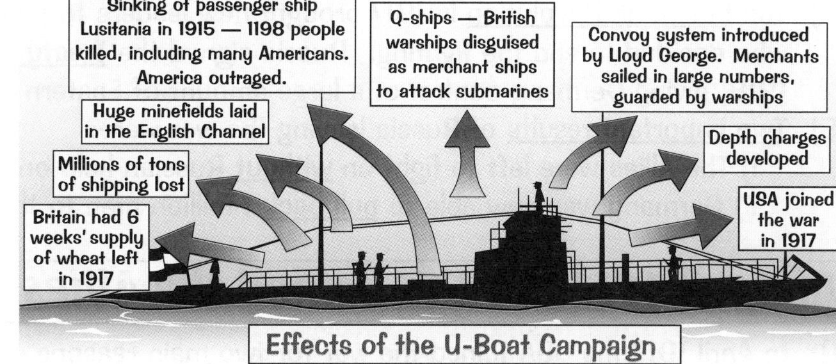

Effects of the U-Boat Campaign

Major Battles were Too Risky

Both sides had raced to build Dreadnoughts — (see p.2). But neither side wanted to risk these expensive ships in too many big battles. The only large-scale battle between the Dreadnought fleets was the Battle of Jutland in May 1916. Around 250 ships clashed. The German Admiral von Scheer wanted to lure part of the British fleet out of their base to attack them. But more British ships came than he expected...

Both Sides said they won at the Battle of Jutland...

1) The British lost 14 ships, and the Germans 11.
2) They fought in the evening, when it was misty, so neither side could fire accurately.
3) The British ships generally suffered more damage than the Germans.
4) The German ships and firepower seemed stronger.
5) But the German fleet left the battle first, and never put to sea in any strength after that.

Meanwhile the U-Boat Seemed to be an Unstoppable Force

1) Over 0.5 million tons of shipping was sunk in April 1917 alone.
2) The U-Boat campaign was trying to starve Britain into submission.
3) To tackle this problem, Lloyd George introduced the Convoy System — where merchant ships travelled together in groups protected by warships — to keep Britain's supplies coming in.

The war at sea — sailing to victory...

Loads of facts here — but you don't need to learn them all. Just make sure you learn the four jobs of the Navy, the reasons for avoiding major battles, and the effects of the U-Boat threat.

The End of the Fighting

The Russians withdrew from the fighting — but the USA joined.

Russia Pulled Out of the War in 1917

1) Tsar Nicholas II of Russia was a poor military commander.
2) To the south, the Brusilov Offensive advanced successfully into Austria-Hungary in June 1916, but was soon pushed back.
3) There was widespread starvation in the winter of 1916, and Nicholas II was forced out of power in 1917. The new Provisional Government continued the war, but was no more successful.
4) The Bolshevik Revolution in 1917 brought new leaders to power who decided to end the fighting. Russia signed the Treaty of Brest-Litovsk with Germany in 1918, giving Germany control of a large amount of Eastern territory in return for peace.
5) Two important results of Russia leaving the war were:
   i) The Allies were left to fight on without Russian help on an Eastern Front.
   ii) Germany was now able to pull back 1 million men to the Western Front.

In April 1917 the USA joined the Allies

1) In April 1917 the USA joined the war for two main reasons — the effects of the U-Boat campaign (100 American citizens were killed when the Lusitania was sunk in 1915), and a German attempt to encourage Mexico to attack the USA. This was a direct threat.
2) By now the fighting in Europe had become even fiercer. The French under General Nivelle had failed to push the Germans back.
3) The Allies fought the battles of Passchendaele and Cambrai in 1917. (The Battle of Passchendaele was also known as the Third Battle of Ypres — over 300 000 Allied troops were killed or wounded to win a few hundred metres of mud.)

Germany had to Attack Before all the Americans Arrived

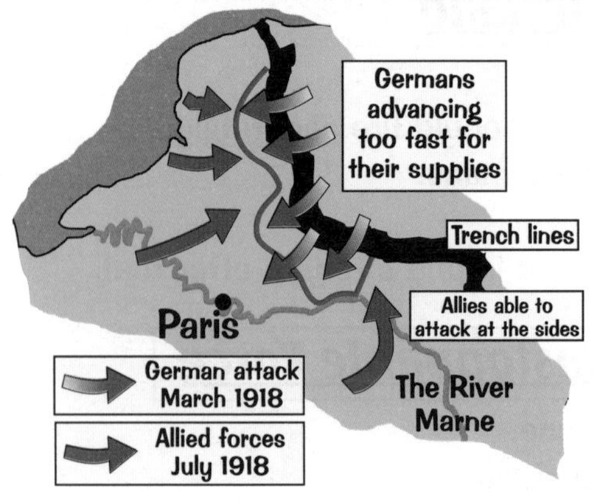

1) The USA wasn't ready to send all its troops, so Germany made a last effort to break through.
2) The Ludendorff Offensive tried to capture Paris in March 1918.
3) It looked like it would work at first — but the Germans advanced too far too fast, and their supplies had not kept up with them.
4) They were beyond their lines in a kind of bulge, so the Allies attacked them from the flanks (sides).
5) Thousands of American troops were soon joining the Allies, and the Germans were pushed back.
6) Kaiser Wilhelm II abdicated and the new government agreed a ceasefire or armistice on November 11th 1918.

US and them — America made all the difference...

Here you go, three key events in the last two years of the war — Russia's withdrawal, the USA joining the struggle and Germany trying a final big offensive. It's important to learn them NOW.

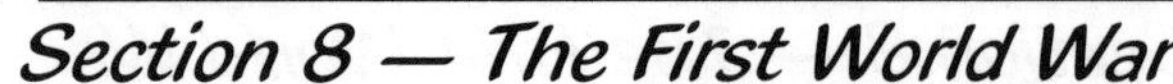

Revision Summary

Don't just turn the page now — you really do need to have a go at these questions. It's the only way you can make sure you know this stuff well — and that's the only way you can guarantee doing well in your exams. See how many you can get right — and revise the stuff you get wrong.

1) List three reasons why the Schlieffen Plan didn't work.
2) How far did the trenches stretch by the end of 1914?
3) Write down four new types of military equipment used during World War 1.
4) When did the Germans first use poison gas against Allied troops?
5) Give a summary of the events of the Battle of the Somme.
6) Write a short paragraph for and against the tactics used by the Allies at the Somme.
7) Give three reasons why the Russian Army did badly when they advanced on Germany in 1914.
8) What was the original aim of the Gallipoli campaign?
9) Give two reasons why the Gallipoli campaign failed.
10) How did the ANZACs get their name?
11) Give four important roles of the British Navy during the war.
12) Name the new type of battleship built by Britain and Germany before the war.
13) Give two reasons why the U-Boats caused Britain so many problems.
14) Why isn't it clear who won the Battle of Jutland?
15) Who was the Russian Tsar who was forced out of power in 1917?
16) What was the name of the treaty made between Germany and Russia in 1918?
17) Give two reasons why USA joined the war in 1917.
18) Why did the Ludendorff Offensive fail in 1918?
19) Here's a list of important battles — put them into the order in which they happened, and note what was important about each one:
    PASSCHENDAELE, MARNE, THE SOMME, 2ND BATTLE OF YPRES

The Weimar Republic

Germany lost the First World War (1914-1918). The peace settlement was harsh on Germany — it said Germany should accept blame for the war and pay £6.6 billion reparations.

A New Government Took Over When the Kaiser Abdicated

1) Kaiser Wilhelm II had ruled the German Empire as a monarch. At the end of the First World War there was a period of violent unrest in Germany — and the Kaiser was forced to abdicate in November 1918.
2) In early 1919, a new government took power led by Friedrich Ebert — it changed Germany into a republic. It was set up in Weimar, because there was violence in Berlin. Ebert became the first President, with Scheidemann as Chancellor.
3) Ebert was leader of the Social Democratic Party, a moderate party of socialists. The new government was democratic — they believed the people should say how the country was run.
4) The new German government wasn't invited to the peace conference in 1919 — and had no say in the Versailles Treaty. At first, Ebert refused to sign the treaty, but in the end he had little choice — Germany was too weak to risk restarting the conflict.

The Weimar Constitution made Germany a Republic

THE WEIMAR GOVERNMENT

REICHSRAT
(Upper house could delay measures passed by Reichstag)

REICHSTAG
The new German parliament (elected by proportional representation)

President
Elected every 7 years.
Head of army.
Chooses the Chancellor.

Friedrich Ebert

Proportional representation is where the number of seats a party wins in parliament is worked out as a proportion of the number of votes they win. This was the system in Germany and it often led to lots of political parties in the Reichstag (German parliament) — making it harder to get laws passed.

The Weimar Republic had Many Problems

1) It was difficult to make decisions because there were so many parties in the Reichstag.
2) It was hard to pick a Chancellor who had the support of most of the Reichstag.
3) The new government had to accept the Versailles Treaty, so they were hated by many Germans because of the loss of territory, the 'war guilt' clause, the reparations etc. (see p.8).
4) Some Germans joined paramilitary groups, such as the Freikorps (Free Corps) — right-wing groups made up of ex-soldiers who saw communists as a threat to peace.
5) Even though the Freikorps were problematic — they were private organisations not under government control — Ebert was happy to use them to suppress communist uprisings.

Weimar — not a kind of sausage...

The Weimar Republic was set up in a time of defeat — which made it unpopular right from the start. Don't forget — many German people didn't accept the peace settlements at the end of the First World War. Scribble a quick paragraph on the Weimar Republic and how it was set up.

Years of Unrest 1919-1923

Germany faced all sorts of problems in the years following the First World War.

Reasons for Discontent

1) Thousands of people were poor and starving. An influenza epidemic had killed thousands.
2) Many Germans denied they had lost the war and blamed the 'November Criminals' who had agreed to the Armistice and the Treaty of Versailles.
3) Others blamed for losing the war included the communists, the government and the Jews.
4) The government was seen as weak and ineffective — the Treaty of Versailles had made living conditions worse in Germany.

Soon there were Riots and Rebellions

1) In 1919 the Spartacists, a communist group led by Karl Liebknecht and Rosa Luxemburg, tried to take over Berlin in the Spartacist Revolt — but they were defeated by the Freikorps.

Wolfgang Kapp

2) In 1920, some of the right-wing Freikorps themselves took part in the Kapp Putsch (Putsch means revolt) — led by Wolfgang Kapp, they took over Berlin to form another government. The workers staged a General Strike — Kapp gave up. The government didn't punish the rebels, because many judges sympathised with people like Kapp.
3) In 1922 Walter Rathenau was killed — he'd been the Foreign Minister who signed the Rapallo Treaty with Russia and was Jewish. Many Germans were now anti-Jewish (anti-Semitic).

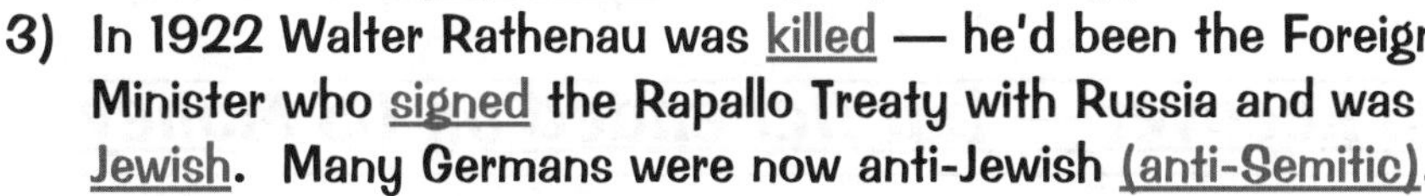

In 1923 Germany Couldn't Pay the Reparations

France and Belgium occupied the Ruhr — the richest industrial part of Germany — to take resources instead. This led to fury in Germany, while workers in the Ruhr refused to work. German industry was devastated again, plunging the economy into hyperinflation.

Hyperinflation happens when production can't keep up with the amount of money there is, so the money keeps losing its value.

Hyperinflation had Three Major Results

1) Wages were paid twice a day before prices went up again.
2) The middle classes lost out as bank savings became worthless.
3) The German Mark became worthless.

Hyperinflation — sounds good for blowing up balloons...

Remember that discontent in Germany got worse when the economy went wrong — but there were lots of other factors too. Scribble a list of reasons why there was so much discontent.

Stresemann and Recovery

In August 1923 Stresemann became Chancellor — he gradually led Germany back to recovery.

Stresemann wanted International Cooperation

Stresemann was Chancellor for a few months, then Foreign Minister. He believed Germany's best chance for recovery came from working with other countries, particularly the US.

1) In September 1923 he told the workers in the Ruhr to return to work, and in November 1923 he introduced a new German Mark called the Rentenmark to make the currency more stable.
2) In 1924 he accepted the Dawes Plan from the US, which reorganised reparation payments.
3) In 1925 the French and Belgian troops left the Ruhr.
4) In October 1925 he agreed to the Locarno Treaty where the western borders of Germany were agreed, but not the eastern. He won the Nobel Peace Prize for his efforts in this field.
5) In 1926, Germany joined the League of Nations, and became one of the permanent members of the Council.
6) In 1928, Germany was one of 65 countries to sign the Kellogg-Briand Pact. They promised not to use violence to settle disputes.
7) In 1929, the US agreed to replace the Dawes Plan with the Young Plan — reparations would be reduced by three-quarters of the amount, and Germany was given 59 years to pay them.

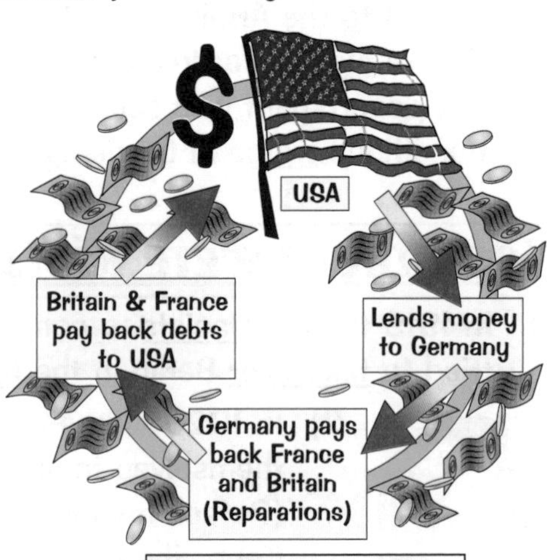

The Dawes Plan

Germany had Begun to Recover — but Depended on US Money

Gustav Stresemann

Life was beginning to look better for Germany thanks to the work of Stresemann. But he died in October 1929, just before the disaster of the Wall Street Crash (see p.14). The plans he had agreed would only work if the USA had enough money to keep lending to Germany — but now it didn't. Things were suddenly going to get worse again.

The Weimar Republic had many Cultural Achievements

1) Germany's capital Berlin became a centre for culture under the Weimar Republic.
2) There were advances in art, architecture, music and literature. German films were successful — e.g. 'Metropolis', directed by Fritz Lang.
3) Some developments were bold and new, like the drama of Bertolt Brecht. The Bauhaus School of design was highly influential.
4) The Weimar Republic encouraged new ways of critical thinking at places like Frankfurt University.
5) Not everyone approved of these cultural changes — the cabaret culture in Berlin was seen as immoral by some. The culture of the Weimar Republic didn't survive under the Nazis...

Stresemann tied Germany's future to the US...

Because it was such a huge economic power, Stresemann believed that by making deals with the US he could make Germany strong again — both the Young and Dawes plans were US led.

The Roots of the Nazi Party

The Nazi Party was a small organisation in the 1920s — but it had big ambitions...

Adolf Hitler was the Nazi Leader

1) Born in Austria in 1889, Hitler had lived in Germany from 1912 onwards.
2) He'd been a brave soldier on the Western Front in World War I, winning the Iron Cross twice. He couldn't accept that Germany had lost the war.
3) In 1919, he joined the German Workers' Party, led by Anton Drexler. It was a tiny party — Hitler was the 55th member. In 1920 the name was changed to the National Socialist German Workers' Party (Nazis).
4) Hitler was a charismatic speaker and attracted new members. He took over the leadership of the party.
5) The party set up its own armed group called the SA — brown-shirted stormtroopers who protected Nazi leaders and harassed their opponents.

Hitler tried to Overthrow the Government in the Munich Putsch

1) In 1923, things were going badly for the Weimar Republic — it seemed weak.
2) Hitler planned to overthrow the Weimar government — starting by taking control of the government in a region called Bavaria.
3) On 8 November Hitler's stormtroopers occupied a beer hall in Munich where local government leaders were meeting. He announced that the revolution had begun.
4) The next day Hitler marched into Munich supported by several thousand armed men. But the revolt quickly collapsed when police fired on the rebels.
5) The number of people involved, including the famous general Ludendorff, made it seem like a big threat to Weimar, but the Nazis had little popular support and it was all over very quickly.

Hitler wrote a Book

1) Hitler was imprisoned for his role in the Munich Putsch.
2) In prison he wrote a book called 'Mein Kampf' ('My Struggle'). Hitler described his beliefs and ambitions.

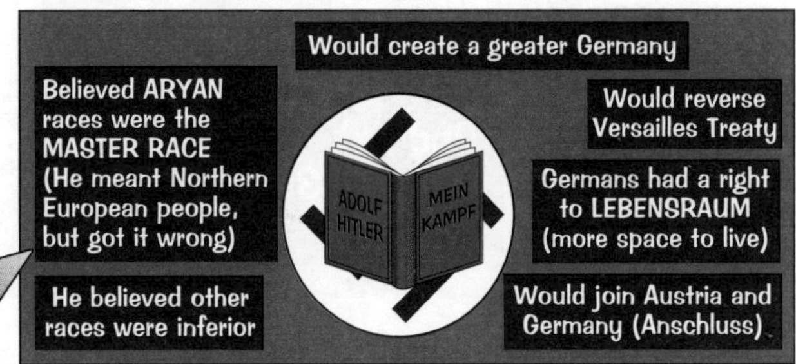

After the Munich Putsch Hitler Changed Tactics

1) The Nazi party was banned after the Munich Putsch. After Hitler was released from prison, he re-established the party with himself as supreme leader.
2) By the mid-1920s, the German economy was starting to recover under Stresemann. As a result, general support for the Nazis declined and overturning the government through a coup no longer seemed realistic.
3) Hitler changed tactics — he now tried to gain control through the democratic system. The Nazi party network was extended nationally, instead of it being a regional party. Propaganda was used to promote the party's beliefs.

The Nazis — ready to sweep to power...

Very few people supported the Nazis at this stage. There were fewer than 30 000 members by 1925, and in the 1928 elections the Nazis had 12 Reichstag members, compared with 54 communists and 153 Social Democrats. All that was about to change though...

The Rise of the Nazis

The popularity of the Nazi Party soared as a result of the Depression.

The Great Depression caused Poverty and Suffering

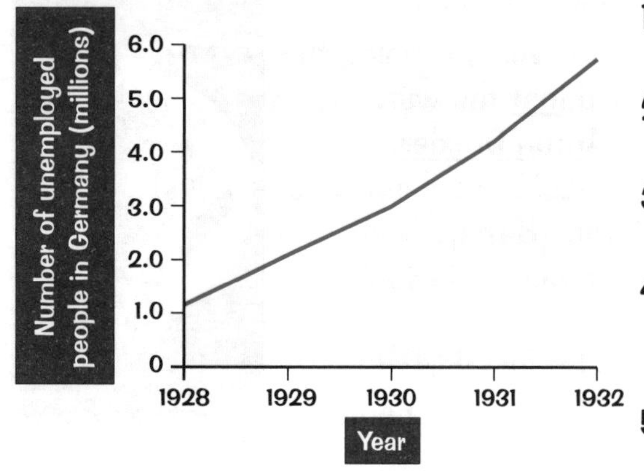

1) The Depression caused massive unemployment in Germany — over 6 million were unemployed by 1933.
2) In 1931, Germany's biggest bank collapsed. This made paying reparations (see p.7) more difficult.
3) Weimar governments kept changing during this time, but none managed to solve the economic problems.
4) The Depression contributed to the collapse of the Weimar Republic. People hoped a new government could sort out the problems.
5) Extremist groups like the Nazis became more popular — they promised strong leadership.

The Nazis increased in Popularity during the Depression

1) The Nazis promised prosperity and to make Germany great again. This appealed to many of the unemployed, as well as to businessmen and young people.
2) Some people supported the Nazis' anti-communist and anti-Jewish views.
3) By 1930 Nazi membership grew to over 300 000.

The Elections of 1930 showed Nazi Gains

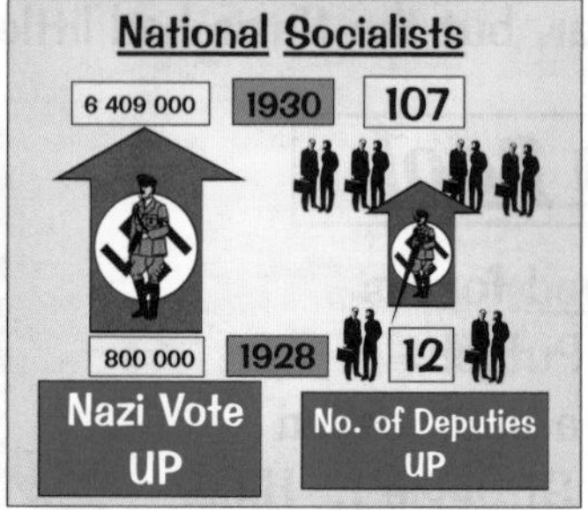

Chancellor Heinrich Brüning couldn't control the Reichstag properly — there was a big increase in seats for both the Nazis (who won 107) and the communists (who won 77). Brüning had to rule by emergency decree as no single party had enough seats to control the Reichstag.

Germany had No Strong Government

1) By April 1932, conditions were serious in Germany. Millions were unemployed, and the country was desperate for a strong government.
2) President Hindenburg had to stand for re-election, because his term of office had run out. Hitler stood against him, and there was also a communist candidate.
3) Hindenburg, a national hero, said he'd win easily but didn't win a majority in the first election — in the second ballot he won 53%, beating Hitler's 36.8% of the vote.

Another depressing page...

In normal circumstances, the Nazis would have stayed a small, extremist group on the fringes of politics. Unfortunately the Depression gave them an opportunity to gain mainstream popularity.

The Rise of the Nazis

The Nazis gained a lot of votes — but they used some underhand tactics to get them...

Hindenburg Refused to give the Nazis Power

1) Hindenburg couldn't find a Chancellor who had support in the Reichstag.
2) He appointed the inexperienced Franz von Papen.
3) In the July 1932 Reichstag elections, the Nazis won 230 seats — they were now the biggest party, but didn't have a majority in the Reichstag. Hitler demanded to be made Chancellor.
4) Hindenburg refused because he didn't trust Hitler and kept Papen.

The Nazis lost seats in the Elections

1) The Nazis lost 34 seats in the November 1932 election — they seemed to be losing popularity.
2) Hindenburg replaced Papen as Chancellor with Kurt von Schleicher. Schleicher tried to cause divisions in the Nazi Party by asking another leading Nazi to be Vice-Chancellor — Gregor Strasser. But Hitler stopped Strasser accepting.
3) Papen knew that Hindenburg would get rid of Schleicher if he failed to get a majority in parliament, so he made a deal with Hitler. They agreed that if Papen persuaded Hindenburg to make Hitler Chancellor, Hitler would make Papen Vice-Chancellor.
4) In January 1933, Papen persuaded Hindenburg to make Hitler Chancellor — Papen argued that they could control Hitler and use him as a puppet. He was wrong.
5) Hitler called another election in March 1933, hoping to make the Nazis stronger in the Reichstag.

The Nazis used Dirty Tricks to Win in 1933

The Nazis did well in the elections because:

1) They controlled the news media.
2) Opposition meetings were banned.
3) They used the SA to terrorise opponents.
4) A fire broke out in the Reichstag building, and Hitler whipped up opposition against the communists, who he said started it. Mass arrests of communists followed.
5) Hitler was allowed emergency decrees to deal with the situation — and used these powers to intimidate communist voters.

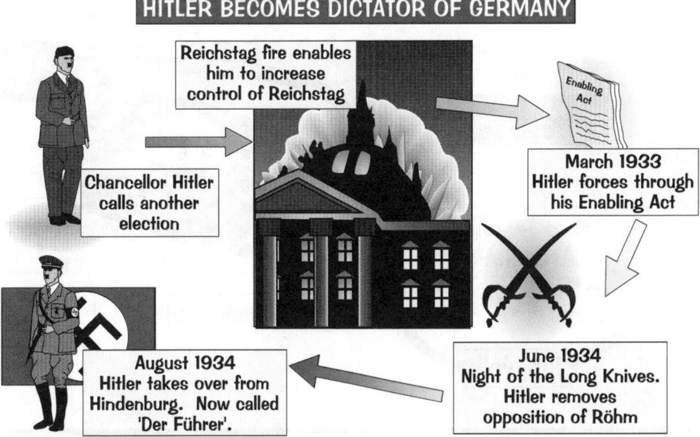

Germany 1930-33 — a state of confusion...

As well as the Depression, the unstable political situation also helped Hitler come to power.

Hitler Comes to Power

Once Hitler was Chancellor he set about strengthening his power...

Hitler Changed the Law to Keep Control

1) The Nazis won 288 seats but no majority — the communists still won 81.
2) So Hitler declared the Communist Party illegal.
3) This gave him enough support in parliament to bring in an Enabling Bill which was passed with threats and bargaining in March 1933.
4) This bill let him govern for four years without parliament and made all other parties illegal. Hitler was almost in full control.

The Night of the Long Knives

1) Hitler still had opposition — and was worried about rivals within the Nazi party.
2) The biggest threat was Ernst Röhm, who controlled the SA (over 400 000 men). On the 29th-30th June 1934, Hitler sent his own men to arrest Röhm and others. This became known as the 'Night of the Long Knives'.
3) Several hundred people were killed, including Röhm, Strasser and von Schleicher. Any potential opposition had been stamped out.
4) A month later Hindenburg died. Hitler combined the posts of Chancellor and President, made himself Commander-in-Chief of the army, and was called Der Führer (the leader). It was the beginning of dictatorship.

Germany was now under Strong Leaders

1) Germany was reorganised into a number of provinces. Each province was called a Gau (plural: Gaue), with a Gauleiter — a loyal Nazi — in charge of each.
2) Above them were the Reichsleiters who advised Hitler, e.g. Goebbels who was in charge of propaganda, and Himmler who was chief of the German police.
3) At the top was the Führer — Hitler himself — who was in absolute control.
4) Every aspect of life was carefully controlled, and only loyal Nazis could be successful.

Joseph Goebbels

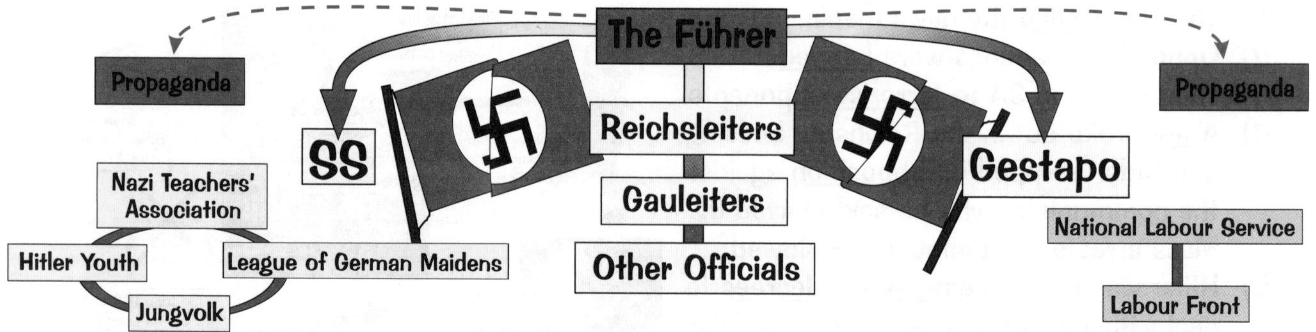

Hitler was obsessed with power...

Once elected the Nazis pretty quickly turned Germany from a democracy into a dictatorship. Hitler set himself up as a supreme ruler — Chancellor, President and army chief combined.

Nazi Methods of Control

The Nazis used many methods to control the German people — from persuasion to violence...

The Nazis used Propaganda

Propaganda means spreading particular ideas and points of view to try to control how people think. Nazi propaganda blamed the Jews and communists for most of Germany's problems.

1) The Nazis took over the media. They controlled radio broadcasts, and also used films and posters to spread their messages.
2) The Ministry of Public Enlightenment and Propaganda (founded in 1933) was led by Dr Joseph Goebbels. All artists, writers, journalists and musicians had to register to get their work approved.
3) The Nazis organised huge rallies of party members to present an image of power and popularity. They also used the 1936 Berlin Olympics as an opportunity for international publicity.

The Nazis used Censorship

1) The Nazis censored books, newspapers and other material.
2) Those who published anti-Nazi material risked execution.
3) The Nazis used censorship to encourage nationalism and anti-Semitism (hatred of Jews). They praised the work of patriotic German composers such as Wagner but banned the work of Jewish composers such as Mendelssohn.

Germany became a Police State

1) The SS (Schutzstaffel) began as a bodyguard for Hitler. It expanded massively under the leadership of Himmler during the 1930s. Its members were totally loyal to Hitler, and were feared for their cruelty. Himmler was also in charge of the secret police — the Gestapo.
2) After 1933 concentration camps spread across Germany and its territories to hold political prisoners and anybody else considered dangerous to the Nazis. Some of these were later turned into death camps (see p.66).
3) Local wardens were employed to make sure Germans were loyal to the Nazis. People were encouraged to report disloyalty. Many were arrested by the Gestapo as a result.

The Nazis saw the Church as a Threat

1) Many Nazis were against Christianity — its teaching of peace was seen as incompatible with Nazi ideas. However, the Nazis didn't want to risk an immediate attack on it.
2) Hitler signed the Concordat (an agreement) with the Catholic Church in 1933. Each side promised not to interfere with the other. However the Nazis did try to curb the influence of the church — and there were some Catholic protests against Nazi policies.
3) Hitler tried to unite the different Protestant churches into one Reich Church. He placed the Nazi Bishop Ludwig Müller at its head. Some church members split off in protest at this state interference. They formed the Confessing Church (see p.65).
4) Many clergy who stood up to the Nazi regime were sent to concentration camps.

This book wouldn't be available in Nazi Germany...

Imagine if the radio and newspapers all covered the same news in the same way, and featured all the same opinions. You might start to think that way after a while.

German Growth Under the Nazis

The Nazis took strict control of the economy.

Hitler gave Work to 6 Million Unemployed

1) Hitler started a huge programme of public works, which gave jobs to thousands of people.
2) From 1933, huge motorways — Autobahns — were started. Unemployment fell dramatically.
3) But — the Nazis also fiddled with the statistics to make unemployment look lower than it really was. E.g. they didn't count women or Jewish people in the unemployment statistics — this is called "invisible unemployment".

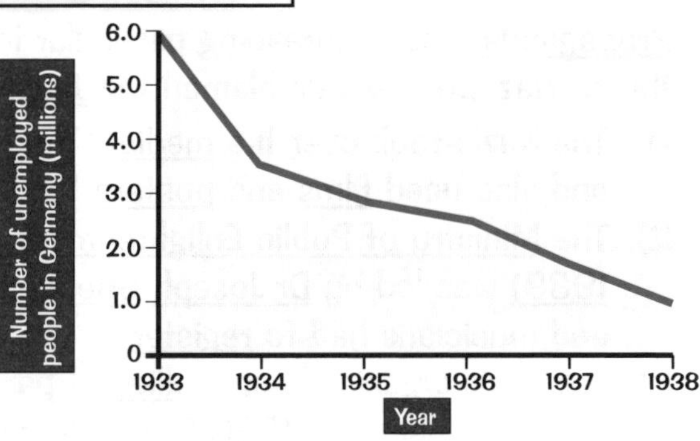

People were Encouraged to Work by Rewards

1) All men between 18 and 25 could be recruited into the National Labour Service and given jobs.
2) The Nazis got rid of trade unions. Instead workers had to join the Nazi's Labour Front.
3) The Nazis introduced 'Strength through Joy' — a scheme which provided workers with cheap holidays and leisure activities. Another scheme, 'Beauty of Labour', encouraged factory owners to improve conditions for their workers.
4) Output increased in Germany, and unemployment was almost ended completely. The Nazis introduced the Volkswagen (the people's car) as an ambition for people to aim for.
5) Wages were still relatively low though — and workers weren't allowed to go on strike or campaign for better conditions.

Hitler Re-armed the German Military

1) Another way to create work was to build up the armed forces. The Nazis did this secretly at first, because the Treaty of Versailles had banned it.
2) Hitler sacked some of the generals, and replaced them with Nazi supporters. Goering was put in charge of the newly-formed Luftwaffe (airforce), which had been banned at Versailles.
3) In 1935, military conscription was reintroduced (drafting men into the army).
4) In 1936, the Nazis introduced a Four-Year Plan to prepare the country for war (see p.67 for more). Industrial production increased — many workers had to retrain in jobs that would help the war effort. The plan was to make Germany self-sufficient, so it wasn't reliant on foreign goods.

Hitler reduced unemployment — and gained popularity...

Hitler provided new jobs and helped Germany recover from the Depression (see p.58). But remember that a lot of the Nazis' economic success was down to the exclusion of women and Jews from the official statistics. Their policies weren't quite as miraculous as they claimed...

Young People and Women

The Nazis believed that to control the future they had to influence children and their mothers.

The Nazis created powerful Youth Groups

1) Hitler knew that loyalty from young people was essential if the Nazis were to remain strong.
2) Boys aged fourteen upwards were recruited to the Hitler Youth, which was compulsory from 1939. Girls aged from fourteen joined the League of German Maidens.
3) Boys wore military-style uniforms, and took part in lots of physical exercise. Girls were mainly trained in domestic skills like sewing.
4) The boys were being prepared to be soldiers, the girls to be wives and mothers.

The Nazis took over Education

1) Schools started teaching Nazi propaganda. Jews were banned from teaching in schools and universities. Most teachers joined the Nazi Teachers' Association and were trained in Nazi methods. Children had to report teachers who did not use them.
2) Subjects like history and biology were rewritten to fit in with Nazi ideas. Children were taught to be anti-Semitic and that World War I was lost because of Jews and communists.
3) Physical education became more important for boys, who sometimes played war games with live ammunition.
4) In universities students burned anti-Nazi and Jewish books, and Jewish lecturers were sacked.

Women were expected to raise Large Families

1) Nazis didn't want women to have too much freedom. They believed the role of women was to support their families at home. Women existed to provide children.
2) The League of German Maidens spread the Nazi idea that it was an honour to produce large families for Germany. Nazis gave awards to women for doing this.
3) At school, girls studied subjects like cookery. It was stressed that they should choose 'Aryan' husbands.
4) Women were banned from being lawyers in 1936 and the Nazis did their best to stop them following other professions. The shortage of workers after 1937 meant more women had to go back to work. Many Nazi men did not like this.

Eight Main Reasons for Hitler's Popularity

It's hard to imagine now, but the Nazis were genuinely popular with many Germans at the time.

1) He gave the Germans jobs after the struggles and unemployment of the 1920s.
2) The people were taught the Nazi way from an early age.
3) He made them proud internationally — Germans had felt humiliated for a long time.
4) People felt much better off as industry expanded.
5) Massive rallies every year gave the impression of a strong, prosperous nation.
6) The army supported his aim to make Germany strong again.
7) Businesses liked the prosperity and the way Hitler attacked the communists.
8) People were frightened to protest against Nazi methods — they knew they'd be arrested.

Hitler Youth — not like your local youth club, then...

Although the Nazis were destroyed in 1945, they expected to be in power a lot, lot longer. That's why they spent so much time and effort on the young — creating Nazis for the future.

Opposition to the Nazis

The Nazis had a tight grip on Germany, but some opposition remained.

Some young people joined the White Rose group

1) The White Rose group was an opposition movement led by students from Munich University between 1942 and 1943. Among the leaders were brother and sister Hans and Sophie Scholl.
2) The group protested against the Nazi discrimination of minorities (see p.66).
3) Some male members of the group had served in the army and had been horrified by the atrocities carried out by the German army, including the mass killing of Jews.
4) They used non-violent methods and distributed anti-Nazi leaflets to encourage opposition.
5) The group were caught and arrested by the Gestapo and several members, including Hans and Sophie Scholl, were tortured and executed.

The Edelweiss Pirates were Difficult to control

1) The Edelweiss Pirates was the name given to groups of rebellious young people which had sprung up across Germany during the 1930s. Groups in different towns each had their own names, including the Navajos and the Roving Dudes.
2) They rejected Nazi values and didn't like being told what to do. They avoided joining the Hitler Youth and some members deliberately got into fights with the Hitler Youth.
3) They were difficult to control because they weren't a single organisation with clear leaders.
4) At first the Nazis mostly ignored them as they had no real political agenda.
5) However, during the 1940s, they started distributing anti-Nazi leaflets. They also helped army deserters, forced labourers and escaped concentration camp prisoners.
6) The Nazis eventually cracked down on the groups. Many were arrested. In 1944, several members of the Edelweiss Pirates in Cologne were publicly hanged.

Members of the Kreisau Circle were Against Violence

1) The Kreisau Circle was an anti-Nazi movement led by Helmuth von Moltke and Yorck von Wartenburg. It was made up of churchmen, scholars and politicians.
2) The group was against violence, so they didn't actively resist the Nazis. Instead they discussed how to make Germany a better country after the Nazis had fallen.
3) Some members of the Circle tried to inform Allied governments about the dangers and weaknesses of Nazi control.
4) In 1944, members of the Kreisau Circle, including Moltke, were arrested and executed.

The Stauffenberg Bomb Plot was an attempt to Kill Hitler

1) By 1944, some German military officers were unhappy with Hitler's leadership — they believed he was going to lead Germany to defeat.
2) Claus von Stauffenberg, along with other German officers, planned to kill Hitler. They wanted to install a moderate government, including members of the Kreisau Circle.
3) On 20 July 1944, Stauffenberg put a bomb in a briefcase and left it in a meeting room by Hitler's chair. However, someone moved the briefcase. Although the bomb exploded, Hitler was unhurt.
4) Most of the plotters, including Stauffenberg, were quickly captured and executed.

Anyone would think Hitler wasn't very popular...

There were plenty of people who weren't keen on Hitler and his policies. Some of them protested peacefully, but others were more violent. Learn all these major movements against Hitler.

Persecution

The Holocaust was the persecution and mass murder of Jewish people by the Nazis.

Hitler believed Aryans were a Super-Race

1) The Nazis believed Aryans (white northern Europeans) were the 'master race' and other ethnicities, like Jewish, Romani ('gypsies') or Slavic people (Russians and Poles), were inferior.
2) The Nazis blamed Jewish people for problems in German society.
3) The Nazis wanted a German population of only 'pure' Aryan people who fitted their ideal. They wanted to eliminate people who were disabled, homosexual, held different beliefs, or weren't 'Aryan'.
4) Hitler was angry when an African-American called Jesse Owens took four gold medals at the 1936 Berlin Olympics, and when the German World Heavyweight Boxing Champion Max Schmeling was beaten by another African American, Joe Louis.

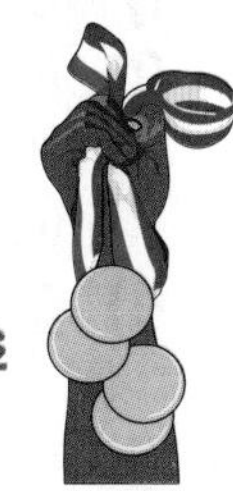

In 1935 the Nazis Passed the Nuremberg Laws

1) These laws stopped Jews being German citizens.
2) They banned marriage between Jews and non-Jews in Germany.
3) They also banned sexual relationships between Jews and non-Jews.
4) These laws were later extended to cover both Romani and black people.

Kristallnacht 1938 — The Night of the Broken Glass

1) A Jew murdered a German diplomat in Paris in November 1938.
2) There was rioting throughout Germany — thousands of Jewish shops were smashed, and thousands of Jews were arrested.
3) Nazi propaganda made people believe that the Jews were bad for Germany, so they should be sent to special concentration camps, or humiliated and maltreated in public.
4) Many people believed the camps were work-camps, where the Jews would work for Germany. Later, Nazi policy became more terrible as they tried to exterminate the Jewish race.

Communists and some Religious Groups were Persecuted

1) Once in power, the Nazis banned communist groups and sent many communists to concentration camps.
2) Some opposition came from religious groups, especially after church land was confiscated.
3) Jehovah's Witnesses were persecuted for not supporting the regime, with many members sent to the concentration camps.
4) Some opponents of the Reich Church joined together as the Confessing Church. Hundreds of clergy were arrested, including Martin Niemöller, one of the Confessing Church's founders.
5) Catholic dissent was more widespread after 1937, when Pope Pius XI sent out a letter protesting at German nationalism and racism, which was read out in Catholic churches.
6) Catholic protesters had some success in reducing Nazi interference with the Church.

Nazi Germany — a climate of cruelty and fear...

The Nazis ruthlessly persecuted their enemies — first the communists and then the Jews and other minorities (see next page). Most people were too scared to stand in their way...

Persecution

The persecution and mass murder of Jewish people by the Nazis is known as the Holocaust.

There was little German Opposition to the persecution

It's hard to understand why so few people protested. Here are some possible reasons:

1) Everybody was scared of the SS and the Gestapo.
2) People were better off after years of hardship, and chose to ignore what they didn't like.
3) Goebbels' propaganda was so effective that people didn't get the whole story about what was really going on — but believed the Nazi government knew best.
4) Opponents, like the communists, had been eliminated.

Jewish people were Moved to Ghettos

1) After the invasions of Poland and Russia more Jews came under Nazi control.
2) From 1940, Jewish people were forced to move into ghettos — separate districts of cities which were usually walled in and policed by armed guards. The largest was in Warsaw.
3) Conditions in the ghettos were terrible. Starvation and disease killed thousands. A rebellion in the Warsaw ghetto in 1943 was ruthlessly put down.
4) When Russia was invaded in 1941, soldiers followed with orders to kill every Jew they came across in the occupied towns and villages.

Other Minority Groups were also Persecuted

1) Romani (gypsies), black people and Slavic people (Russians and Poles) were also seen as racially 'impure'. Some were forcibly sterilised. Eventually, people from these groups were sent to concentration camps.
2) Homosexual people were sent to concentration camps in their thousands. In 1936, Himmler, Head of the SS, began the Central Office for the Combating of Homosexuality and Abortion.
3) In the early 1930s the Nazis began to sterilise disabled people (preventing them from having children). By the late 1930s they had also begun a 'Euthanasia Programme' — killing people suffering from mental or physical disabilities.

The Nazis began the Final Solution in 1942

1) The Final Solution was the Nazis' plan to destroy the Jewish people.
2) Death camps were built in Eastern Europe. Gas chambers were built for mass murder.
3) Mainly Jewish people were killed, but other groups were targeted as well, for example Slavs, Romani people, black people, homosexuals, disabled people and communists.
4) Heinrich Himmler, head of the SS, was in overall charge of this 'final solution'.
5) Some death camps were: Auschwitz, Treblinka, Sobibor, Chelmno, Belzec.
6) By the end of the war, approximately 6 million Jewish people had been killed by the Nazis. The Nazis were also responsible for the deaths of over 200 000 Romani people and around 200 000 mentally and physically disabled people.

Nazi racial policy ended in mass murder...

The Jewish people suffered terribly at the hands of the Nazis. Although most victims of the concentration camps were Jewish, remember that other groups were also persecuted.

Impacts of the Second World War

The Second World War had a big impact on German society.

The War forced Changes in the German Economy

1) In 1936, Goering introduced a Four-Year Plan to prepare the German economy for war.
2) The Nazis built up industries like weapons and chemicals at the expense of domestic goods.
3) By the outbreak of war, a quarter of the work force was working in war industries, especially weapons. Two years later, this had become three-quarters. Unemployment fell.
4) During the war, working hours increased to over 50 hours a week, and wages were lower than they had been under the Weimar Republic. Despite this, the German industry was not producing enough, and there were not enough workers.
5) Industry suffered as a result of the bombings. Industrial plants were bombed, particularly in the Ruhr, meaning factories had to be rebuilt.
6) In 1943, Albert Speer was appointed Minister for Armaments and Production. He reorganised industry and rapidly increased production, but the German industry still couldn't produce enough.
7) A lot of working age Germans were conscripted into the army, so the Nazis used foreign workers to help keep the economy going. By 1944, around 20% of the workforce were foreigners — either civilians from occupied territories or prisoners of war.
8) At the start of the war, the Nazis had encouraged women not to work. However, by 1944 about 50% of the workforce were women.

The War Affected German Civilians

Bombings killed many civilians

1) From 1942, the Allies began to bomb German cities more heavily. Around half a million German civilians were killed, and many more were made homeless.
2) The bombing was often relentless — the US bombed by day and Britain bombed by night.
3) The German cities of Dresden, Berlin and Hamburg were all badly affected by bombing.

Rationing affected quality of life

1) Food and clothes rationing began in 1939, but while Germany was winning the war, most goods could still be acquired easily.
2) By 1942, German civilians were living off much less than British civilians. Civilians lived off rations of bread, vegetables and potatoes — these rations decreased as the war progressed.
3) It became nearly impossible to buy new clothes or shoes.

Propaganda encouraged loyalty to the Nazis

1) Nazi news media only reported wartime successes. This made the Nazis appear strong, but the public were misinformed.
2) Nazi propaganda warned Germans against non-Nazi groups, such as the Bolsheviks. Some people supported the Nazis because they were made to fear the alternatives.
3) In the last days of the war, Nazi propaganda encouraged members of the Nazi party, boys and old men to defend Berlin from the Russians to the last man.

The Second World War was tough on everyone...

There were very few people who were left unaffected by the War. War dominated daily life.

Revision Summary

Phew — it's question time again. Now's your chance to show off what you've learned — and to find out what you still need to practise. Germany between the wars is a tricky subject — make sure you know about the long-term consequences of the Versailles Treaty, and the reasons for the weakness of the Weimar government. Most difficult of all, you've got to be able to give clear arguments for why Hitler was able to come to power. Remember — it doesn't matter if you can't answer all the questions first time. Go over the section again and keep trying, until you can answer every one first time. And there's no point in cheating by looking back — that won't help you in the exams. So let's get going.

1) What was the name of the first President of the Weimar Republic? Which party did he belong to?
2) What was the name of the parliament in the Weimar Republic?
3) Name the force which was started to keep the peace in Germany.
4) Give three reasons for discontent in Germany after World War I.
5) Where did the Spartacist Revolt and the Kapp Putsch take place?
6) Give the main results of the French occupation of the Ruhr in 1923.
7) Write a paragraph outlining the work of Gustav Stresemann.
8) Which party was responsible for the Munich Putsch? Who was its leader?
9) What was the title of the book Hitler wrote in prison?
10) Who beat Hitler in the Presidential elections of April 1932?
11) How did Hitler use the Reichstag Fire?
12) What did Hitler's Enabling Bill allow him to do in March 1933?
13) What was the Night of the Long Knives?
14) What title did Hitler give himself on the death of Hindenburg in 1934?
15) Which Nazi was put in charge of propaganda? Write about some of the methods he used.
16) What was the SS? What was the Gestapo?
17) Give an achievement of the Nazi programme of public works.
18) What was the 'Strength through Joy' programme? What organisation did workers have to join instead of trade unions?
19) Name the leading Nazi who was put in charge of the Luftwaffe.
20) In what ways did the Nazis make sure that young people followed their cause?
21) Which organisation did teachers in Nazi Germany have to join?
22) Give eight reasons why the German people followed the Nazis.
23) Name two groups who opposed the Nazis.
24) Describe the Stauffenberg bomb plot.
25) What were the Nuremberg Laws? What did they do?
26) Describe what happened on the 'Night of Broken Glass'.
27) What was the name of the church set up by Protestants who opposed the Reich Church?
28) Give two reasons why opposition was weak under the Nazis.
29) Name four groups of people who were persecuted under the Nazis.
30) Describe a problem faced by the German economy during the Second World War.
31) When was rationing introduced in Germany?

The USA's Reaction to World War One

After the First World War (1914-1918), the USA chose not to get involved in international affairs. This policy was known as isolationism.

The League was the idea of the American President

Woodrow Wilson

1) The League of Nations was largely the idea of the American president Woodrow Wilson. It was one of his Fourteen Points (see p.6) — fourteen principles on which he thought a peace settlement could be based.
2) He thought a League of Nations could act like a world parliament where the representatives of all the major powers would meet to discuss matters of international importance.
3) He was sure that such an organisation could prevent another world war.

But America Never Joined the League of Nations

1) A League of Nations was set up following the end of the First World War, as part of the Treaty of Versailles.
2) Wilson wanted the USA to join the League of Nations, but he needed the approval of the US Congress.
3) The problem was that most Americans didn't want to join.
4) The majority of the American people favoured 'isolationism' — they wanted the USA to remain isolated from foreign entanglements.

Americans Didn't Trust the League of Nations

1) Many Americans had been against the USA getting involved in the First World War and were upset by the loss of American lives.
2) They were worried that if America joined the League of Nations they would be obliged to interfere in conflicts that most Americans thought were none of their business.

3) The USA had a lot of citizens who were German or Austrian immigrants. These people saw the League as linked to the hated Treaty of Versailles (see p.7). They were opposed to the USA joining an organisation that was forcing Germany to pay vast amounts in reparations (damages for the war).
4) Some Americans were suspicious of the French and the British. They were sure that the League would come under British and French control and that America would be called upon to help these countries defend their colonies. Many Americans felt that colonies didn't fit in with their ideas about freedom and democracy and should not be supported.
5) Other Americans were concerned that joining the League of Nations could cost them money. They were worried that the League would drag America into lots of expensive wars. Many businessmen contended that the US had grown prosperous by staying out of European affairs and that it should remain isolated from Europe.

The USA thought it was better off alone...

Perhaps it was a bit selfish of the USA to reject the League of Nations, but they probably did save themselves a lot of trouble and expense, at least in the short term. Make sure you learn all the reasons for their decision not to join.

Growth of Isolationism

America just wanted to be alone.

The USA Entered Late and Gained From World War One

1) The American economy boomed as a result of the First World War.
2) The USA exported weapons and food to Europe during the war.
3) The USA joined the Allied side in 1917 — but no fighting happened on American soil.
4) After the war, European countries whose industries had been damaged bought American goods with the help of American loans.

Cheap European Imports were seen as a Threat

1) American businesses were afraid that the USA would be flooded with cheap European imports.
2) Unemployment was higher in Europe so European workers were willing to work for lower wages. Businessmen were worried American consumers would start buying European products rather than the more expensive American ones.

   This would mean:
   - The loss of American jobs.
   - Lower profits for US companies.
   - Less money in taxes for the US government.

Warren G Harding raised tariffs to protect US Industry

President Harding

1) Harding was elected President in 1921. He brought in the Emergency Tariff Act of May 1921. A tariff is a tax on imported and exported goods. The act increased the tariff rates on imported farm products.
2) In 1922, the Fordney-McCumber Tariff gave the President the power to raise and lower the tariff rates.
3) Harding used the Fordney-McCumber Tariff to raise duties on both factory and farm goods.
4) He hoped to protect America from "unfair" European competition.

Immigration Control was increased

Before the First World War, America had followed an 'Open Doors' policy that allowed almost anybody to move to the USA. But some Americans started demanding that this 'door' be closed. The most powerful and wealthy cultural group in America at this time were people with mainly British ancestors — later known as the White Anglo-Saxon Protestants (WASPs).

1) Many WASPs believed that people such as anarchists and communists were coming into the USA and undermining the American way of life.
2) They were also alarmed at the number of Asian, Catholic and Jewish people who were entering the USA.

The WASPs had great influence in Congress (the American parliament).
As a consequence President Harding decided to place strict limitations on immigration, especially from Eastern and Southern Europe.
In 1921, Congress passed an act which introduced a quota system.
Annual immigration was reduced from over one million to about 150 000 in 1929.

Isolationism — it's tariffic...

After the First World War, Europe had lots of problems, while America had relatively few.
By limiting imports and reducing immigration, the US sought to secure its peace and prosperity.

Prosperity in the 1920s

The 1920s were a time of huge economic growth in the US.

The 1920s were a Time of Plenty

This decade was a 'boom time' for many — incomes rose and standards of living improved.

1) There was low inflation, low unemployment and low interest rates.
2) Cities were rebuilt with tall skyscrapers, and major road building programmes were undertaken.
3) There was a consumer boom. More people could now afford items such as radios, refrigerators, washing machines, vacuum cleaners and telephones.
4) Advertising encouraged more spending and became a big business in itself, expanding into radio and film commercials.
5) Hire purchase (buying in instalments) was introduced to make cars affordable to average earners who could only buy them on credit. It encouraged more spending on luxury goods.

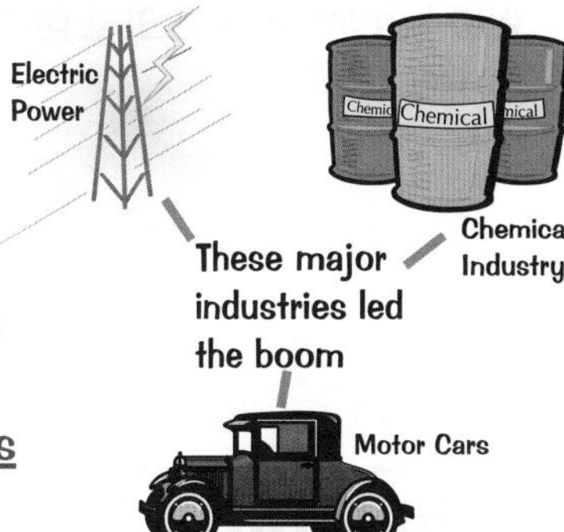

6) Republican government policy contributed to prosperity. The reduction of income tax left people with more money to spend. The government also promoted cheap credit through the Federal Reserve Board (central banking system). They encouraged banks to lend money on easier terms, which (in the short term) contributed to the boom.

The Stock Market boomed

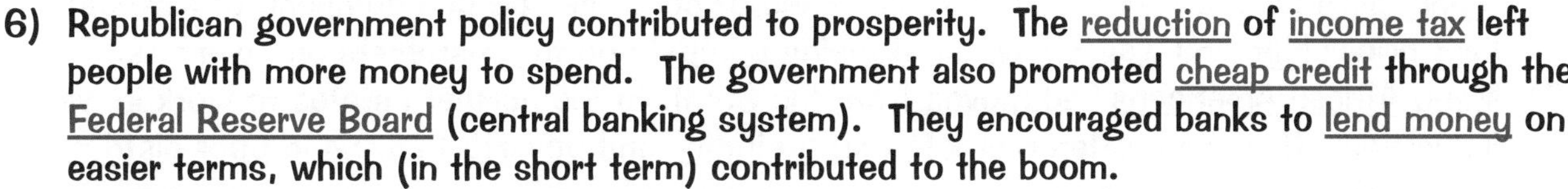

1.5 million Americans bought shares in the 1920s. Before the price of shares began to rocket unrealistically in 1928, there were sensible reasons for buying them — people were investing in a real boom in production and consumption. It only started to go bad when people took to buying shares on credit in the hope of selling them at a profit (see p.76).

The Motor Industry led the way

1) The jobs of 1 in 12 workers were linked to motor car production.
2) Car production boosted other industries — steel, petrol, chemicals, glass and rubber.
3) Cars became more affordable — the Model T Ford cost less than $300.
4) Production of cars became dominated by the big three companies — Ford, Chrysler and General Motors.
5) Ford's factory used an assembly line system. It divided manufacturing tasks among a group of workers spaced alongside a moving belt. It made production far more efficient, which allowed for a huge reduction in price. By 1929, there was one car for every five Americans.

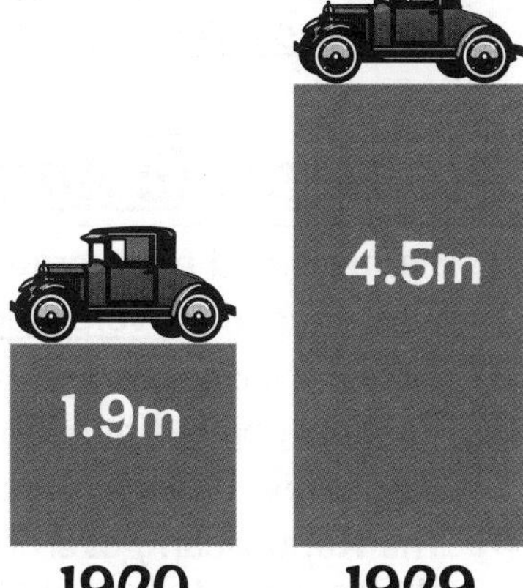

Annual car production

Boom in the US — revise this and prosper...

This page is really important. It shows you how the American economy really took off in the 1920s. Make sure you learn some of these statistics — they'll impress the examiners.

Poverty in the 1920s

While there was a boom for many Americans, for others life remained a struggle.

There was still Poverty

Wealth wasn't distributed evenly — there was a big gap between rich and poor in the USA.

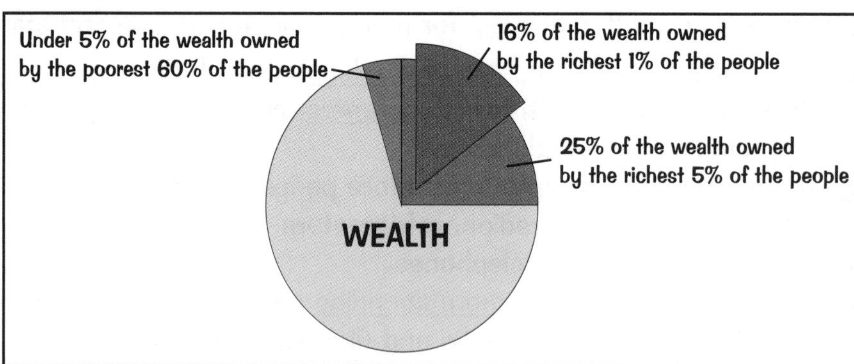

Some poverty was in Urban Areas

1) Monopolies (where a whole industry is owned or controlled by one company or alliance) kept prices high and wages low, by stopping competition for customers and workers.
2) Many African Americans had moved from the South to the northern states to work in war industries. They were often restricted by prejudice and poverty to living in poor districts.
3) Some urban poverty was produced by the pressure of numbers — many people moved to cities because of rural hardship.

"Old" industries Suffered

1) The coal industry did badly. Coal mining suffered from competition with oil. Cars and trucks began to take over from the railways, which were a major user of coal.
2) About 10% less coal was mined in 1929 than in 1919. More efficient mining technology also caused workers to be laid off, and those that remained saw their wages decrease. The mining towns suffered acute hardship.
3) In 1920 the wartime cotton boom collapsed. In 1921 the boll weevil — a beetle that feeds off cotton plants — destroyed 30% of the crop. In the mid 1920s the opposite problem, overproduction, caused prices to plunge.

Problems in Agriculture led to Rural Poverty

1) Farmers had prospered during the war. But during the 1920s, they grew more food than was needed. Overproduction led to falling prices and so to falling profits.
2) Taxes, mortgages and wages were rising, further reducing farmers' profits.
3) Foreign competition increased during the 1920s. European agriculture recovered from the war, while Canada, Russia, Argentina and Australia also competed on the world market.
4) The Republican government didn't believe in direct help to farmers. When Congress passed the McNary-Haugen bill, to allow the government to buy up farmers' crops, President Coolidge vetoed it twice — he thought it would encourage more overproduction.
5) For the first time ever, the American farm population began to shrink.

The Jazz Age wasn't all Bentleys and champagne...

There are always winners and losers — the 1920s were no different. It's important to remember that some people struggled through what are often thought of as the 'good times'.

Intolerance in the 1920s

Some groups in 1920s America suffered discrimination and persecution.

Prejudice against Immigrants led to the Red Scare

1) There was prejudice against newer immigrant groups and worries about communist agitators entering the country. In 1919 the authorities used a series of bombings across the country to whip up a 'Red Scare'. They deported over 4000 people, mainly Russians.
2) During the Red Scare, two Italian anarchists called Nicola Sacco and Bartolomeo Vanzetti were convicted of murder and robbery. There were protests by people who argued it was a miscarriage of justice, and that the judge was prejudiced. But they were executed in 1927.

- From 1917 immigrants had to pass a 'literacy test' to enter.
- A quota system was introduced in 1921. This was replaced in 1924 by the National Origins Act which strictly limited immigration. This act discriminated against immigrants from Southern and Eastern Europe, and Asia.

The racist Ku Klux Klan (KKK) Expanded

1) First formed in the 1860s, the Ku Klux Klan gained new popularity in the early 1920s.
2) The KKK was a white supremacist organisation based in the Southern states of the USA.
3) They opposed African Americans being given more rights. They were also prejudiced against immigrants, Jewish people and Catholics. They used intimidation and violence.
4) KKK membership had grown to around 4 million by 1925.
5) In 1925, there was a scandal involving Indiana KKK leader D.C. Stephenson (he was convicted of kidnapping and second degree murder). The organisation lost much support, and never regained such significant cultural and political power.

Some Laws were Racist

1) The 'Jim Crow Laws' was a collective name for laws that discriminated against African Americans. These were more common in the Southern states of the USA.

DRINKING FOUNTAIN
WHITE ONLY

2) Some laws made it difficult for African Americans to vote. For example, it was law in some states that voters had to show that their grandfathers had voted — this excluded many African Americans whose ancestors were slaves with no voting rights (slavery was only abolished in America in 1865).
3) Some laws forced white and African American people to use separate facilities, e.g. different schools, transport, parks, cafes and theatres. This was called segregation. Although the facilities were supposed to be "separate but equal", the ones provided for African Americans were usually much worse.

There was Prejudice against some Scientific Ideas

1) In 1925, a teacher called John Scopes was arrested for teaching Darwin's theory of evolution — which was against Tennessee state law.
2) He'd deliberately chosen to take a stand against the law.
3) The 'Monkey Trial' became headline news. On appeal, Scopes's defence argued the law broke US Constitutional Amendments on free speech and separation of church and state.
4) Scopes was found guilty — but his lawyers had succeeded in making the law look very foolish.

There was an ugly, violent side to American society...

Remember — there were many groups who were discriminated against in 1920s USA.

Prohibition and Organised Crime

In January 1920 it became illegal to manufacture, distribute or sell alcohol. This was Prohibition.

In 1920 America tried to turn Teetotal

1) Pressure for Prohibition had built up over a long time. Some states were "dry" by 1917.
2) Temperance movements had been campaigning for Prohibition since the 19th century — they were popular in rural areas, and were often Christian. They claimed alcohol led to violence, immoral behaviour, and the breakdown of family life.
3) The middle class often blamed alcohol for disorder among immigrants and the working class. Businessmen blamed alcohol for making workers unreliable.
4) The First World War (which the USA joined in 1917) resulted in more support for Prohibition. Many breweries were owned by German immigrants — and the USA was fighting Germany.
5) Opposition to Prohibition was mainly in urban areas — especially cities in the northern states.

Saloons were closed down. Buying alcohol illegally was expensive, which caused consumption to decrease — especially among the poor. The US authorities recruited over 1500 agents (later increased to 2800+) to enforce the law.

Organised Crime 'took over' the distribution of alcohol

1) Millions of dollars were made trading in illegal alcohol. Prohibition saw a massive rise in organised crime and gangsterism as rival gangs fought for control of the business.

Prohibition Crime

Hijackers: Stole smuggled alcohol

Rum-runners: Smuggled alcohol from Europe, the West Indies, Canada and Mexico

Moonshiners: Made their own liquor

Speakeasies: Illegal drinking clubs sprang up with secret passwords at the door

Bootleggers: Sold on redistilled industrial alcohol

2) In Chicago 1926-29, gang warfare led to 1300 murders. Al Capone was a gang leader:

Al Capone worked for Johnny Torrio, a leading Chicago gangster.

→ Taking over from Torrio in 1925, the ruthless Capone was making \$60m a year from alcohol and \$45m from gambling, dance halls and race tracks.

→ He used a private army to intimidate voters and fight rival gangs. In 1929, 7 members of a rival gang were machine-gunned in the St Valentine's Day Massacre.

→ Capone was sentenced to 11 years in prison for tax evasion in 1931. In poor health, he retired to his Florida mansion and died in 1947.

Prohibition finally ended in 1933

1) Enforcing Prohibition proved impossible because there was still a public demand for alcohol.
2) Prohibition led to corruption — judges and policemen took bribes from gangsters. Some policemen even got involved in bootlegging themselves. In 1930, George Cassiday, a bootlegger, revealed that he'd sold alcohol to most of Congress (the US parliament).
3) In his 1932 presidential campaign, Roosevelt (see p.78) promised to repeal Prohibition. Congress repealed Prohibition in December 1933.

Prohibition — a tee-total disaster...

When prohibition began, criminals quickly got involved — there was big money to be made.

Social Developments

American society underwent big changes in the 1920s.

Many people had More Money to spend on Leisure

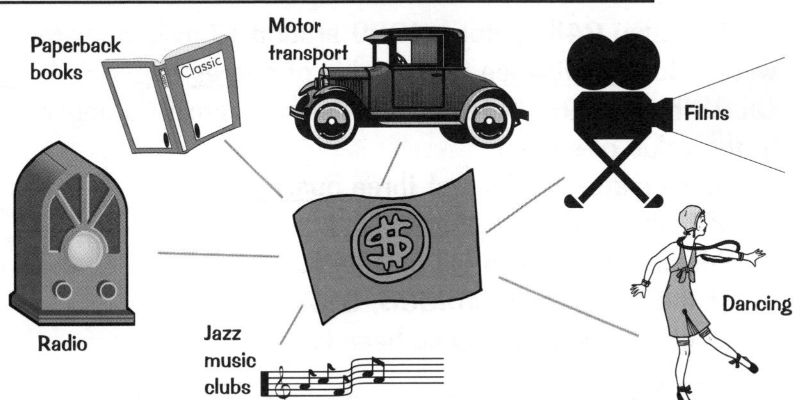

1) Film became the essential mass entertainment — and a multi-million dollar industry. Huge cinemas were built which could seat up to 4000 people. Films were silent until 1927, when the first "talking" picture was released. Hollywood was the major film-making centre.
2) Radio also boomed. In 1921 there was just one licensed station. Two years later there were 508. Millions of sets were sold. By 1929, $850m was spent on sets and parts every year. The NBC (National Broadcasting Company) was set up in 1926. By 1929 it had made $150m from advertising.

There were changing Manners and Morals

1) Young people enjoyed smoking, dancing and cocktail parties. Some women started to wear lipstick, shorter skirts and high heels (these women were called flappers).
2) Church attendance fell and the divorce rate increased.
3) But many people felt that permissiveness and sexual freedom had gone too far.

Women gained more Freedom and Independence

1) Films, popular songs and paperbacks encouraged new fashions and freedom.
2) Some feminists encouraged liberation, but had only limited success.
3) Women were encouraged to gain economic independence — some learned a trade or trained as typists or secretaries. New office jobs provided employment for many women.
4) Household gadgets gave some relief from domestic drudgery.
5) Rising high school and college attendance meant women were better educated than before.

But Traditional Views continued

1) Some books and magazines tried to set 'decent' standards.
2) Women were still expected to be homemakers.
3) In employment there was continuing discrimination against women.
4) The vast majority of working class women continued in low skilled, low paid jobs.
5) Traditional male values continued to emphasise the superiority of men in the 'public sphere'.

Sport also became a huge part of US life in the 1920s...

The 1920s were when sports became a big part of American life — millions watched baseball every year, making stars of players such as Babe Ruth. Another big-hitter was boxer Jack Dempsey, whose fights drew a live audience of tens of thousands, with millions tuning in on the radio.

The Wall Street Crash

Wall Street is the major financial centre in New York. Stocks and shares are bought and sold there.

On Black Thursday share prices Plummeted

On Thursday 24th October 1929 around 13 million shares were sold. Confidence in the value of shares began to be lost. On 28th and 29th October, a series of sharp falls began in the value of shares.

- Some major stocks lost three quarters of their value.
- Prices continued to fall for years.
- At the lowest point in 1933, 83% of the stock market's value had been lost.

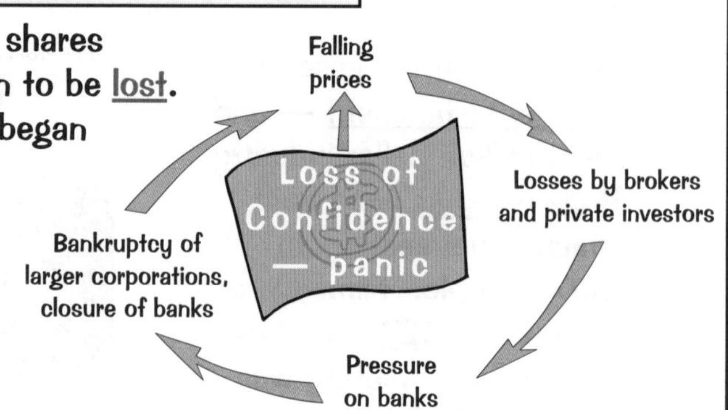

Efforts to Shore Up prices Failed

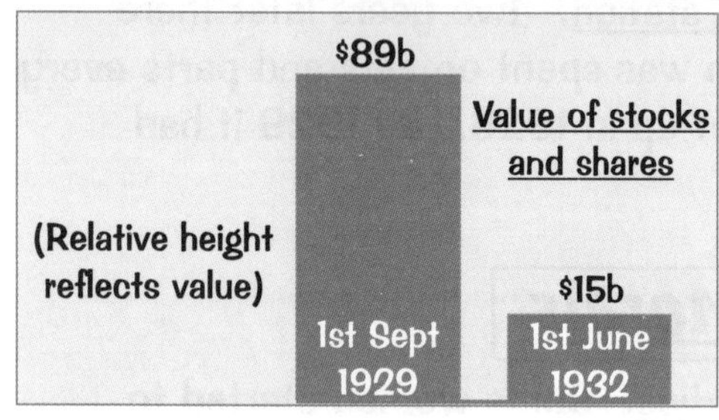

Most early losers were large-scale speculators. Leading financiers met to pool $240m. They used this to buy shares in an attempt to restore confidence and stop panic.

They failed — panic selling led to further falls.

- Investment trusts were unable to meet their obligations.
- Defaulting on debts led to other investors going bankrupt.
- People rushed to withdraw their savings from banks, causing many banks to go bust.

Underlying Economic Problems contributed to the Crash

Though the 1920s had been a 'boom time' for many, there were serious problems with the economy. Prosperity depended on people continuing to spend. But many people had run up large debts, or had already bought the consumer goods they needed. After 1927 there was a downturn in demand.

This situation was made even worse for a number of reasons.

1) Wealth was distributed unequally — rising profits were not passed on to workers, so most people were too poor to spend more. This meant demand did not rise as fast as production.
2) There was overproduction — industry was producing more than people wanted to buy. By 1929, unsold stock was building up and manufacturers reduced production. They started to lay off staff and unemployment increased.
3) Banks were largely unregulated. They were unstable and gambled depositors' money on the stock exchange.
4) Brokers provided expensive loans to enable investors to buy shares. When the stock market crashed, investors could not pay back their loans.
5) There were barriers to trade (such as high tariffs) between the USA and Europe — partly because of the USA's policy of isolationism (see p.70). Plus European countries had suffered economically because of the First World War. This meant Europe couldn't provide a good market for America's surplus goods.

Wall Street '29 — a crash course in things going wrong...

Speculating on the stock market means trying to make money by buying and selling shares. When it all went wrong, everybody suffered because of the awful effect on the economy...

Consequences of the Wall Street Crash

The crash destroyed confidence. People lost money and savings and there was no recovery in sight. A second long decline from mid-1931 to early 1933 resulted in even more bankruptcies.

The Depression hit all walks of life

1) The effects of the Wall Street Crash were immediate — from late 1929 to 1930, around 700 banks closed. By mid-1932 around 5000 banks had folded — losing over $3 billion of deposits.
2) The national income fell from over $80bn to just under $70bn in the first year. By 1933 it had fallen as low as $40bn.
3) The price of goods continued to fall. From 1929 to 1931 industrial production dropped by a third — wages fell and workers were laid off. 9% of workers (about 4.7 million) were unemployed by 1930. By 1933 a quarter of the workforce (about 13 million) were unemployed. Around 20 000 US businesses folded in 1932 alone.
4) The price of agricultural products fell 60% because of over-production and declining demand. It cost farmers more to harvest and transport their produce than they could make by selling it — fruit rotted, sheep were killed and burnt, wheat was not harvested and debts increased. Many bankrupt farmers were evicted or became tenants, losing their independence.

The Depression caused Terrible Poverty

1) Poverty led to undernourishment. A typical diet included bread and coffee for breakfast and bread, carrots and soup for dinner.
2) Thousands were made homeless. Some of the homeless built shanty towns to live in. These were nicknamed Hoovervilles after President Hoover.
3) Many people moved to seek work. Some fathers abandoned their families in the search for work.
4) Migrant farm workers roamed the countryside looking for work. Their situation was made worse by a period of drought in the Midwest, partly caused by overuse of the land.
5) Marriages were delayed and the birth rate fell.

Attempts were made to Help People

The Depression was a shattering and demoralising experience. Some people fought hard for survival and to keep their pride. State and charitable agencies tried to help people keep going.

Private charities, religious groups → RELIEF AND HELP → Temporary homes and shelter
State governments → RELIEF AND HELP → Supply of food and clothes bread lines and soup kitchens
Federal relief agencies → RELIEF AND HELP → Offers of jobs

President Hoover helped by introducing some important economic policies:

- The Emergency Relief and Construction Act — this established the Reconstruction Finance Corporation, which provided loans to help businesses. The Reconstruction Finance Corporation was so successful that it continued under Roosevelt.
- The Federal Home Loan Bank Act — this gave banks access to low cost funds to encourage them to offer more mortgages. This meant that fewer people lost their homes, because they were able to remortgage when they got into financial difficulty. More mortgages also helped increase the demand for houses, which meant more jobs in construction.

John Steinbeck wrote a novel about the Depression...

'The Grapes of Wrath' tells the story of a family of farmers trying to survive during the Depression. If you haven't got time to read it, try to find a copy of the film to watch instead.

Election of Roosevelt (FDR)

The Republican President Hoover tried to deal with the Depression — but he failed.

Not all of Hoover's Measures were Successful

1) He set up the Federal Farm Board which was meant to help farmers work together to stabilise crop prices, but it failed to stop farmers from over-producing, so crop prices stayed low.
2) Hoover agreed to the Smoot-Hawley Tariff — a tariff that increased the cost of importing goods into the US, to make goods manufactured within America more popular. This tariff actually harmed US recovery because other countries raised their own tariffs in response, to protect their own industries. US exports to Europe more than halved between 1929 and 1932.
3) Hoover oversaw the creation of the National Credit Corporation. All the major banks were meant to pay into a fund that would make loans to struggling banks to stop them going bust. However, the scheme was unsuccessful because most banks didn't want to help their rivals.

For many people Hoover's efforts were 'too little, too late'. He persisted in his belief in 'rugged individualism', believing that if the right conditions could be created, people would be able to work themselves out of poverty without direct assistance from the government. He therefore refused to offer any financial relief to individuals. This was very unpopular.

FDR was Elected in 1932

1) FDR (Franklin Delano Roosevelt) had been a popular governor of New York. He ran a well organised and energetic election campaign supported by wealthy backers. Influential supporters helped him with ideas and well written speeches. So FDR looked like a winner.
2) Hoover wasn't helped by the 'Bonus Army' protests in June 1932. These 'Bonus Marchers' were 15 000 First World War army veterans who gathered in Washington to demand extra bonus payments not due until 1945. Two protesters were killed by police, and many more were injured in army action to clear their encampments.
3) The Democrats swept to power, with FDR gaining 22 million votes and Hoover 15 million.

Election Promises

- Immediate action after the election
- Relief and help for small banks and homeowners
- A flexible approach for practical results
- An end to prohibition

FDR thought that Federal Government should act and lead on the economy

FDR had 3 Main Aims

This was to be a 'New Deal' for the American people.

Relief — to help to improve the lives of people.
Recovery — to begin to rebuild US industry and trade.
Reform — to change conditions to ensure future progress.

Happy times are here again...

The Great Depression was a terrible time. Hoover tried to help big business and the economy as a whole, but he did little to help ordinary people. That's why he lost to FDR in 1932.

The New Deal

Roosevelt now had to deliver his 'New Deal' to the American people.

Confidence had to be restored in Banking and Finance

1) There was a four-day 'bank holiday' closure.
2) Healthy, sound banks reopened. Weak banks were reorganised under Federal supervision.
3) Laws were introduced to insure deposits and limit speculation.
4) The stock market was to be monitored more closely.
5) The USA was taken off the 'gold standard'.
6) Bank failures fell — deposits rose — and confidence began to return.

The 'Hundred Days' Launched Many New Measures

The "Hundred Days" was the first period of Roosevelt's term in office, during which he introduced many new acts. Much work was carried out by special Federal agencies (often called 'alphabet agencies' because they were known by their initials). The most important were:

FERA The Federal Emergency Relief Administration made $500m available to state and local government for emergency relief. This was used to give direct assistance to the poor, for example: for dole payments and soup kitchens.

CCC The Civilian Conservation Corps provided work for thousands of unemployed men in forestry, water and soil conservation projects. This was followed by the Public Works Administration (PWA) which provided work building roads, bridges, hospitals, schools and housing.

AAA The Agricultural Adjustment Administration paid farmers to limit food production. This raised prices and increased incomes. The AAA also helped farmers modernise and rebuild their businesses.

NRA The National Recovery Act drew up codes of fair competition, set minimum wages and a maximum eight-hour day. Trade unions were encouraged. This was a cooperative effort and relied on the voluntary agreement of business.

TVA The Tennessee Valley Authority. See page 80 for details.

HOLC The Home Owners' Loan Corporation helped people who were in danger of having their homes repossessed. It provided new long-term loans.

The Economy Strengthened a bit but Problems remained

1) Some agencies gave out money too slowly.
2) Stricter regulations on hours, wages and child labour hurt small businesses and farmers.
3) Tenant farmers continued to suffer — 3 million were displaced from the land (1932-5).
4) There was some opposition to Federal control — for example by the 'Liberty League' (1934-6). The Supreme Court raised constitutional objections, which delayed several of FDR's measures.
5) After an initial increase in industrial production the NRA encountered much opposition from business and was unable to secure continued recovery. Some argue that FDR didn't put enough money into reviving industry.
6) The severe drought and heat, on top of overfarming, led to the erosion of topsoil in large areas of the Midwest. Parts of Kansas and Oklahoma became 'dust bowls'.

But the fall in wages and prices was halted. Employment rose and, despite criticisms that Roosevelt was not being radical enough, the measures were very popular.

Learn this and you can have an ice cream — a new deal...

Roosevelt gave speeches on the radio known as 'fireside chats'. These urged listeners to have faith in the New Deal. Overall, he gave the American public a big old charm offensive.

The TVA and the Second New Deal

There were still problems left that needed action...

The Tennessee Valley Authority (TVA)

1) The Tennessee Valley was one of the poorest regions in the country. Overcultivation had led to soil erosion and this had turned the land into a near desert.
2) Agriculture was in a dreadful condition and industry almost non-existent. Many local people were leaving the area to find work further west.

The huge area covered by the TVA

TVA brought Construction Projects

1) The TVA built a large number of dams to prevent the flooding that had been causing so much damage and to provide irrigation in times of drought.
2) Trees were planted to prevent more soil erosion.
3) The TVA constructed power stations which brought electricity to the area.

There was a huge improvement in the region's economy. The massive building projects provided thousands of jobs for local people. Agriculture began to prosper.

The Second New Deal focused on Social Welfare

The Second New Deal began in 1935 and took the new ideas about social welfare and the responsibilities of the state even further. Roosevelt introduced new measures that would benefit the elderly, the sick and the unemployed.

The Social Security Act was passed in 1935

1) This began America's state system of old age pensions. Americans over 65 received a government pension.
2) It also set up a plan for unemployment benefit. Both employers and employees paid into a fund so that the worker received a small amount of unemployment benefit if they lost their job.
3) It also set up schemes to help the sick and the disabled.

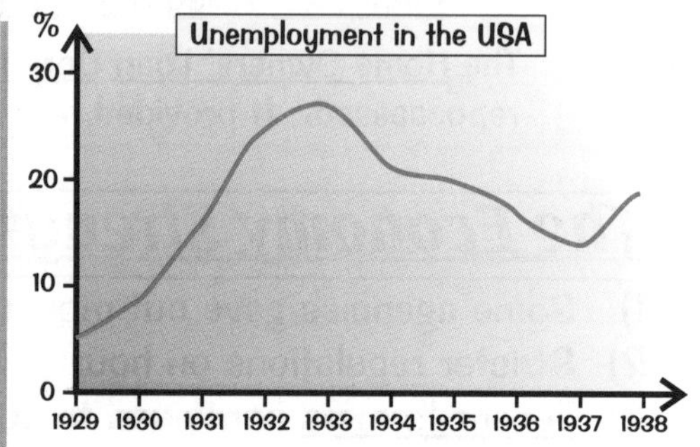

The Wagner Act, 1935

This act gave workers the right to join a trade union. Companies were now forced by law to allow their employees to become members of a trade union.

The Works Progress Administration (WPA), 1935

This was very like the Public Works Administration, but it also created jobs for actors, artists, photographers and musicians. However, the USA still lagged behind countries like Britain and Germany in social welfare provision.

A new New Deal for y'all to remember...

A big change brought about by the New Deal was the acceptance that the state had a role in relieving the hardship of individual citizens. This was what the second New Deal was all about.

Opposition to the New Deal

Although many Americans supported the New Deal, some people opposed Roosevelt's policies.

Some thought the New Deal had Not Gone Far Enough

Some people wanted to do more to help the poor:

- Senator Huey Long of Louisiana wanted to tax the rich and give the money to the poor. He called this plan 'Share Our Wealth' and claimed that it would give every family an income of $5000 a year. The families would spend the money and this would create a bigger demand for goods and services and therefore more jobs. Huey Long planned to stand against FDR in the 1936 presidential elections — but he was assassinated in 1935.
- Father Charles Coughlin hosted a popular radio show in the 1930s, which was very influential. Coughlin originally supported Roosevelt's New Deal, but he turned against it because he thought it hadn't gone far enough and it didn't focus enough on helping the working classes.
- Dr Francis Townsend recommended a plan by which every American over 60 was given a pension of $200 per month (a huge amount in the 1930s) on condition that they spent the lot within one month. Dr Townsend said that this would boost the economy and get unemployment down.

Some thought the New Deal had Gone Too Far

1) Roosevelt's critics said that the New Deal made Americans too dependent on government help. These people believed that it was wrong for the government to create work and give Americans pensions and sickness benefits — individuals should provide for themselves.
2) Some business people were angry that the New Deal allowed trade unions into the workplace. They said this was unnecessary government interference in their business affairs.
3) Some people condemned the New Deal measures as 'socialist' and therefore un-American.
4) It was claimed that it was wrong to tax the rich to pay for the New Deal. The rich had earned their wealth through their own efforts and enterprise. By taxing the rich you discouraged them from wishing to create more wealth. This was a strongly capitalist viewpoint.

There was also Opposition from the Supreme Court

1) Most of the Supreme Court judges were Republicans and therefore opposed Roosevelt.
2) They used the Schechter Poultry 'sick chicken' case in 1935 to undermine Roosevelt:

- Schechter Poultry had broken some of the business codes in Roosevelt's New Deal.
- These codes were supposed to ensure fair wages and fair competition.
- The Supreme Court felt that the President didn't have the power to tell people how to run their businesses — they declared that parts of the New Deal were unconstitutional.

3) Roosevelt asked the Congress to allow him to put six Democrats on the Supreme Court so that this would not happen again. However, many Americans felt that this would be a violation of the constitution and Roosevelt was forced to back down.
4) The Supreme Court began to take a more lenient view of the New Deal and the argument died down. However, the objections did succeed in delaying some of FDR's policies.

Money, money, money...

America was (and to a great extent still is) attached to ideas of free enterprise and minimal state intervention in the affairs of individuals. This largely explains the opposition to FDR.

How Successful was the New Deal?

The New Deal had mixed success — no American president had promised anything like this before.

The New Deal really was New

1) The New Deal was a new idea — it was the first time the US government had seriously intervened in the US economy to help the poorest Americans.
2) President Hoover had been more traditional — he didn't think the government should interfere with businesses. He promoted self-reliance and cooperation. He wanted people to work their own way out of debt and help others do the same — without relying on direct government help.
3) FDR was more radical — he thought the government should be actively responsible for helping struggling US citizens caught up in the Depression. That's why he introduced the New Deal.

The New Deal had considerable success in its Main Aims

Give aid to the needy

1) The FERA did a good job in providing the needy with much-needed emergency aid.
2) From 1935 onwards, the elements of a basic welfare state were established — unemployment benefit and pensions were introduced, and the government intervened to ensure better working conditions and a minimum wage.

Restore stability to America's banking and financial system

1) Roosevelt successfully resolved the banking crisis with the Emergency Banking Act (EBA).
2) This restored people's confidence in the banks and people began to deposit their money in them once again.

Reduce unemployment and restore prosperity

1) The New Deal created millions of jobs through the various agencies such as the CCC and the PWA. When Roosevelt became president in 1933, unemployment stood at 13 million. In 1940, the figure was 8 million.
2) However, though the 1940 figure is an improvement on the one for 1933, it is important to remember that there were only 1.5 million people out of work in 1929. So the New Deal did not actually bring back the low unemployment levels of 1920s America.
3) In 1937, another depression hit the American economy and unemployment rose in 1938 to over 10 million. The New Deal therefore failed to solve America's unemployment problem.

World War Two solved the Unemployment Problem

It was the outbreak of the Second World War in Europe that brought the jobless total down.

1) In March 1941 the Lend-Lease Act authorised the President to lease or sell military equipment and supplies to the British and other countries on the Allied side for their fight against Germany. From then on, the US geared production to war needs, eventually supplying her allies with $50 billion worth of food, armaments and equipment.
2) America's entry into the war in December 1941 increased the demand for military equipment. This, together with recruitment into the armed forces, put an end to high unemployment.

The end of the Depression — I feel better already...

Roosevelt's New Deal couldn't end the Depression but it did relieve the worst of the hardship.

Revision Summary

You've read the section, now try these revision questions, just to check that you've got the whole thing stored safely in your brain. Don't forget — if you get any wrong, look back through the section, learn it properly and then try again...

1) Write a short paragraph explaining why many people in America didn't want to join the League of Nations.
2) Who became President in 1921?
3) What did the Fordney-McCumber Tariff allow the US President to do?
4) How did the Republican government's policies encourage the economic boom in the 1920s?
5) Explain how the motor industry contributed to American prosperity in the 1920s.
6) Why did agriculture not share in the boom?
7) Why were there protests about the trial of Sacco and Vanzetti?
8) What did the Ku Klux Klan believe in? Who did they persecute?
9) Why was John Scopes prosecuted in the so-called 'Monkey Trial'?
10) When was Prohibition introduced?
11) Explain the following terms: speakeasy, rum-running, moonshine.
12) What crime was Al Capone convicted of in 1931?
13) Name two forms of entertainment which first became popular in the 1920s.
14) Explain how the social position of women changed in the 1920s.
15) What year did the Wall Street Crash happen?
16) Explain four economic problems that contributed to the Wall Street Crash.
17) How many Americans were unemployed by 1933?
18) What were Hoovervilles?
19) Explain why Hoover lost the 1932 election.
20) Who won the 1932 election? What were his three main aims?
21) Name three 'alphabet agencies' and explain how they helped America through the Depression.
22) What does TVA stand for?
23) Name two acts passed in 1935 as part of the 'Second New Deal'.
24) Why did Huey Long oppose the New Deal?
25) Explain why some businessmen and members of the Republican party opposed the New Deal.
26) How successful was the New Deal in achieving its three main aims?
27) What finally solved America's unemployment problem?

Russia Under the Tsars

Before the First World War, the Tsar held supreme power in Russia.

The Government of the Russian Empire was Unpopular

Tsar Nicholas II

Absolute ruler: His dynasty had ruled Russia for 300 years. Increasingly unpopular.

Peasants: 85% of people. Poor people using old, inefficient farming methods.

Industrial workers: Had low wages and poor working conditions. Industry was growing.

1) The Tsar was all-powerful — he ruled without a parliament, and most of the country's wealth and land was owned by a small noble class. The Church taught that the Tsar must be obeyed.
2) Peasant villages were controlled by the mir — a local council who interfered in everyone's business and had the power to decide whether a peasant was allowed to own or rent land.
3) The growth of industry meant there was a large working population in the towns — but conditions in the towns were cramped and the workers were badly paid.
4) In 1905 Russia was defeated in a war with Japan.
5) Poor conditions led to strikes and demonstrations — on 'Bloody Sunday' troops fired into a crowd of peaceful demonstrators in St Petersburg. There was nearly a popular revolution.

The Tsar allowed some Change and set up a Parliament

1) In the first Duma of 1906, the liberal Constitutional Democratic Party (known as the Cadets) won a majority. They demanded control of taxes, as the Tsar had promised them.
2) Instead he dismissed the Duma and many Liberals fled to Finland. New elections were held.
3) This time the Duma was even more radical — members of the Marxist SDLP (Social Democratic Labour Party — see p.86) won some seats from the Cadets. When the Tsar wanted to arrest several SDLP members as terrorists the Duma refused — so the Tsar dismissed it too.
4) The next two Dumas obeyed the Tsar (1907-1914). The SDLP were not allowed to run as candidates and any known 'troublemakers' were arrested and imprisoned.
5) The press was censored and a secret police was used to spy on people the Tsar feared.
6) The situation of the people hadn't improved and there was still a lot of discontent among the poor working classes.

Attempted Reform hit Problems — 1906 to 1911

1) Prime Minister Stolypin wanted economic reforms — he was afraid that badly run industry could get out of control.
2) He ended the control of the mir over how land was distributed. Hard-working peasants could now rent or buy land to farm themselves — helped by special Peasant Banks. These better-off peasants were known as kulaks.
3) The mir system continued but became less efficient when the kulaks left — causing problems for the country's food supply.
4) Peasants in the mir farms resented the wealth of some kulaks.
5) Reform needed peace, but Europe was heading for war (see section 1).
6) Stolypin was murdered in 1911 by a revolutionary.

Countdown to Revolution

Attempts were made to fix Russia's problems, but World War I made everything more difficult.

Russia entered World War One

1) When Austria-Hungary declared war on Russia's ally Serbia, Russia entered the war.
2) At first the war actually increased patriotism and loyalty to the Tsar — the Russian people unified, hoping for a short and victorious war.
3) However, military leadership was bad and early casualties were high:

- At the Battle of Tannenberg, August 1914, a grudge between Russian generals led to a split in the Russian forces. The Germans took advantage, and out of 150 000 Russian soldiers only 10 000 escaped being killed or captured.
- At the Battle of the Masurian Lakes, September 1914, Germany attacked the rest of the Russian force that had split at Tannenberg. The Russians were outnumbered — by the end of the battle they had lost more than 100 000 men.

4) Shocked by these defeats, the Tsar made himself commander in chief in 1915. This meant he was often away at the Eastern Front — leaving his unpopular wife in charge in the capital.

Tsar Nicholas' wife was influenced by a 'Holy Man' called Rasputin who claimed supernatural powers to treat the Tsar's son for haemophilia — a disease where the blood won't clot. Rasputin became powerful and even sacked and appointed government ministers. He was killed by angry nobles in 1916 — but the Tsar's authority had been undermined.

Rasputin

The First World War caused more Problems

1) High casualties continued — 1 800 000 Russian soldiers were dead by the end of 1917.
2) There was a shortage of rifles and equipment. Poor transport slowed supplies to the front.
3) The Russian army was pushed back by the Germans and there was a stalemate.
4) Inflation meant that prices at home went up massively.
5) There was widespread hunger and food and fuel shortages at home.

The 'February' Revolution of 1917

1) Demonstrations and food riots suddenly broke out in the capital city of Petrograd.
2) The Tsar had lost support and control — when his soldiers were ordered to fire on the mobs many refused or deserted to join the rioting workers.
3) The Tsar gave up the throne. A Provisional Government was formed under the leadership of Prince Lvov until July, and then Kerensky. Russia was now a republic.
4) The main revolutionary parties were taken by surprise — this was a real people's revolution caused by sudden risings of workers and soldiers sick of the war, shortages and high prices.
5) This meant that the new government could face opposition from the revolutionaries, who wanted power for themselves — among them, a group from the Social Democratic Labour Party (SDLP) called the Bolsheviks.

The end of Tsarism — the people were revolting...

The Tsar made some bad moves that helped lead to his fall — like taking command of the army.

The Bolsheviks

The Bolshevik Party wanted power in Russia — it held Marxist beliefs.

Marxism said Capitalism was Wrong

1) Capitalism is the economic system based on business — selling things to make a profit.
2) Marx, a 19th-century political thinker, said this was unjust because thousands of workers were receiving low wages for labour that made a tiny elite class very rich.
3) According to Marx, history is a process of development towards an ideal society — change comes because of class struggle between the middle class and working class.
4) This would in time lead to a violent revolution by the workers. After the revolution, the means of production would be used for everyone's benefit and shared — this is called communism.

The SDLP were the Marxist Party in Russia

In the late 1890s and early 1900s, the SDLP encouraged the industrial workers in the towns to protest against their terrible living conditions. They hoped to create a situation where a Marxist revolution could take place. Many of them were exiled by the Tsarist government — this was one reason they weren't involved in the February Revolution.

The Bolsheviks came out of the SDLP

Lenin

1) At the Social Democrat Conference of 1903, the SDLP quarrelled over whether to become a mass party (open to anyone) or to remain a small party of dedicated members working towards revolution.
2) The party split into Bolsheviks who wanted a small party and were led by Lenin, and Mensheviks led by Martov who wanted a mass party.

Vladimir Ilyich Lenin was the Bolshevik leader. He was a clever thinker and a practical man — he knew how to take advantage of events.

The Bolsheviks were a Small Party

1) At first, the Bolsheviks were too small a party to make much impact on the workers.
2) During the war, Lenin was in exile in Switzerland. When the February Revolution came he returned to Russia to rally the Bolshevik cause.
3) The Germans helped him to return in a sealed train in April 1917, because they hoped he would cause another revolution and that Russia would end the war.

Lenin's 'April Theses' Urged Revolution

1) Lenin issued a document called the April Theses, promising 'peace, bread, land and freedom'.
2) He called for an end to the 'capitalist' war, and demanded that power should be given to the Soviets — elected committees of workers, peasants and soldiers which had started up in 1905 and had given leadership to the people during the February Revolution.
3) He demanded a revolution against the Provisional Government as soon as possible.

Peace + Land + Bread

Learn your theory — it's easy Marx...

Make sure you know how the Bolsheviks were formed and what they stood for. The April Theses are important too — no one expected Lenin to attack the Provisional Government.

The Provisional Government

The situation was very tricky for the Provisional Government.

The Provisional Government had Problems

1) It wasn't supposed to stay in power — but the economic crisis made elections impossible.
2) Inflation grew even worse. Prices were ten times higher than 1914 by November 1917.
3) Food shortages became worse and peasants began to seize land from noble estates.
4) The new government didn't end the war — soldiers and sailors began to mutiny.
5) A network of Soviets was established — the Petrograd Soviet became an alternative government. Key workers were told to strike to undermine the Provisional Government.
6) The Petrograd Soviet issued 'Order No. 1' which said that soldiers shouldn't obey orders from the Provisional Government if they were opposed by the Soviet.

The Soviets demanded an end to the war, but the army attacked the German forces in June 1917. After early Russian success the Germans counter-attacked, forcing a retreat and the collapse of morale and discipline in the Russian army.

The Bolsheviks Prepared for Further Revolution

The Bolsheviks gained increasing support among workers and soldiers with their slogan:

1) In July 1917 the Bolsheviks tried to take control of the government but were defeated and Lenin was forced to leave the country and flee to Finland.
   Kerensky had turned public opinion against him by accusing him of being a German agent.
2) Leon Trotsky led the Red Guards — a Bolshevik military force. At the same time, the Bolsheviks won control of the Soviets, and Trotsky was Chairman of the Petrograd Soviet.
3) Peasants attacked kulaks and took land from the Church and nobles.
4) Many soldiers started to desert from the army and returned home.

General Kornilov Attempted a Military Coup

1) In September 1917, the Russian Commander in Chief, General Kornilov, turned his army back from the Front and marched against the Provisional Government determined to seize power.
2) Kerensky had to give weapons to the Bolsheviks and the Petrograd Soviet to save his government from a military takeover.
3) Bolshevik railway workers and Red Guards were waiting to stop Kornilov's advance — but all his soldiers deserted him and he fled.
4) The Bolsheviks were now the real power in Russia, and Lenin encouraged Trotsky to prepare plans for seizing power.

The Bolshevik Press — it was red all over...

There's lots to learn here. Make sure you know what problems the Provisional Government was facing and understand why the Bolsheviks were becoming powerful and popular.

The Bolsheviks Seize Power

The October Revolution of 1917

The Bolshevik Central Committee under Lenin voted for revolution. Detailed plans were made by Trotsky to seize important buildings in Petrograd and arrest Ministers. The revolution started on 24th October and the Bolsheviks were in control by the next day.

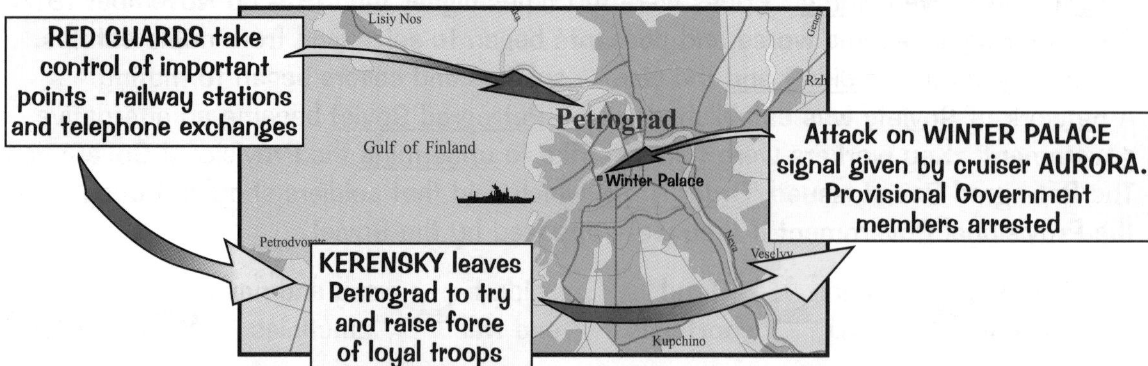

There were only 250 000 Bolsheviks in Russia, controlling a small part of the country — civil war was inevitable as there were many people who were opposed to Bolshevik rule.

Lenin was ruthless and determined to keep power. He knew a strong government was needed — so the ideals of communism had to wait.

The Bolsheviks Established Control

1) The All-Russian Congress of Soviets gave power to the Soviet Council of People's Commissars under Lenin, on 26th October 1917.
2) Soldiers were sent into the countryside to seize grain to feed the towns.
3) The Bolsheviks controlled the main centres of power and used telegraph communications to spread their revolutionary message to local groups.
4) Elections were held for a new constituent assembly. Bolsheviks won 168 seats out of 703, with most seats going to the Socialist Revolutionary Party (SRP), who had peasant support.
5) After one day the Red Guards closed down the Assembly — January 1918.
6) The Bolsheviks became the Communist Party, the only legal party in Russia.
7) Lenin made two decrees (orders) — the Decree on Land nationalised all land in Russia and the Decree on Peace called for peace with Germany.

The Reasons for the Bolshevik Success

1) They were strong in key political and administrative centres — especially Petrograd.
2) They had their own trained military force — the Red Guards.
3) They were ruthless and planned clear strategies — they were prepared for swift action.
4) They were practical — they recognised that the time for a true Marxist revolution was a long way off and so they changed their policies in order to seize power at the first chance. They claimed they ran a socialist government which was trying to create the right conditions for communism in the long term — so in the short term they could do whatever they liked.
5) The continuing problems of war and famine, and the breakdown of law and order, weren't dealt with by the Provisional Government, who had become a weak target.
6) The vision and ability of Lenin — he was a quick-thinking leader who inspired his party.

"Learn it all well" — Lenin's Decree on Revision...

Because Russia used a different calendar to the rest of Europe, the October Revolution is also known as the November Revolution and the October/November Revolution, but they're all the same thing.

1918 — Ending the German War

The Bolsheviks took Russia out of one war, and prepared for another one.

The Germans were Advancing

1) The Bolsheviks signed an armistice with the Germans, hoping to delay the peace treaties because they thought there might be a communist revolution in Germany too.
2) This didn't happen, and the German armies advanced — so the Bolsheviks quickly agreed to the harsh terms of the Treaty of Brest-Litovsk in March 1918.

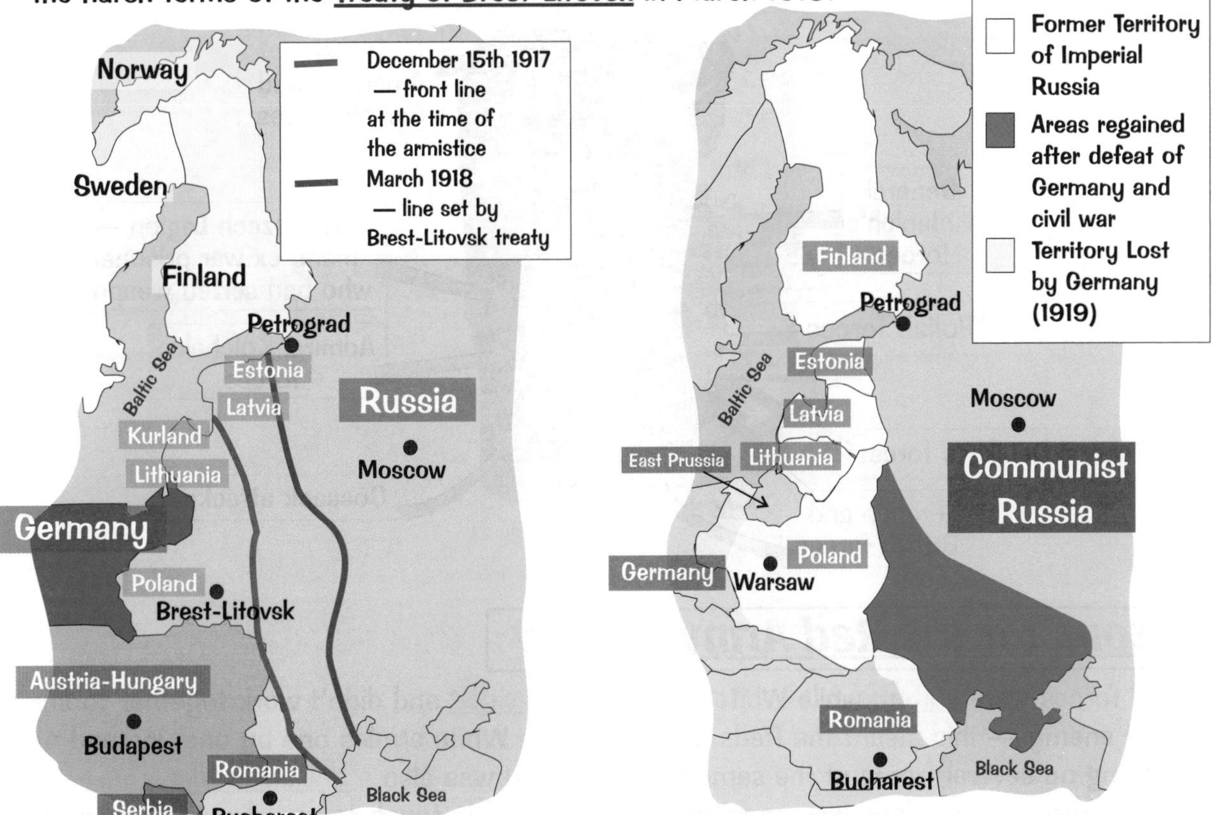

Germany was defeated by the Western Allies later in 1918 and some lands were regained.

A Civil War was Inevitable

Lenin and Trotsky were prepared for this. The reasons the civil war broke out were:

1) The communists had seized power suddenly and repressed the elected Constituent Assembly — they had also outlawed political opposition, so many people saw them as a danger.
2) Anti-communist army officers were no longer fighting Germany — many were royalists and wanted the return of the Tsar — and now they could attack the communists.
3) Communism wanted a world revolution — the Comintern (the Communist International) was formed under Zinoviev to promote revolution abroad and to encourage friendly governments in nearby European countries.

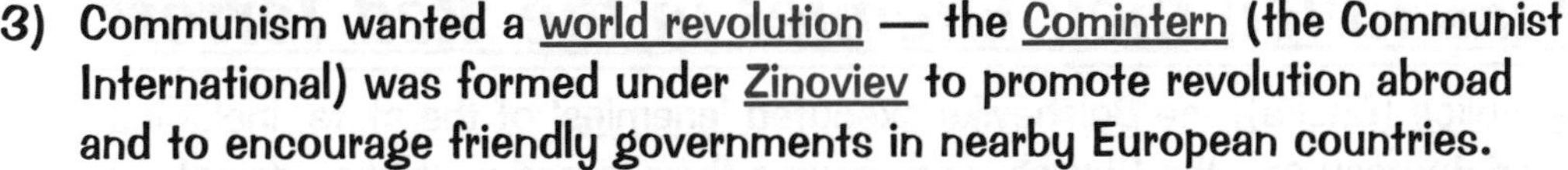
The government moved from Petrograd to Moscow in 1918 — Leon Trotsky began to build an efficient Red Army to fight the civil war.

The civil war — not a very polite affair...

Remember — a civil war was the last thing Russia needed after the disasters of the First World War, but the communists knew it was coming, which was why they made peace with Germany at any cost. Scribble down the names of the lands lost by Russia.

The Civil War 1918-1921

The first big challenge for the new Bolshevik government was the brutal civil war.

Anti-Communist forces surrounded Red Russia

1) These armies were called the 'Whites' — the colour of the Tsarist state.
2) There were many White groups who often had different aims and purposes — a key problem.
3) Britain, France and the USA sent troops to help the Whites — trying to restart the Eastern Front against Germany, and worried by communist ideas of world revolution.

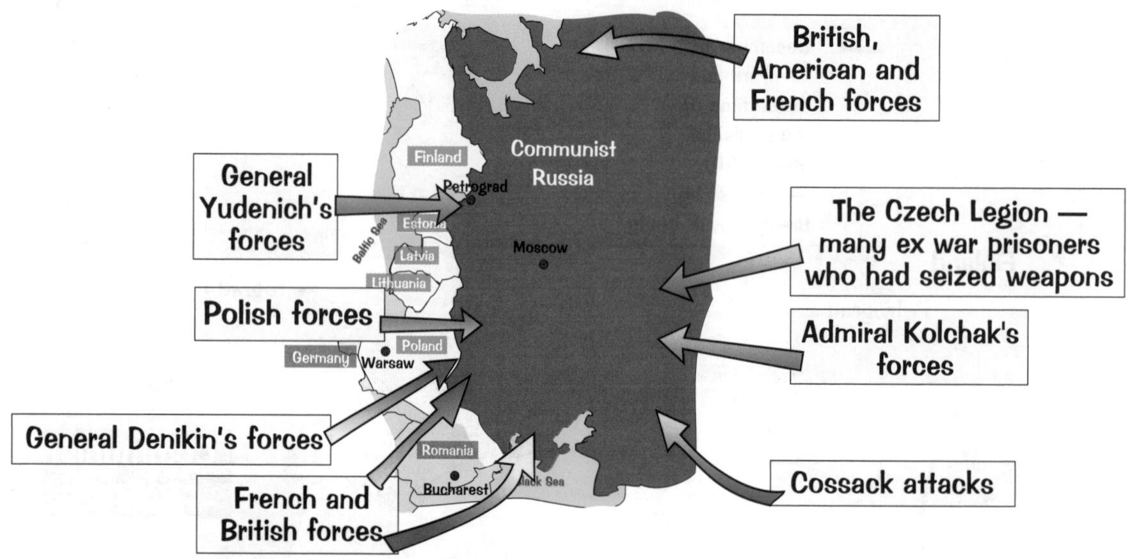

Reasons for the Red Army Victory

1) Red forces were united, while White forces were divided and didn't work together to surround their enemy — this meant the Reds could fight the White armies one by one, instead of fighting on several fronts at the same time. Trotsky was also a brilliant leader.
2) White forces were a long way apart and couldn't stay in touch to coordinate attacks. Some had different political opinions — which meant they didn't want to work together.
3) Patriotic Russians supported the Reds — the Whites were led by nobles and foreign armies.
4) Foreign military support was soon withdrawn as it became clear the Reds would win.
5) The communists controlled the main cities and communications systems — and the railways.
6) The strict and ruthless laws of War Communism helped obtain supplies for the Reds.
7) When the Red Army had defeated its enemies in Russia it carried on and pushed into Poland, hoping to link up with communists in Germany to spread revolution throughout Europe — but it was defeated by the Poles outside Warsaw in late 1920. The war ended with a treaty in 1921.

The Bolsheviks Killed their Enemies in the 'Red Terror'

1) Using the secret police (Cheka), the Bolsheviks executed 'enemies' of the state, including members of the aristocracy and the Church, and anyone they feared might be against them.
2) This included the Tsar and his entire family who were executed by the Bolsheviks in 1918 because Lenin feared that they could become a symbol for the opposition.
3) The 'Red Terror' lasted until 1922. It's estimated that up to 500 000 Russians died.

Reds vs Whites — nope, not football this time...

Plenty for you to learn here — looking at the map you'd have thought the Whites would win easily. Focus on the Whites' lack of coordination and the strength of communist control.

War Communism and Mutiny

War Communism — a Strict System to Win the War

1) Farms and factories were put under state control — private trade was banned.
2) Food was taken for soldiers and industrial workers — peasants who refused to hand it over to the Red Army were shot or sent to forced labour camps.
3) Industrial workers weren't allowed to strike or be absent from work. They could be sent to any region. Experts were brought in to improve efficiency.
4) All adults had to work except for the sick and pregnant women.
5) The results were famine and decline.

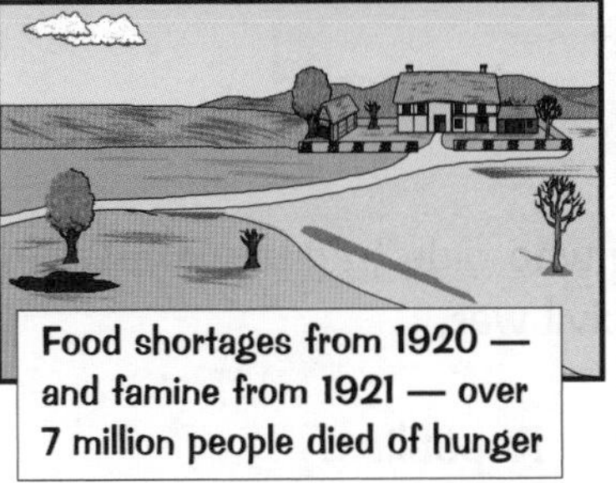

Food shortages from 1920 — and famine from 1921 — over 7 million people died of hunger

Worthless currency abandoned — wages paid in fuel and food

Workers leave cities, little food in towns. Industry declines

The Kronstadt Naval Base Mutinied

The sailors were unhappy with the lack of progress, the famine and the terror. They mutinied and seized the base near Petrograd, in February 1921.

Kronstadt rebels demands

Free speech and press

Sale of peasant grain

Free elections for Soviets

Free trade unions

Ballot Box

1) The Kronstadt sailors had supported the communists in 1917 — especially Trotsky's leadership in Petrograd.
2) Despite this, Lenin and Trotsky were worried that dissent might spread when the ice around the island base thawed and let the sailors leave.
3) Trotsky ordered the Red Army to put down the mutiny.
4) The Red Army attacked, losing many men, but captured it in a brutal battle.
5) Many rebels were killed in the fighting — those who were left were either executed or imprisoned as traitors.

There were other revolts — peasants in Tambov Province robbed food convoys and many factories suffered strikes and unrest.

Lenin Decided to Change Communist Policy

1) Communism was pushing ahead 'too fast' — Trotsky had recognised the economic crisis in 1920 and suggested a change of policy to encourage businesses. Lenin rejected this at first.
2) Now the civil war was won, the communists needed to keep control of public opinion.
3) This meant a policy of complete party unity — no dissent or splits allowed.
4) In 1921 Lenin introduced the New Economic Policy (NEP) to restore order and increase prosperity after the chaos of revolution, civil war and War Communism.

War Communism — not an overwhelming success then...

The Bolsheviks survived in part due to Lenin's willingness to change a failing policy.

The New Economic Policy

The New Economic Policy Reversed War Communism

1) Peasants could sell surplus food produce and pay tax on profits.
2) Small businesses, like shops and small factories, no longer had to be state-owned — they could therefore make a profit.
3) Vital industries such as coal, iron, steel, railways, shipping and finance stayed in state hands. But here experts were brought in on higher salaries, and extra wages were paid for efficiency.

The NEP allowed economic recovery — by 1928 industrial and food production levels were about the same as in 1914, and some people grew rich.

Communist political Control Grew

1) A 'purge' in 1921 expelled about a third of Party members — those who didn't agree with Lenin.
2) Communist governments were imposed in areas recaptured in the civil war, against the will of independent nationalists such as in the Ukraine.
3) A new constitution established the USSR — Union of Soviet Socialist Republics.
4) Each Republic had a government with some policy freedom, but they all had to be communist, and the system was run centrally by the Politburo — the senior council.

Lenin Died on Jan 21, 1924

1870	Lenin born.
1898	First Congress of the SDLP.
1903	Bolsheviks (majority) split from Mensheviks (minority).
1917	February — First Revolution — Provisional Government (Kerensky).
	April — Lenin outlines plans to overthrow government.
	July — Bolshevik rising defeated.
	October — Bolshevik communist revolution and takeover.
1918	March — Peace treaty with Germany (Brest-Litovsk)
1918-21	Civil war. Reds vs Whites.
1921	Famine. Kronstadt rebellion. New Economic Policy.
1922	Lenin ill after a stroke. Policy led by Stalin, Zinoviev and Kamenev.

Lenin died in 1924. Stalin organised his funeral, and against Lenin's own wishes, his body was embalmed and placed on public display in Moscow. Petrograd was renamed Leningrad in his honour.

Lenin's Key Strengths as a Leader

1) His organisation and leadership of the Bolshevik party transformed it.
2) He had a pragmatic and realistic approach to problems.
3) He was able to 'seize the moment', which was vital in the Bolsheviks gaining power.
4) He could be ruthless — he set up the Cheka (secret police) and the labour camps. He also wasn't afraid to use force to put down the Kronstadt mutiny.
5) He was able to change his policies — e.g. he was able to adopt War Communism to win the civil war, and then to introduce the NEP afterwards to help the economy recover.

The New Economic Policy — so new it wasn't even communist...

The NEP reversed War Communism. The easiest way to get them learned is to compare the two. Scribble a list of the main details of each policy — especially the differences between them.

The Struggle for Power

Lenin's death meant that there was a vacancy at the top of the Party.

Several Leaders Struggled to Succeed Lenin

1) TROTSKY was the most able, and popular with the army and Party members. He led the Red Army brilliantly during the civil war, but some people thought he was too arrogant and he lacked support in the Politburo. He had been a Menshevik and he often made enemies.
2) ZINOVIEV and KAMENEV were left-wingers who agreed with Trotsky's ideas about state control of land and continuing the revolution. But they were determined to stop Trotsky becoming Party leader. Zinoviev was a popular man and had been a friend of Lenin.
3) STALIN didn't seem likely to lead the party. He had accumulated power through good organisation 'behind the scenes' in his work as General Secretary of the Party.

Lenin's testament talked about who might succeed him — he said Trotsky was arrogant but able and said Stalin should be removed from office because he was too rude and ambitious.

Trotsky and Stalin Had a War of Ideas

Leon Trotsky

...wanted revolution to spread to other countries — he called for the USSR to work for a world revolution.

Joseph Stalin

...and most of the Party wanted a period of peace and rebuilding in the USSR — 'Communism in one country'.

How Stalin Made Himself All-Powerful

1) Stalin controlled the Communist Party — he appointed people loyal to him to senior positions.
2) This meant Stalin's rivals had no support in the Party, and he suppressed Lenin's testament.
3) Only Party members could hold government positions and they were chosen by Party voting. It was a one-party state.
4) By the late 1920s Stalin had enough Party support to have his rivals voted out of power.

Stalin Destroyed the Leftists and the Rightists

1) Stalin joined Zinoviev and Kamenev against Trotsky — who was dismissed as Commissar for War in 1925. 'Socialism in one country' became Party policy in 1925.
2) Trotsky was isolated — and thrown out of the Communist Party in 1927.
3) New members were elected to the Politburo, loyal to Stalin. At this time Stalin supported the NEP and gradual reform of the economy. The 'leftist' Zinoviev and Kamenev were dismissed from the Politburo because they believed in fast economic modernisation (one of Trotsky's main ideas). They joined Trotsky to protest against Stalin and were expelled from the Party.
4) Trotsky was exiled to Kazakhstan in 1928, and forced to leave the USSR in 1929.
5) But in 1928 Stalin adopted fast modernisation instead of the NEP. This swing to the left meant he could now remove the leading figures on the right of the party, such as Bukharin and Rykov who supported the NEP, and could have been a threat to his position.
6) By 1929 he was in complete control as leader of the Communist Party and the USSR.

Stalin was a spin doctor — he changed the revolution...

The key factor in Stalin's rise was Party control. Remember, the Party wasn't the same as the government. But the USSR's constitution could be abused by anyone controlling the Party.

The Terror and the Purges

Stalin was single-minded on his way to the top — and terrifying when he got there.

Stalin was Ruthless in Destroying Rivals

1) Born in 1879 in the Republic of Georgia, his real name was Joseph Jughashvili. He had studied to become a priest, but became a Bolshevik. He changed his name to Stalin ('man of steel') when he was imprisoned as a revolutionary.

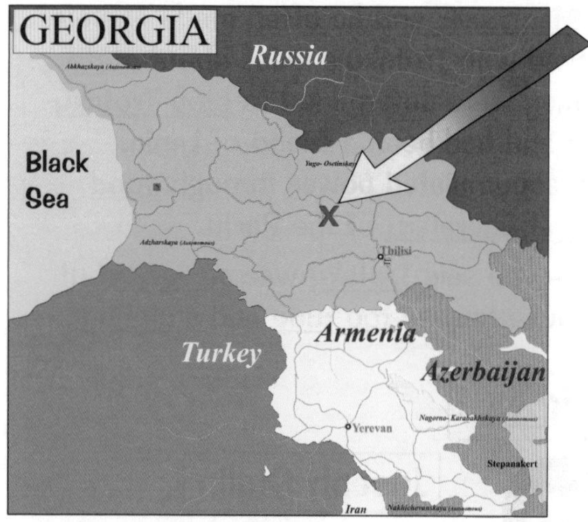

2) He was an organiser who began by making speeches, and organising strikes and bank raids to aid Bolshevik funds. He was efficient at routine organisation which many thought was dull.
3) His power base came from being General Secretary of the Party after 1922 — by controlling Party appointments he could control who was given government roles, and chose people loyal to him.
4) By 1930 he was undisputed leader of Russia, but he became terrified that others wanted to overthrow him — this made him determined to get rid of rivals.

The Kirov Murder Began a Purge

1) Kirov was the popular head of the Party in Leningrad — he was murdered in 1934.
2) Some historians think Stalin was responsible for his death — in 1956 Stalin's successor, Khrushchev, blamed Stalin for the murder, but there is no clear proof.
3) Immediately Stalin ordered a purge of people he believed were involved in a conspiracy against Kirov and against himself — but Kirov's murderer was never put on trial.
4) In 1935-6, many 'old' communists like Zinoviev and Kamenev were arrested and charged in 'show trials'. They were forced by torture or threats to confess to betraying Stalin.
5) No one knows exactly what was true and what was invented by Stalin's torturers.
6) One claim was that the exiled Trotsky was plotting with senior leaders to take power.

Soon the Purges Reached Ordinary People

1) Anyone suspected of disloyalty to Stalin was taken away by the NKVD (the new secret police).
2) Most were shot or sent to labour camps.
3) People who wanted to avoid arrest did so by providing information about others — even if it was false.
4) Stalin's wife killed herself (or was murdered) after a purge at the university where she was a teacher.
5) The exiled Trotsky condemned Stalin's purges from his home in Mexico, calling for a new revolution. In 1940 he was murdered by one of Stalin's agents.
6) The total number of people killed by Stalin's regime is uncertain — but some estimates are as high as ten million.

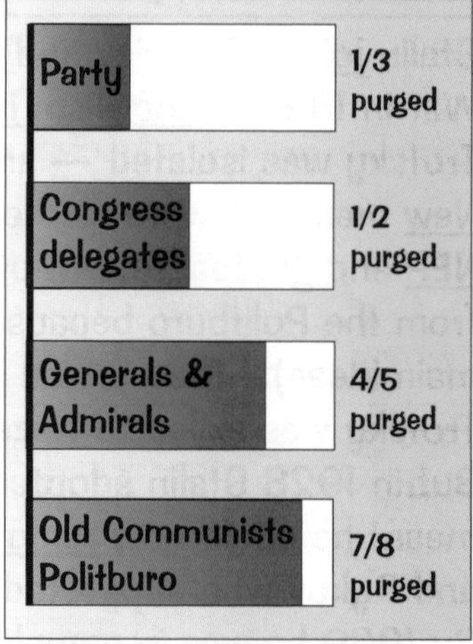

The purges — a vicious circle...

Confusing stuff — but you need to get it straight. Under torture people invented all sorts of things to try to save themselves. Stalin started to believe there really was a plot against him.

Stalin the Dictator

Stalin tightened his brutal grip on the USSR.

Stalin Controlled all Information

1) Artists and writers had to follow the Party line, creating 'useful' art for the workers.
2) Newspapers, cinema and radio spread propaganda about the heroic workers' struggle and Stalin's great leadership and personality. Criticism was banned.
3) History was rewritten so that Stalin became more important in the story of the October Revolution than he really had been at the time.
4) Trotsky became a 'non-person' — his name was removed from history books and articles, and his picture was rubbed out of old photos as though he had never existed.
5) Photographs were altered to show Stalin as a close friend and ally of Lenin.

Top Tip: source material in the exams could be propaganda — opinion and not just fact. To get top marks you've got to say which points are true and which aren't, and explain what opinion the source expresses.

The Purges Weakened the USSR

The terror slowed down by the end of the 1930s, but it had serious consequences:

1) Many of the most gifted and able citizens had disappeared — killed or sent to camps.
2) The army and navy was seriously weakened by the loss of most senior officers.
3) Industrial and technical progress was hampered by the loss of top scientists and engineers.
4) In 1936 a new constitution was brought in — every four years there were elections and only official Party candidates were allowed to stand. Power was kept in the Politburo.

The Communists Attacked the Church

1) The Russian Orthodox Church had been a powerful supporter of the Tsar.
2) The communist government began to take Church property and land — these were valuable assets for the Party. Christians were persecuted as a political threat to communism and priests were murdered or exiled.
3) In 1929 the Church was banned from any activity except leading worship.
4) By 1939 a few hundred churches remained active — the state claimed the promise of free conscience in the 1936 constitution was being honoured.
5) Many people were still believers — nearly half the population in 1940.

Stalin's Russia was a Dictatorship

1) Stalin ran everything — his policies were often completely different from communist ideas.
2) Party 'apparatchiks' — members loyal to Stalin — received privileges like holidays, flats etc.
3) Most people lived in fear but were unable to speak out.

Stalin got stronger — the USSR suffered...

Sources often mix facts with opinions. Your job is to separate the two, and find out why a source gives a particular opinion, and why it may ignore some of the facts. Think about who wrote it, why they wrote it, and when they wrote it — how much they really knew.

The Five-Year Plans

The Party used targets to increase the pace of industrialisation.

The USSR still had a Poor Economy

1) The NEP had made some progress, but more rapid growth was needed for the USSR to catch up with the industrialised West and their economies.
2) Stalin adopted Trotsky's ideas for a programme of fast state-controlled modernisation to speed up production. Lenin's policy of the NEP was dropped.
3) The state took over planning for industry and agriculture with a commission called Gosplan to set targets for achievement.

The First Five-Year Plan was started in 1928

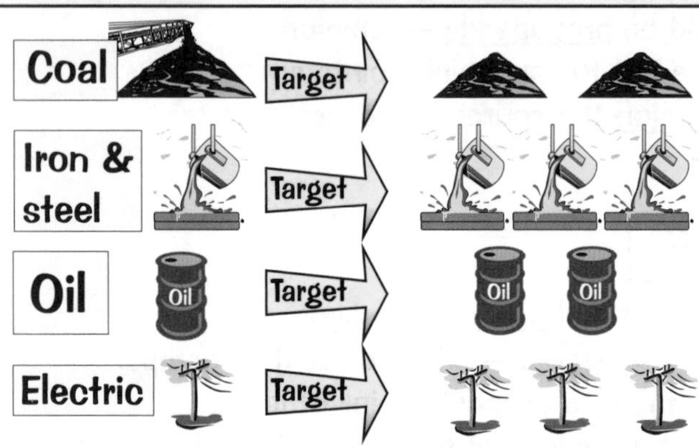

1) A Five-Year Plan set targets for all basic industrial factories and workers.
2) The plan concentrated on basic heavy industry — coal, steel, railways, electricity, machinery.
3) Actual production figures were lower than the targets, but remarkable growth in output was achieved.

In 1933 a Second Five-Year Plan was Started

1) Some parts of the second plan were achieved, but fear at the rise of Adolf Hitler in Nazi Germany meant more development took place in the armaments industry than any other.
2) A third Five-Year Plan started in 1938, but was even more disrupted by war preparation and the German invasion of 1941.

> In under 10 years, the USSR had almost doubled its industrial output — the price was misery and low living standards for Soviet workers.

There were Serious Problems with the Plans

1) New towns, cities and industrial zones were set up — often with poor quality housing.
2) Long hours were worked for low pay, and higher wages were offered to foreign workers with special skills required to work on new schemes.
3) Bonuses were given for workers who could improve upon production targets as an inspiration to others — e.g. Alexei Stakhanov, whose coal mining team dramatically increased its output — but these were often unrealistic targets for most workers.
4) Much of the work was done by forced labour camps of criminals and political prisoners.
5) The targets were propaganda tools — the government said they'd been broken but often it's hard to tell how much was really achieved and how much was just propaganda.

Five years — I've got a cunning plan...

Communist Party propaganda used Stakhanov as an image of a heroic worker in the press and news reels. A 'Stakhanovite' movement began which encouraged workers to match this ideal.

Collectivisation

Communism was forced on the countryside.

Food Production had to be Increased

1) It was vital to increase the food supplies to workers in the towns and cities or the five-year plans wouldn't succeed.
2) Millions of peasants hid food away and didn't support the communists.
3) They were often poor and had no time-saving equipment.
4) Many richer peasants, or kulaks (see p.85), were influential in the villages, which annoyed the local Communist Party secretaries.

In 1929 Stalin began Collectivising All Farms

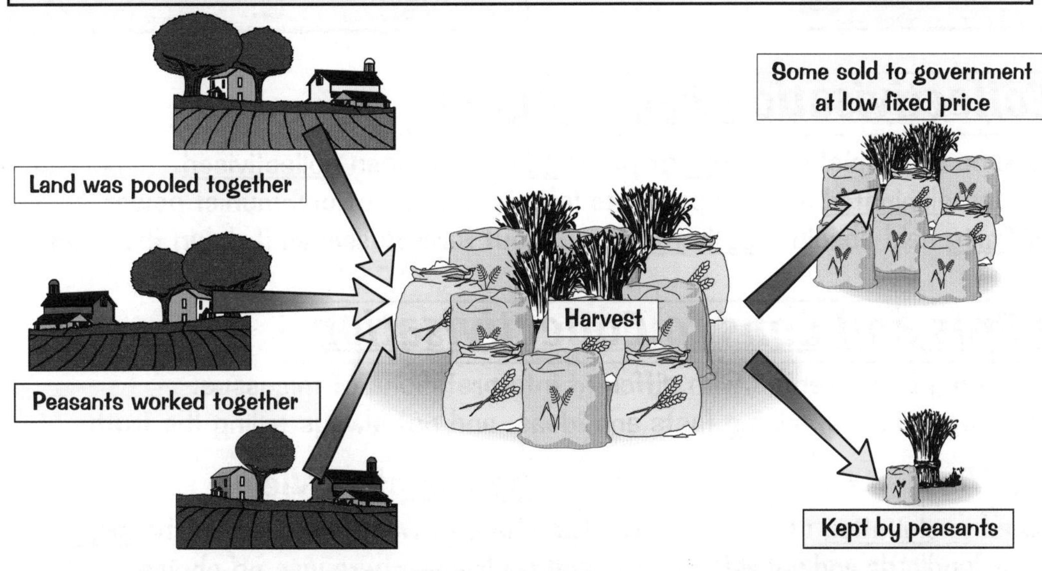

Peasants were forced to collectivise — they could keep small plots of land of their own for fruit, vegetables and animals. There would now be extra machinery for use on the larger farms.

There were Problems with Collectivisation

1) The speed of change required would destroy the traditional peasant way of life.
2) The peasants resisted this change and didn't want to give up land — especially the kulaks.
3) The collectives were forced to grow particular crops needed for industry, export or food for workers and they had to supply a specific amount to the state, whether the harvest was good or bad. Party officials were brought in to run collectives — this was resented.

Stalin Declared War on the Kulaks

1) Some of the peasants refused to collectivise, and Stalin blamed the kulaks.
2) Stalin sent troops to attack what he called these 'enemies of the people'.
3) An estimated 3 million kulaks were killed. Some were shot. Others died from starvation or cold either on the way to labour camps or during their time working there.
4) Some villages were surrounded and destroyed — many kulaks burned their own crops and killed livestock in protest. This contributed to a famine in the Ukraine — around 5 million people died.
5) 1930 saw famine and a poor harvest, and collectivisation was halted briefly.

Putting the farms together — a collective disaster...

This is all pretty vicious I'm afraid — and it's going to get worse. Collectivisation is a really important topic — it was intended to help the five-year plans but the effects were horrific. Don't forget to learn the main problems with collectivisation. And remember that when things went wrong Stalin looked for someone to blame — the kulaks were scapegoats here.

The Results of Collectivisation

Collectivisation brought agriculture under communist control — but at a cost.

The Famine Continued into 1932-33

Millions were dead or deported. Grain production was down and animal numbers had fallen.

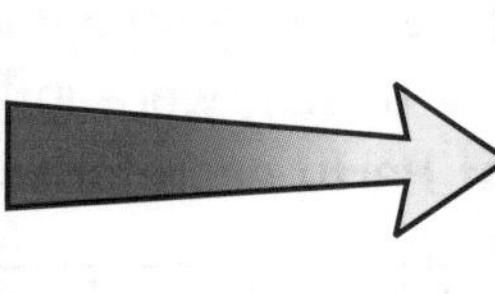

After 1931 Collectivisation Began Again

1) By 1939 it was almost complete — 99% of farming land had been collectivised.
2) The kulaks had been eliminated and the peasants left were afraid of communist power.
3) The Communist Party held absolute authority throughout rural Russia as it did in the cities.

There were Pros and Cons to Collectivisation

In exam questions you may be presented with different interpretations of this issue. Remember often these are opinions, mixing facts and ideas, and not always telling the truth:

The Positive View

1) It ended the forced exploitation of peasants by greedy landlords and got rid of the greedy and troublesome kulaks.
2) It helped peasants work together.
3) It provided large-scale organisation of food production for the farms.
4) This was communism in practice.
5) Soviet propaganda showed collective farms as a triumph for the state, and created a myth of the happy worker.

The Negative View

1) The changes were enforced by the army and by law — there was no choice.
2) The kulaks were scapegoats for inefficient food production in the past.
3) The policy led to the murder and imprisonment of millions of people.
4) The new system didn't work at first and a bad harvest combined with kulaks destroying crops and animals caused a serious famine — killing more people.

State Farms were an Extension of Collective Farms

1) Land was owned completely by the state, and peasants worked as labourers — so they received wages even if the farm did badly.
2) Food was delivered to the state, and farm workers bought food with their wages.
3) This was closer to the communist ideal than the collective, but they were very expensive to establish and run. Few farms of this type existed by 1940.

Propaganda and scapegoats — Stalin's key tactics...

Another important page for you to learn here — two views of collectivisation. Remember that neither side is giving pure facts — they're mixing them with opinions. It'll be up to you to tell opinions and facts apart in the exam, and use them to give a balanced answer to the question.

Life in the Soviet Union

Everyday life was difficult for many citizens of the USSR, but some did better than others.

Conditions were Harsh for millions of people

1) Life was hard, but it was dangerous to grumble — people feared being taken away by the secret police. Millions were shot or taken to labour camps during the purges (p.94).
2) Life in the cities was tough. Discipline was strict in the factories, and wages were low.
3) However, as a result of the rapid industrialisation there was almost no unemployment.
4) Life was probably worse for those in the countryside as a result of the forced collectivisation. Most people lived in rural areas, and in general they were far poorer than those in the cities. Only about a quarter of Party members were of peasant origin.

Some groups were "More Equal" than others

Communism was supposed to be about equality, but some people were better off than others.

1) What people could buy depended on a system based on social grouping — farmers, factory workers, engineers and Party managers had different places in the hierarchy. Those high up in the Party got the best goods and services. This also decided the standard of medical treatment people received.
2) Social mobility did increase as a result of the technical colleges which were opened during the first Five-Year Plan. Thousands of workers achieved promotion through education.

There were mixed fortunes for the Ethnic Minorities

1) Early Bolshevik ideology supported the rights of ethnic minorities, but the USSR didn't grant any real political independence to its non-Russian republics.
2) Some minorities suffered forcible population transfers. Stalin ordered mass deportations of ethnic Poles during the 1930s and of people from the Baltic states after 1940. Many were sent north-east to Siberia.
3) The USSR followed a policy of 'decossackisation'. The Cossacks — a military people who had mostly fought against the Bolsheviks during the civil war (see p.90) — were forced from their traditional homeland.
4) Although communism was against anti-Semitism, Stalin distrusted Jews — partly because his enemy Trotsky was Jewish. Many victims of the purges were Jewish.

Women were supposed to be Equal

1) The revolution gave women legal equality. Divorce was simplified. The state provided many communal creches, kitchens and laundries, to help women to work outside the home on an equal basis with men.
2) During 1919-30 the Women's Department of the Communist Party — the Zhenotdel — organised political training conferences attended by millions of women. But there were always far fewer women than men in the Party.
3) In the 1930s Stalin introduced legislation to restrict divorce and reduce women's independence. The emphasis was increasingly on stability and discipline, rather than on equality. Women were expected to go out and work, while still fulfilling traditional roles when they got home.

Not an easy time to be Russian — or Ukrainian, Georgian...

Communist rule didn't affect everybody in the same way. Although it was terrible for many millions of people, for others there were opportunities they'd never have had under the Tsar.

Revision Summary

And now it's time for your favourite part of every section — those sublime revision questions. I bet you can't wait — but remember that this is a really big topic. Make sure you know the order of events and be careful about mixing facts and opinions — especially with source questions. Give all sides of the story.

1) What was the name of the last Tsar?
2) What was the Duma?
3) Who was Rasputin?
4) Explain the impact that the First World War had on Russia.
5) What were the main beliefs of Marxism?
6) Why were communists split into Bolsheviks and Mensheviks?
7) What did the 'April Theses' promise?
8) Why was Kerensky's government 'Provisional' — and what does this mean?
9) Give three problems the Provisional Government faced.
10) Which General marched against the Provisional Government in September 1917?
11) How did the Bolsheviks seize power in 1917?
12) Give four reasons for the Bolsheviks' success?
13) Why were the Bolsheviks prepared to agree to the Brest-Litovsk Treaty?
14) Consider the events of the civil war — why did the 'Reds' win and the 'Whites' lose?
15) What were the results of the civil war on the economy, farming and industry?
16) What was the Kronstadt rebellion and how was it dealt with?
17) Write down the main features of the New Economic Policy, and its results.
18) When did Lenin die?
19) Write a short summary of Lenin's achievements.
20) What was the main difference in ideas between Stalin and Trotsky?
21) Why was Joseph Stalin able to win the struggle for power?
22) What were the purges?
23) What was the NKVD?
24) How were religion and the Church changed by Stalin's rule?
25) Explain or make a diagram to show the aims of the first Five-Year Plan.
26) Why did Stalin want to get rid of the 'kulaks' in the countryside?
27) Make summary notes/diagrams to explain how a collective farm worked.
28) Why were many peasants opposed to a collective farm system?
29) Why was the early 1930s a time of famine?
30) Why were people afraid of complaining about working conditions in Stalin's Russia?
31) Which element of the first Five-Year Plan helped increase social mobility?
32) What was the name for the policy the USSR brought against the Cossacks?

The Impact of the Cold War

The Cold War was a long period of hostility between the USA and USSR post-1945. No direct fighting took place between the two sides — but the situation was very tense.

The USA and USSR became Rivals after World War 2

1) The USA and USSR were allies during the Second World War. After the war, they were the two biggest powers in the world — often called superpowers. They soon became rivals.
2) Ideologically, they were very different. The USA was capitalist. The USSR was communist.

Early events in the Cold War

1) In the aftermath of the war, the USSR developed a sphere of influence in Eastern Europe. Most Eastern European countries had communist governments installed by the USSR.
2) In 1947, US President Truman promised support to countries threatened by communist takeover — this became known as the 'Truman Doctrine'.
3) Truman also gave economic aid to Western European countries — hoping that this would help protect them from communist influence. This was called the Marshall Plan.
4) There was a crisis in Berlin in 1948-1949. The USSR, USA, France and Britain each had a zone they controlled in post-war Berlin. The USSR was angry when the other three decided to combine their zones. The USSR stopped supplies getting by land to West Berlin — so supplies had to be airlifted in (see p.27).
5) In 1949, the North Atlantic Treaty Organization (NATO) was formed — a defensive alliance between America and Western European countries.

Events in the Far East made the Cold War worse

1) Communists came to power in China in 1949. They were led by Mao Tse-tung.
2) In 1950, communist North Korea invaded non-communist South Korea. The United Nations intervened to stop the communists taking over South Korea.
3) Once the UN forces had pushed them back past the original border, the communist Chinese sent an army to help the North.
4) The US General MacArthur, in charge of the UN forces, wanted to hit back at China itself. President Truman, afraid of starting World War 3, refused and insisted on a limited war.
5) In 1953 the Korean War ended with the pre-war border restored.

General MacArthur

Americans' Fear of Communism increased

1) American suspicions of the USSR grew — they thought it wanted world domination.
2) Under the 1947 Federal Employee Loyalty Program government employees were subjected to security checks. Their loyalty was questioned if they belonged to organisations with liberal ideas on race, disarmament or workers' rights.
3) Alger Hiss, a former senior member of the US State Department, was accused of spying and imprisoned for lying in court in 1950. This was an embarrassment to the US government.
4) By the 1950s, concerns about communism had started to cause a climate of fear and panic in the USA — this was called the Red Scare.

I spy — communists everywhere...

In the 1950s, there was huge fear and suspicion of communists in the USA. To understand why, you need to learn this stuff about the Cold War and what was going on in the world.

McCarthyism and the Red Scare

There was a 'Red Scare' in the 1950s — people were panicked by the communist threat.

The HUAC hunted for American Communists

1) The House Un-American Activities Committee (HUAC) was set up to investigate subversive activities. During the 1940s and 1950s it became focused on finding communists in the USA.
2) In 1947 HUAC began investigating the film industry, asking suspects at its hearings, "Are you now or have you ever been a member of the Communist Party?"

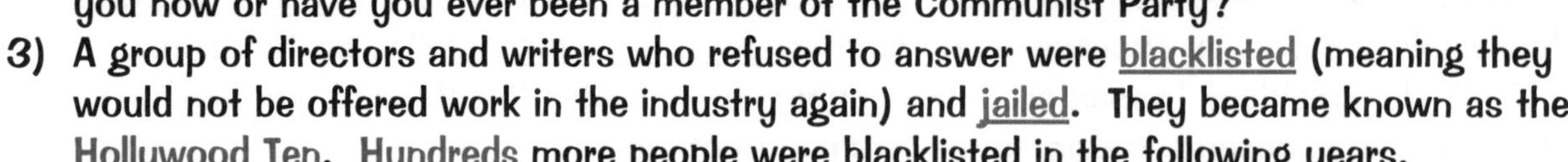

3) A group of directors and writers who refused to answer were blacklisted (meaning they would not be offered work in the industry again) and jailed. They became known as the Hollywood Ten. Hundreds more people were blacklisted in the following years.
4) Some famous actors like Humphrey Bogart supported the Hollywood Ten — but it didn't make any difference in the end. Some of those blacklisted went to Europe to find work.
5) Blacklisting also happened in broadcasting, schools and universities.

The FBI also investigated communists in America

J Edgar Hoover, director of the Federal Bureau of Investigation (FBI), was obsessed with "subversives". He kept thousands of secret dossiers on left-wing activists and thinkers, including six Nobel Prize-winning authors. The FBI conducted loyalty probes of millions of government employees.

McCarthy made Accusations with little evidence

1) In 1950, Senator McCarthy gave a speech during which he waved what he claimed was a list of 205 communists in the State Department (the US Foreign Office). He claimed some were giving information to the USSR — putting America at risk.
2) No one ever got a look at the list and many of the accusations were never proved. But newspapers published his allegations, and many people believed him.
3) McCarthy investigated possible communists. During Senate hearings he intimidated witnesses and pressured people to accuse others. He destroyed the careers of thousands of people.

McCarthy's activities were made possible by an already existing climate of fear. China had gone communist. The Russians had the bomb. And in 1951 two members of the US Communist Party, Julius and Ethel Rosenberg, were convicted of passing atomic secrets to the Russians. They were executed in 1953.

McCarthy Lost Popularity because of his Bullying Tactics

1) In 1953 McCarthy turned on the Army, accusing it of covering up communist infiltration. In the televised Army-McCarthy hearings in 1954, his bullying of witnesses turned public opinion against him. His Senate colleagues finally voted 67-22 to censure him in December 1954.
2) However, anti-communist feeling remained strong. The Communist Control Act in 1954 allowed dismissal from the civil service for political beliefs.

Red Scare — BOO!

The playwright Arthur Miller was blacklisted for refusing to give information to HUAC. He wrote a play called 'The Crucible' about a 17th century witch hunt — a symbol for McCarthyism.

The Vietnam War

There's a lot to learn about the Vietnam War, so here's a rundown on the whole thing.

The First Vietnam War was fought against the French

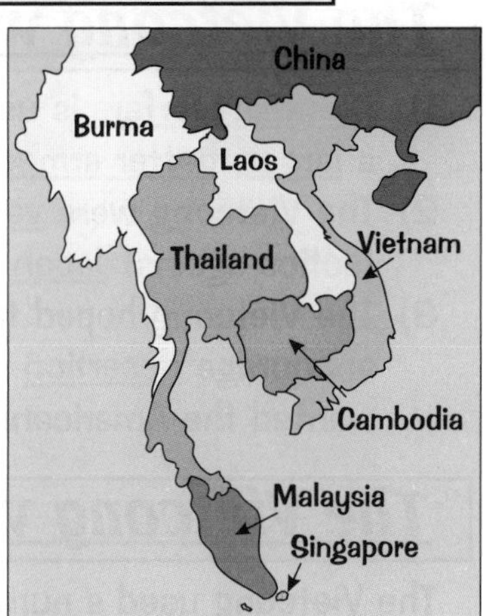

1) In the 19th century, Vietnam was ruled by the French. During World War Two, a communist group called the Viet Minh were formed — they wanted Vietnam to become independent.
2) Between 1946 and 1954, the Viet Minh fought the French for independence. The USA supported France because they feared that if Vietnam became independent, communism would spread in the Far East. This was known as the 'domino theory' (see p32).
3) By 1954, many French forces were based in a military stronghold at Dien Bien Phu. They hoped to draw the Viet Minh into a battle and defeat them once and for all.
4) The Viet Minh attacked but the French had underestimated their strength. After weeks of fighting, the French were defeated and they left Vietnam. The country was split into two — North Vietnam became communist, while South Vietnam had a pro-western, anti-communist government.

Kennedy Increased US Involvement in Vietnam

1) The US had given military help and advice to the French to help prevent the spread of communism.
2) After the split, the US supported the president of South Vietnam, Ngo Dinh Diem, despite the fact that he was very corrupt. The US provided his regime with financial help and political and military advice.
3) In 1960, the communist National Liberation Front was formed in opposition to Diem's government. The military arm of this group became known as the Vietcong.
4) US President Kennedy was determined to stop the spread of communism in Asia. He sent financial aid, military equipment and over 12 000 military advisers to South Vietnam.

The US sent More Troops to Vietnam

1) After Kennedy was assassinated, Lyndon B. Johnson became the new president of the USA.
2) In 1964, US ships were attacked by the North Vietnamese. This became known as the Gulf of Tonkin Incident (see p.106), and it led to full-scale war in Vietnam. President Johnson sent aircraft to attack North Vietnam and ground troops to South Vietnam.
3) By 1965, Johnson increased the number of ground troops to 125 000 men. By 1968 there were over 500 000 US troops in Vietnam.
4) The US troops found it hard fighting the Vietcong in the jungle — so they used tactics such as heavy bombing and chemical weapons instead (see p.105).
5) In 1968, the Vietcong and the North Vietnamese Army (NVA) launched an all-out attack on the South — the Tet Offensive. Although the US recovered most of their losses after three days, fighting continued for several weeks. Eventually, the US defeated the Vietcong and NVA forces.
6) The Tet Offensive was a victory for the US, but it had taken them by surprise, and had led many Americans to oppose the war. After Tet, the new president, Richard Nixon, promised to withdraw US troops from Vietnam and negotiate 'peace with honour'.

The US and Vietnam — in for a penny, in for a pound...

During the 1960s and 1970s, the USA feared the spread of communism. That's what drove the US to support South Vietnam, but the more support it gave, the harder it was to pull out.

The Vietcong

The Vietcong were supported by the NVA — but they weren't a trained army. They weren't as well armed as the US troops, but they turned out to be a tough enemy to fight.

The Vietcong were experienced Guerrilla Fighters

1) Guerrilla warfare is used when small military units want to avoid open battle with a larger, better armed opponent. It involves tactics such as raids and ambushes.
2) The Vietcong were very experienced in guerrilla warfare — the Viet Minh had used guerrilla tactics against Japan and France during World War Two and the First Vietnam War.
3) The Vietcong hoped that guerrilla warfare would exhaust the US troops, lower morale, encourage desertion and encourage South Vietnamese soldiers to defect. The Vietcong wanted the Americans to leave so that they could unify Vietnam as an independent country.

The Vietcong were Hard to Pin Down

The Vietcong used a number of guerrilla tactics that made fighting them very difficult.

1) They worked in small groups and launched surprise attacks on US troops. They knew the land well, so they could choose when and where to attack.
2) In the jungle, they used hidden traps to kill or injure US soldiers. For example, explosives triggered by tripwires and covered pits filled with bamboo spikes.
3) They hid in underground tunnels. These tunnel systems were very complex, and some even had army barracks and hospitals.
4) They blended in easily with Vietnamese villagers. This made it difficult for the US troops to identify Vietcong soldiers.
5) The Vietcong often returned to areas where the US had driven them out. The US army seemed to be making little progress.

The Vietcong's tactics made them strong, but the US army had weaknesses. Most US troops in Vietnam were very young — in their early twenties. Many had been drafted (conscripted) and didn't want to be there. Most only served one year. This gave them little time to gain experience of fighting in the jungle.

The Ho Chi Minh Trail was Crucial for the Vietcong

1) The Ho Chi Minh Trail was a North Vietnamese supply route. It passed through Laos and Cambodia.
2) The trail allowed soldiers, supplies and weapons to be sent from North Vietnam to support the Vietcong in South Vietnam.
3) The trail was used throughout the war and it allowed the Vietcong to keep on fighting.
4) The US tried to bomb the trail but never managed to break it. It was difficult to bomb paths in the jungle as new routes could easily be created. Also, the trail was actually a system of trails which were often added to. Some trails were just decoy routes to confuse the Americans.

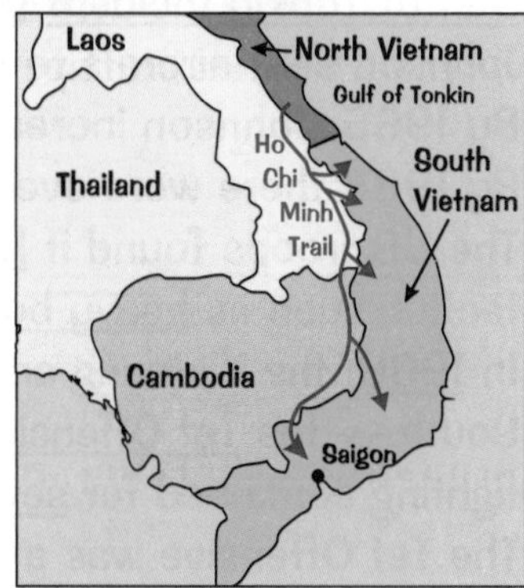

The US couldn't fight them if they couldn't find them...

The US had a massive amount of military power, but in the jungle they weren't able to use it to its full potential. Make sure you learn the tactics the Vietcong used and why they were so effective.

Fighting the Vietcong

The US troops needed ways to overcome the Vietcong's guerrilla tactics.

The US launched Major Military Operations

The US used a variety of methods to try to combat the guerrilla tactics of the Vietcong.

Operation Rolling Thunder

1) Operation Rolling Thunder was a huge bombing campaign against North Vietnam which ran from March 1965 until 1968. It was meant to destroy North Vietnam's industry and stop supplies arriving from China.
2) The US hoped that if North Vietnam was weakened, it wouldn't be able to supply the Vietcong.
3) The operation wasn't successful. Vietnam's economy relied on farming, not factories, so it wasn't badly affected. Supplies from China continued to arrive.

'Search and Destroy'

1) 'Search and destroy' was a tactic which focused on killing enemy troops. Instead of securing territory, US forces would simply hunt the Vietcong and clear them out of villages. Villages suspected of supporting the Vietcong were often destroyed. Afterwards, the US troops would move on to another village or return to base.
2) It was difficult to spot Vietcong soldiers from ordinary villagers, so innocent people were sometimes interrogated or even killed. This made the US unpopular.
3) US troops sometimes made brutal attacks to get revenge for their losses. This also made the US unpopular around the world.

Chemical Weapons

1) Napalm was a burning chemical jelly which stuck to people and objects. It was used to destroy hidden targets and burn areas of jungle. It caused many civilian casualties, and its use was widely criticised.
2) Agent Orange was a chemical which destroyed trees and plant life. The US used it to try to remove big parts of the jungle where the Vietcong hid. It was also used to destroy food supplies. It was used on trees and crops, but it was very harmful, and caused cancer and birth defects.

'Hearts and Minds'

1) The US wanted to win South Vietnamese 'hearts and minds', so they wouldn't help the Vietcong.
2) They did this by providing free health care and training programmes for Vietnamese villagers.
3) It wasn't very successful because South Vietnamese civilians had been badly affected by the USA's 'search and destroy' tactics and chemical weapons.
4) The US was also unpopular because it supported the corrupt South Vietnamese government.

'Search and Destroy' led to the My Lai Massacre

1) In March 1968, a 'search and destroy' mission in the village of My Lai led to the murder of over 300 unarmed civilians, including women and children.
2) At first, the US Army tried to cover up the incident — early reports claimed that around 20 civilians had been accidentally killed.
3) But the massacre was revealed by the media in autumn 1969. The news horrified the public and led to a high profile investigation (see p.106).

The conflict in Vietnam had devastating consequences...

Both the Vietcong and the US troops used increasingly brutal tactics as the war raged on. But it was the sheer scale of the damage caused by US tactics that caused the most outrage.

TV and Media Coverage

Hundreds of journalists covered the war in Vietnam. Their reporting was very influential.

Media Coverage led many people to Oppose the War

1) The presence of the media in Vietnam meant that the US public could see what the war was really like.
2) During the 1960s, more and more people owned televisions. A lot of Americans watched news about the war every night, so they knew that the death toll was rising.
3) Reporting was mostly upbeat until the Tet Offensive in 1968 (see p.108). Footage of the Tet Offensive, including scenes showing the Vietcong inside the walls of the US embassy, made many people think that the US was losing the war.
4) A famous photograph from the Tet Offensive shows a South Vietnamese police chief shooting a handcuffed Vietcong soldier in the street. This made many people think that the US and the South Vietnamese were just as brutal as the enemy.
5) Walter Cronkite was a respected news reporter. After the Tet Offensive, Cronkite said that the situation in Vietnam was at a 'stalemate'. His opinions made some US citizens pessimistic about the war.

The Tonkin Incident was Exaggerated

Lyndon B. Johnson

1) On the 2nd August 1964, a US ship, the USS Maddox, was attacked in the Gulf of Tonkin by North Vietnam.
2) Two days later, more attacks on the USS Maddox and the USS Turner Joy were reported. However, there was no proof that these attacks took place.
3) President Johnson announced these suspected attacks, and the story was printed in US newspapers. Johnson made the attacks seem very serious, and he wanted to take action to appear tough.
4) The attacks gave Johnson public and political support for taking further action in Vietnam. Congress (the US parliament) passed the Gulf of Tonkin Resolution, which gave Johnson permission to use 'all necessary steps' to 'prevent further aggression'.

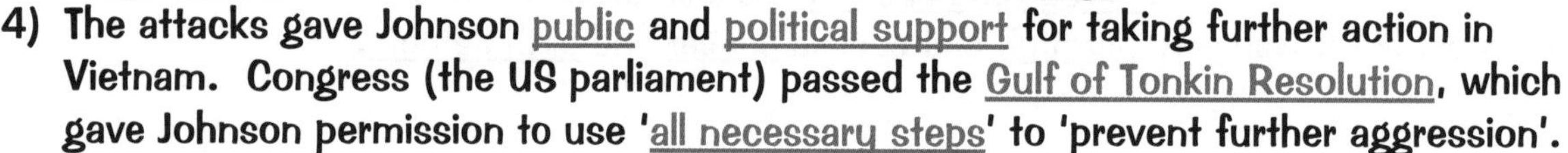

5) In the late 1960s, it was revealed that the second attacks may not have happened. This made many Americans feel that they'd been tricked into the war.

Evidence from My Lai was released in the press

1) In 1968, over 300 Vietnamese civilians were killed in the My Lai Massacre (see p.105). Photographs of the incident were printed in the media in 1969.
2) Public opinion about My Lai was divided — many Americans were horrified by the massacre, and the news increased anti-war feeling. Others believed that the massacre was an unfortunate consequence of the war, and that the My Lai villagers were probably helping the Vietcong.
3) In the early 1970s, several of the soldiers who had taken part in the massacre were brought to trial. Only one officer, Lieutenant William Calley, was convicted. He was sentenced to life in prison, but he was released in 1974.
4) Opinion polls showed that most Americans believed that Calley had just been following orders. Despite this, other polls showed that a majority of Americans opposed the war in Vietnam.

Vietnam — the first TV war...

The media played a crucial role in encouraging people to support the war, and then to oppose it.

Anti-War Protests

During the 1960s, a strong culture of protest movements developed in the US.

Many Anti-War Demonstrations were held

Chicago Anti-War Protests

1) In 1968, the Democratic Party held its convention in Chicago.
2) The Democrats chose Hubert Humphrey (Johnson's Vice President) as their presidential candidate. Anti-war protestors believed that Humphrey would continue Johnson's Vietnam policies.
3) Violent demonstrations took place and were broadcast on television. 12 000 police and over 5000 National Guardsmen dealt with the protests — over 500 arrests were made.
4) The Republican candidate, Richard Nixon, promised to secure 'peace with honour' in Vietnam, and put an end to the violent protests at home. Nixon won the 1968 election, but it was very close.

Vietnam Veterans' Protest

1) The Vietnam Veterans Against the War (VVAW) was an organisation of soldiers who had fought in Vietnam and wanted the war to end.
2) In April 1971, the VVAW held a week of protests in Washington DC. Over 1000 veterans threw their medals onto the steps of the Capitol — the building where US Congress (parliament) meets.
3) The VVAW protests divided public opinion. Some people felt that Vietnam veterans were worth listening to. Others felt that the demonstrations were unpatriotic.

The Kent State University protest ended in Tragedy

1) Nixon's decision to invade Cambodia (see p.108) sparked off several student protests, including one at Kent State University, Ohio, in May 1970.
2) The Governor of Ohio used the National Guard to deal with the protestors. The students were angry that soldiers had been used and violence broke out.
3) The National Guard used tear gas, and when this didn't disperse the students, they opened fire. Four students were killed. The incident outraged many people and caused riots at other universities across America. Some believed that the protestors were to blame for the outbreak of violence, but some believed that they had a right to protest.

The Fulbright Hearings were a media sensation

1) Senator Fulbright was chairman of the Senate Foreign Relations Committee. Among other things, the committee discussed ways to end the war in Vietnam.
2) In 1971, Fulbright organised a series of hearings from people who both supported and opposed the war. One of the most important testimonies came from John Kerry (a member of the VVAW).
3) In his testimony, Kerry spoke about the Winter Soldier Investigation. In this investigation, several veterans had admitted to committing offences in Vietnam such as rape, torture, and the destruction of entire villages and the people who lived there.
4) The hearings were widely covered in the news. Kerry was the first veteran to speak so publicly about the war and his testimony was a media sensation. Many saw him as a hero for revealing the truth, but others believed he had betrayed the army and the US.

War — what is it good for?

It's difficult to know how most US citizens felt about Vietnam. Despite the large number of protests, President Nixon believed that the 'silent majority' of US citizens supported the war.

Trying to End the War

As the war in Vietnam progressed, it became more and more unpopular in the US.

The Tet Offensive worried the US Public

1) The Tet Offensive (January 1968), was the biggest attack of the war by the Vietcong and the North Vietnamese Army (NVA). Around 80 000 Vietcong troops attacked US bases throughout South Vietnam, including the capital Saigon.
2) The NVA and the Vietcong hoped that the South Vietnamese citizens would join them when they saw the attack and they could force the US out of Vietnam.
3) However, the South Vietnamese did not support the attack. The Vietcong and the NVA were pushed back after three days of fighting. The Vietcong was almost completely destroyed.
4) This was a clear victory for the US. The US Commander, General Westmoreland, believed that the US could soon 'finish the job'.
5) However, the attack had taken the US by surprise. The US public saw images of mass destruction and death. The Tet Offensive made the Vietcong seem strong.
6) Many Americans wanted to end the war. When General Westmoreland requested 200 000 extra soldiers it was very unpopular with the public.
7) President Johnson didn't run for re-election. The new president, Richard Nixon, promised to end the war. He wanted peace without it looking like the US was admitting defeat.

Vietnamisation was Nixon's New Strategy

Richard Nixon

1) Nixon had promised to withdraw US troops from Vietnam. This meant that the South Vietnamese Army (the ARVN) would have to fight the North Vietnamese alone.
2) The US invested money in the ARVN to recruit more troops and provide training and weapons. This was called Vietnamisation.
3) Vietnamisation was largely unsuccessful because ARVN troops lacked discipline. The remaining US troops were also demoralised — they felt that the US wasn't committed to Vietnam, and they were simply waiting to be sent home.

Nixon tried to Pressure North Vietnam to make Peace

Along with Vietnamisation, Nixon used aggressive tactics to force peace talks.

Cambodian Campaign

1) In 1969, Nixon began a bombing campaign in Cambodia to try to destroy the Ho Chi Minh Trail and pressure North Vietnam to make peace.
2) He also sent in 30 000 US ground troops to destroy communist bases and supplies.
3) However, crossing into Cambodia led to more anti-war demonstrations (see p.107).
4) Anti-war feeling led Congress to cut military spending and cancel the Gulf of Tonkin Resolution (see p.106). This made it difficult for Nixon to carry on the war.

Laos Campaign

1) In 1971 the South Vietnamese Army attacked the Ho Chi Minh Trail in Laos.
2) US troops couldn't enter Laos, but they provided air support.
3) Although many communist supplies were destroyed, the South Vietnamese army was quickly driven out of Laos.

President Nixon — bombing his way to peace...

Nixon hoped that heavy bombing would pressure North Vietnam into signing a peace agreement.

Peace and Defeat

A peace deal for Vietnam took a long time to negotiate, and the peace didn't last very long...

Initial Peace Talks were Unsuccessful

1) Peace talks with North Vietnam were first held in Paris in 1968, under President Johnson. In 1969, Nixon also held secret peace talks — but both were unsuccessful.
2) North Vietnam was in no hurry to make peace, and it refused to withdraw its troops from South Vietnam. The North Vietnamese government believed that anti-war protests in the US and military spending cuts would soon force Nixon to make peace.

Peace was agreed at the Paris Peace Conference

On 27th January 1973 both sides signed the Paris Peace Accords. The key agreements were:

- The president of South Vietnam, General Thieu, could stay in power.
- The NVA could stay in areas of South Vietnam which it already controlled.
- All US prisoners of war would be released.
- All US troops would leave Vietnam within two months.

Both sides wanted to Reach a Deal

North Vietnam

1) The US had improved its relations with China and the USSR. These countries were North Vietnam's allies. They encouraged North Vietnam to make peace.
2) In December 1972, the US launched its 'Christmas bombing' of North Vietnam. The renewed bombing made North Vietnam eager for the US to leave.
3) The North Vietnamese government wanted a chance to recover and rebuild, and then mount a final assault on South Vietnam.

USA

1) The war was becoming increasingly unpopular in the US.
2) It was difficult to finance the war after Congress cut military spending.
3) It seemed the war would drag on for a long time.

The Fall of Saigon showed that Peace had Failed

1) US troops were gradually being withdrawn from 1969, but once the peace treaty was signed, all remaining troops left Vietnam.
2) By 1974 the US had withdrawn all its troops, and Congress had stopped all financial help to the country as well — South Vietnam was left to defend itself.
3) North Vietnam invaded South Vietnam in late 1974. They advanced rapidly against the weak and disorganised South Vietnamese forces. In April 1975, they took control of the South Vietnamese capital, Saigon.
4) Helicopters landed on the roof of the US embassy to pick up the last remaining diplomats. This evacuation was broadcast on television. Many Americans who watched it felt that the chaotic scenes were an embarrassment for their country.

Saigon, 1975 — a not quite honourable exit...

Some argued that the US evacuation was a success, with thousands of people lifted to safety. Others believed it was chaotic and disorganised and that evacuation should have begun earlier.

Civil Rights for African Americans

In the 1940s and 1950s, African Americans were still denied the rights promised by the American constitution. Many states were still segregated (see p.73) and racist attitudes were common.

African Americans fought in World War 2

1) World War 2 started in 1939, but the USA didn't join the fighting until December 1941.
2) About a million African Americans fought in the American armed forces during the war.
3) The army was segregated — African Americans served in separate military units to whites.
4) African Americans saw action on all fronts and often distinguished themselves in the fighting, for example in the Battle of the Bulge in 1944 and at Iwo Jima in 1945.
5) However, because of racism, no African Americans were awarded the Medal of Honor.
6) Some concessions were made for the sake of military efficiency. African Americans were admitted to the Marine Corps for the first time. The first African-American fighter pilots flew combat missions.
7) African American soldiers fought for freedom abroad — but returned home to a society in which they were oppressed and discriminated against.
8) After the war, in 1948, President Truman ended segregation in the armed forces.

African Americans remained Second-Class Citizens

In 1941, President Roosevelt had signed an executive order banning racial discrimination in defence industries. This caused resentment from some white workers. Race riots broke out in the industrial city of Detroit in 1943 — during which 25 African Americans and 9 white Americans were killed.

In the South of the USA, segregation was enforced by law in most aspects of daily life — schools, restaurants, theatres, workplaces, public transport and public toilets. Most white people thought this was normal and unremarkable. In the North, there was some informal segregation — reflecting and reinforcing African Americans' lower social status. Average wealth and living standards remained comparatively low for African Americans across the whole country.

The Ku Klux Klan (see p.73) was a secret organisation that believed in white supremacy — and used violence to intimidate African Americans. It had declined in popularity by the 1940s but was still active — and many people still shared its beliefs.

Civil Rights — in the land of the not yet free...

Despite gaining freedom from slavery after the civil war, African Americans were still heavily oppressed in the South. See page 73 for more on how prejudice was rife in pre-war America. Make sure you learn about the impact of World War 2, and how bad things remained at home.

Civil Rights for African Americans

With the help of the Supreme Court, the African Americans began to gain civil rights.

Justice lay in Enforcing the Constitution

The USA's Declaration of Independence and Constitution promise all citizens certain rights, including equal protection by the law. One strategy for gaining civil rights for African Americans was to appeal back to these iconic American documents. This approach, combined with non-violent protest, was pursued by organisations such as:

- The NAACP — National Association for the Advancement of Colored People, founded in 1909 — funded court cases challenging discrimination.
- CORE — the Congress of Racial Equality, founded in 1942 — dedicated to non-violent protest.
- The SCLC — Southern Christian Leadership Conference, founded in 1957 by Martin Luther King and Ralph Abernathy — used the churches' strength for protests.
- The SNCC — Student Nonviolent Coordinating Committee, formed in 1960 (see p.117).

The Supreme Court ruled against Segregated Education

1) Following campaigns by the NAACP, the US Supreme Court — which interprets the Constitution — ruled in the case Brown v Board of Education of Topeka (1954) that racial segregation in state schools was unconstitutional.
2) Since the Constitution is the highest law of the land, the federal (central) government was obliged to intervene when it was contradicted by local state law.
3) In 1957 President Eisenhower ordered 1000 paratroopers to the Central High School campus at Little Rock, Arkansas, to enforce the admission of nine African-American pupils in the face of local mob violence.
4) In 1962, James Meredith, an African American, had to have the protection of Federal troops as he registered as a student at the University of Mississippi.
5) In both the above cases the state governor, backed by passionate public support from white people for segregation, did all he could to defy the federal authorities.

The Montgomery Bus Boycott — a victory for Integration

Rosa Parks

1) In 1955 in Montgomery, Alabama, Rosa Parks refused to give up her seat on the bus for a white man. She was arrested.
2) Black ministers, led by 26-year-old Martin Luther King, organised a bus boycott in protest. African Americans supported the boycott by walking to work or sharing cars for a year, until the Supreme Court finally ruled that Alabama's bus segregation laws were unconstitutional.
3) The success of this peaceful protest was inspirational to all who opposed segregation in the South.

The Civil Rights Acts of 1957 and 1960 were ineffective

1) The 1957 act created a Civil Rights Commission to investigate obstruction of voting rights.
2) The 1960 act increased record-keeping and supervision of voting procedures.
3) Neither act achieved much in practice, but a small beginning had been made by Congress.

All men are created equal...

... or so says the Declaration of Independence which, along with the Constitution, has a lot to say about freedom and equality — but African Americans still had to struggle to achieve theirs.

Civil Rights for African Americans

Martin Luther King, the first president of the SCLC, was committed to non-violent struggle.

Non-Violent Protest won support

1) Martin Luther King and other activists used peaceful protests like marches, sit-ins and freedom rides (see box below) — gaining publicity and sympathy for the cause.
2) Many peaceful protests were undertaken by civil rights activists:

- In 1960, four African-American students started a series of sit-ins at segregated lunch counters at the Woolworths in Greensboro, North Carolina. These protests spread and some succeeded in forcing the desegregation of facilities.
- The Freedom Rides of 1961, organised by CORE and the SNCC, saw groups of African Americans and white Americans sitting together on bus trips into the South. Segregation on bus services had been ruled unconstitutional by the Supreme Court. There was a violent reaction to the Freedom Rides by some white people in the South — such as the burning of a bus at Anniston, Alabama.

The Birmingham victory convinced the President

1) President Kennedy (who came to power in 1961) at first gave limited support for African-American civil rights. He didn't want to alienate Southern white voters.
2) King and the SCLC organised protests in Birmingham, Alabama in April 1963. Protesters were met by police with fire hoses, truncheons and police dogs. Images of the harsh treatment of the protesters in the media gained support for their cause. King and hundreds of others were jailed. But in the end the Birmingham authorities gave way and agreed some concessions.
3) President Kennedy decided it was time to send a major Civil Rights Bill to Congress.

Next came Pressure on Congress

1) In August 1963, 250 000 demonstrators marched on Washington, where King spoke of his dream of a non-racist America.
2) But when Kennedy was assassinated in November 1963, his Civil Rights Bill had still not passed. He was replaced by President Johnson.
3) Despite the fact that Kennedy was from liberal Massachusetts in the North, and Johnson from segregated Texas in the South, it was Johnson who was more effective in achieving civil rights.

Martin Luther King

Important Acts were passed in 1964 and 1965

1) The Civil Rights Act of 1964 empowered the federal government to enforce desegregation in all public places. This was a big victory for the civil rights movement.
2) Voting rights were still a problem. In theory, African Americans could vote, but in the South all kinds of local rules were invented to stop them.
3) In the "Freedom Summer" of 1964 thousands of student volunteers spent vacations in Mississippi in a drive for voter registration. Three of these students were murdered.
4) In March 1965 the police in Selma, Alabama, used clubs and tear gas on civil rights marchers and again the brutality was televised. In response, King — who had been awarded the Nobel Peace Prize in 1964 — led a march through Alabama from Selma to Montgomery.
5) In August 1965 Johnson signed the Voting Rights Act. Federal registrars would now enforce voting rights. This was another major success for the civil rights movement.

Civil Rights — a victory for non-violence...

King was influenced by Gandhi who used non-violent civil disobedience against the British in India.

Civil Rights for African Americans

The late 1960s and early 1970s saw the rise of a more confrontational approach to civil rights.

There was still Discrimination and Unrest

1) Formal civil rights weren't enough to help African Americans trapped in poverty.
2) The Vietnam War began to absorb funds which might otherwise have been available for more spending on social programmes.
3) Some African Americans became impatient with King's leadership and non-violent methods.
4) There were many inner-city riots by African Americans in the mid-1960s. 34 people were killed in a 6-day riot in the Watts district of Los Angeles in August 1965. The 8-day Detroit riot of July 1967 left 43 dead.

Martin Luther King was Assassinated in 1968

1) In 1966 Martin Luther King went north to Chicago to organise marches against discrimination in housing — a problem not dealt with by the 1964 Civil Rights Act.
2) The government gave no support because President Johnson was angered at the "ingratitude" of black leaders who had criticised his Vietnam War policy.
3) Congress did pass an effective Civil Rights Act for housing after King's assassination in April 1968 had triggered more riots in more than 100 cities.

Some groups favoured Violent Protest

Malcolm X, an African-American Muslim, rejected integration and non-violence. He called the peaceful march on Washington the "farce on Washington". His preaching drew converts to the African-American separatist organisation, the Nation of Islam. Malcolm X developed more 'inclusive' views and left the Nation of Islam in 1964. He was killed by Nation of Islam members in February 1965.

In 1966 SNCC chairman Stokely Carmichael popularised the "Black Power" slogan. Under his leadership, the SNCC expelled its white members. In Newark in 1967, after a riot in which over 20 African Americans had been killed by police, a Black Power conference passed resolutions calling for a separate African-American nation and militia.

The Black Panther Party was founded in 1966 by Huey P. Newton and Bobby Seale. Its members wore uniforms and went on armed patrol, claiming to defend African Americans from police violence. They also carried out programmes of education and healthcare for African Americans.

Affirmative Action gave African Americans opportunities

1) President Johnson sought to combat the under-representation of African Americans in many areas of employment with a preferential hiring policy.
2) Under President Nixon, people began to criticise this policy as "reverse discrimination".
3) However, from 1969 Nixon encouraged the growth of African American-owned businesses with the Small Business Administration's set-aside programme. This guaranteed that a proportion of government contracts would be awarded to ethnic minority owned firms.
4) During the 1970s attempts were made to integrate schools by "busing" children from different areas to make sure schools were ethnically mixed. It caused much resistance — many white Americans moved out to the suburbs or put their children in private schools to avoid it.

There was a protest at the Mexican Olympics in 1968...

Two African American athletes raised their fists in a "Black Power" salute on the winners' podium. It was an iconic moment — but they were expelled from the US team.

Civil Rights of Hispanic Americans

African Americans weren't the only group in the USA who struggled against discrimination.

People emigrated from Latin America to the USA

The Mexican-American border

1) The states bordering Mexico — Texas, New Mexico, Arizona and California — attracted much immigration from Mexico and other countries in Latin America.
2) To help the wartime labour shortage, from 1942 the Bracero Program allowed Mexican labourers to work temporarily in the US. The scheme lasted till 1964.
3) Millions more came as illegal immigrants — the 2000-mile border was difficult to police.
4) Mexican Americans faced segregation in schools, housing and employment.

The war sparked an era of Progress

1) Hundreds of thousands of Hispanic Americans served in the US armed forces in World War 2.
2) There was some racism against Hispanic Americans. In 1943 Los Angeles erupted in the Zoot Suit Riots — American sailors spent 10 days seeking out and beating up Latino teenagers.
3) After the war, the League of United Latin American Citizens and the American GI Forum mounted legal challenges to overturn school segregation in California and the exclusion of Mexican Americans from Texas juries.
4) In 1954 the Supreme Court in the case Hernandez v Texas declared that the 14th Amendment outlawing racial discrimination applied not just to African Americans but to all races.
5) Founded in 1968, the Mexican American Legal Defence and Educational Fund (MALDEF) became the most prominent Mexican-American civil rights organisation.

Cesar Chavez led the farm workers

1) Cesar Chavez, the grandson of Mexican immigrants, formed the United Farm Workers union in 1962. From 1965 he organised a 10-year campaign to improve the pay and working conditions of migrant workers, including a nationwide grape boycott in 1967.
2) In 1975 the Agricultural Labor Relations Act protected the right of farm workers to unionise. Chavez's success played a part in raising awareness of the wider struggle for Hispanic-American rights.

United Farm Workers' flag

The 1965 Immigration Act loosened restrictions

1) US immigration rules were based on a system of national quotas designed to reflect the existing ethnic structure of the USA. In the 1960s liberals denounced this as race bias.
2) The 1965 Immigration Act set preference categories based less on country of origin and more on kinship relations and occupation. Immigration from Latin America and Asia increased.

The Zoot Suit Riots — a fashion crime...

Zoot suits were over-sized suits popular with Latin American teenagers in the 1940s. Some people said they wasted material — bad in wartime. But hardly justification for a riot...

Civil Rights of Native Americans

Native Americans suffered discrimination. Traditionally many tribes had led a nomadic lifestyle on the plains — but white settlers in the 19th century had forced them off much of the land.

Native American Land and Independence was under Threat

1) The 1934 Indian Reorganisation Act had halted previous attempts to break up tribes and enforce assimilation. Now substantial self-government was offered to tribes who wanted it, in an effort to restore their sovereignty and cultural autonomy.
2) After World War 2, Congress reverted to the earlier goal of complete assimilation. Under this 'termination' policy, started in the 1950s, the government withdrew benefits from many tribes. Many reservations (areas set aside for Native Americans) were absorbed by the states, becoming new counties. 'Terminated' tribes now had to pay state taxes and obey state regulations. Many had to sell land or mineral rights to outside interests, and were left poorer than before.
3) In the 1960s the Supreme Court began issuing decisions supporting Native American sovereignty and recognising the tribes' legal status as higher than that of the states, which limited the power of the states over the reservations.

AIM struggled for Native American Rights

1) The American Indian Movement (AIM) was formed in 1968 in response to police harassment in Minneapolis. It became a national organisation concerned also with issues such as living standards and treaty rights.
2) In 1972 AIM members joined with seven other organisations in the Trail of Broken Treaties, a march on Washington. The protesters vandalised the headquarters of the Bureau of Indian Affairs (BIA) — the federal agency which manages the reservation system.
3) Civil disobedience 'fish-ins' brought success in the 1974 Boldt Decision in favour of Native American fishing and hunting rights.
4) By 1980 Native Americans had succeeded in forcing the government to return some important tribal lands and to provide compensation for some confiscated lands.
5) The 1978 Indian Religious Freedom Act guaranteed protection for forms of religious worship and access to sacred sites.

There was conflict at Wounded Knee in 1973

1) A faction at the Oglala Sioux reservation, opposed to corruption in the way the reservation was managed, invited AIM to join a protest.
2) The protesters seized the village of Wounded Knee at gunpoint. Soon they were surrounded by a military cordon. The siege lasted for 71 days. Shots were exchanged and two people were killed.
3) The symbolism of the site — scene of an 1890 massacre of Sioux by the Army — ensured national media attention.
4) Eventually, after a negotiated settlement of the local issues, the siege ended in a triumph for AIM.

Russell Means — one of AIM's leaders in the '70s

Native American Rights — AIM to learn the whole page...

Wounded Knee is a place with very heavy significance in Native American history. The 1890 massacre of Sioux is generally regarded as the final event in the Native American struggle against the expanding USA. So the siege there in 1973 made people sit up and take notice.

Women's Rights

The feminist movement gained momentum in the 1960s — and won better rights for women.

Women began to challenge Discrimination at Work

1) In 1960 women usually worked in low-paid jobs such as nursing, teaching, and clerical and domestic work. During the 1960s, women made up around 33-43 per cent of the total workforce, but their average earnings remained around 60 per cent that of men.
2) Eleanor Roosevelt pressured President Kennedy into creating a Presidential Commission on the Status of Women (1961) with herself as its head.
3) The 1963 Equal Pay Act made it illegal to pay women less than men for the same job. But the Equal Employment Opportunity Commission was understaffed and there was little to stop employers giving different job titles to men and women doing the same activities.
4) Title VII of the 1964 Civil Rights Act prohibited discrimination in employment on the basis of sex. But enforcement was slow to follow.
5) Available from 1960, the contraceptive pill ('the Pill') made it easier for women to postpone having children while they started a career.

Eleanor Roosevelt

The campaign group NOW was formed in 1966

1) Betty Friedan in 'The Feminine Mystique' (1963) criticised the isolation of women in the household — saying many felt trapped in the homemaker role.
2) Friedan was one of the founders of the National Organisation for Women (NOW) — founded in 1966 to campaign for women's legal, educational and professional equality.
3) NOW pressured Congressmen into passing the Equal Rights Amendment (ERA) in 1972 — but the Amendment failed to achieve ratification by the necessary three-quarters of states.
4) Opposition to the ratification of the ERA included women who wanted a return to "traditional" femininity. Conservative activist Phyllis Schlafly organised a group called "Stop ERA".
5) However, the objectives of ERA were largely achieved by other means — especially a more vigorous enforcement of Title VII of the 1964 Civil Rights Act.
6) Title IX of the Educational Amendments Act (1972) forced government-funded educational establishments to provide equal facilities and opportunities for both sexes.

Feminists began to campaign against the objectification of women. Feminists protested at the 1968 Miss America beauty pageant — they crowned a sheep their own 'Miss America'.

The right to Abortion was a Controversial Issue

Feminists argued that women had the right to choose abortion. The Supreme Court ruled in the case Roe v Wade (1973) that state laws banning abortion were unconstitutional. But in response to pressure from religious groups, Congress passed the Hyde Amendment in 1976. This stopped Medicaid (the medical assistance programme for the poor) from funding abortions.

Women's liberation — get learning NOW...

The women's movement achieved a lot for women — including basic rights we take for granted nowadays like equal pay and equal educational opportunities.

Student Protest and Youth Culture

The 1960s were a decade of student protest and youthful discontent.

There were some Big Political Issues in the 1960s

1) The civil rights movement was at a peak in the 1960s (see p.112-113). Students and young people were often involved in the protests and campaigns.
2) The American government was also stuck in a long war in Vietnam (see p.103-109). Many young people were opposed to the US's motives and the tactics it used in the war.

3) Young people were the group most affected by the war because of the draft (conscription).
4) In October 1967, over 50 000 students and others opposed to the war took part in a march on the Pentagon during Stop the Draft Week.

Student Groups organised major Protests

The SDS

1) The Students for a Democratic Society (SDS) was formed in 1959. In the early 1960s many of its members worked for civil rights — which taught them protest tactics.
2) As the Vietnam War continued, the SDS became a leading group for anti-war protests.
3) In April 1968 the SDS led a student takeover of Columbia University to protest against the Vietnam War and against segregation. The takeover lasted for 8 days and resulted in around 700 arrests.

The SNCC

1) The Student Nonviolent Coordinating Committee (SNCC or 'snick') was formed in 1960 by students who wanted to campaign for civil rights.
2) The SNCC helped organise the Freedom Rides (see p.112) as well as the Albany Movement — a series of sit-ins in Albany, Georgia between 1961 and 1962.
3) From 1966 the SNCC strongly opposed the war in Vietnam and organised increasingly militant protests, particularly against the draft.

The 'Swinging Sixties' challenged traditional values

1) Many young people experimented with new lifestyles involving rock music, psychedelic drugs, sexual freedom and religious experimentation.
2) Events included the San Francisco "Summer of love" (1967) and the Woodstock Music Festival (1969).
3) Protest singers, such as Bob Dylan, wrote songs about political issues like the Vietnam War and the civil rights movement.
4) By 1967 there were hippy areas in most American cities — populated by "drop-outs" from mainstream life. Not all young people took part though — some still had traditional values.

Stop the draft — it's getting chilly in here...

The 1960s were a time of fervent student protest and activism. There were big cultural changes too — the 'swinging sixties' were a break with what had gone before...

Revision Summary

It's another glorious revision summary. It's the usual drill — answer all the questions, then see what you got wrong and revise any weak spots. You'll be an old hand at it by now.

1) What was the Marshall Plan?
2) What was the name of the American general in charge of UN forces in the Korean War?
3) What was the 'Red Scare' in the 1950s?
4) Who was the director of the FBI during the Red Scare?
5) Where were the French finally defeated in the First Vietnamese War?
6) What was the name of the type of warfare that the Vietcong used?
7) What was the name of the supply route that connected North and South Vietnam?
8) Name two chemical weapons used in the Vietnam war and describe their effects.
9) What was the Gulf of Tonkin incident?
10) What was the name of the massacre that journalists revealed in 1969?
11) What does VVAW stand for?
12) At which US university were four students killed in anti-war protests in May 1970?
13) What was Vietnamisation and why was it unsuccessful?
14) Give two reasons why the North Vietnamese government were willing to make a ceasefire deal in 1973.
15) In which year did the North Vietnamese army take control of Saigon?
16) What was segregation?
17) What does NAACP stand for?
18) What was the ruling in the case Brown v Board of Education of Topeka (1954)?
19) What act of resistance did Rosa Parks make against segregation in 1955?
20) What were the 'Freedom Rides'?
21) When was Martin Luther King assassinated?
22) How did Malcolm X's approach differ from Martin Luther King's?
23) Why was President Johnson's preferential hiring policy criticised?
24) What were the Zoot Suit Riots?
25) Who founded the United Farm Workers union in 1962?
26) What does AIM stand for?
27) Describe the events at Wounded Knee in 1973.
28) What Act made it illegal to pay women less than men for the same job?
29) What was the name of Betty Friedan's famous 1963 book?
30) What was the ruling about abortion in the case Roe v Wade (1973)?
31) What was the SDS?
32) What was the SNCC?

The Need for Reform

In the 1890s many people in Britain weren't just poor, they were desperate.
There was no government help for the old, ill or unemployed.

Poor People faced serious hardship in the 1890s

1) The only help available for very poor people was workhouses run by local councils. They provided basic food and lodging in exchange for long hours in brutal conditions. Many people saw going to the workhouse as shameful.
2) There was serious unemployment in some industries, and no 'dole' or unemployment benefit.
3) Old people who had no savings or family suffered very badly — there were no government pensions. The only option for many old people was the workhouse.
4) Housing in poor areas was damp, cold and didn't have proper sewage systems. It was easy to get ill in these conditions, which meant missing work, and maybe losing your job.
5) Many people couldn't afford doctors or medicine.
6) Many children had to go to work from an early age, and so missed getting an education.
7) Large numbers of people couldn't even afford to eat properly. Out of all the men recruited to fight in the Boer War (1899-1902), half were malnourished.

Two reports said a Third of British people were Poor

Not everybody believed that poverty was all that bad — especially rich people.
Two reports said that poverty was serious, and that it affected large numbers of people.

Charles Booth published the first edition of Life and Labour of the People in 1889. This showed that 30% of people in London were living in severe poverty, and that it was sometimes impossible for people to find work, however hard they tried. He also showed that wages for some jobs were so low that they weren't enough to support a family.

Seebohm Rowntree had a factory in York. He didn't believe the problem was as bad there as in London — so he did a survey of living conditions. The report of his findings, Poverty, a Study of Town Life (published 1901) showed that 28% of people in York were so poor that they couldn't afford basic food and housing.

Public Opinion on helping poor people began to Change

There was no way you could put a third of the population into the workhouse. Britain needed a new approach to deal with poverty. Many people had an opinion on how it should be done.

1) Popular and well-respected writers like George Bernard Shaw, J. Galsworthy, Charles Dickens and H. G. Wells wrote about how poor people lived. They said the poor needed help, and the government should pass laws to make sure it happened.
2) People involved in public health and medicine said the government should get more involved in health issues.
3) Socialists argued that wealth should be more equally spread between working people and people like factory owners and land owners, who were traditionally the richest.
4) The Labour Party was the only mainstream socialist political party. They argued that the government should give financial help to the poorest members of society. Labour was attracting more and more working-class supporters.

Rowntree — social reformer AND inventor of Fruit Gums...

Learn the examples of the problems facing poor people, the two reports, and the new ideas on helping the poor. Scribble them down, and check you've got them right.

Conservatives, Liberals and Labour

Pressure was growing for the government to deal with poverty. The main parties — the Liberals and Conservatives — traditionally felt it wasn't the government's role. But things were changing.

The political parties had Different Attitudes to Poverty

The oldest, most powerful political parties — the Liberals and the Conservatives — didn't really agree with giving government help to people. They believed that:

1) the government should interfere as little as possible in people's lives
2) it was wrong to raise taxes as people should decide how to spend their own money
3) giving poor people money was morally wrong as it undermined their independence.

The Labour Party didn't have many MPs before 1906, but they did have growing support from working people. They believed that:

1) the poorest people in society should get government help
2) the government should get the cash to pay for this from taxes
3) the government should also take over (nationalise) the major industries and make use of the profits.

Some Liberals and some Conservatives were more open to the idea of the government helping the poor — especially if it helped their party win votes from Labour.

A Royal Commission investigated Poverty

In 1905 the Conservative government set up a Royal Commission to look at the Poor Law. This was the 19th-century law which set up the workhouses and other help for the poor. The Commission was supposed to decide whether the help given by the Poor Law was good enough. But the members of the Commission couldn't agree about what caused poverty so they published two reports:

The Majority Report (what the majority of the commission thought)

- If people were poor it was their own fault.
- They made themselves poor by gambling and drinking — so they didn't deserve help.
- Enough was being done for the poor already.

The Minority Report (what the minority of the commission thought)

- People couldn't help being poor.
- Illness, old age and a shortage of jobs made people poor.
- They thought more should be done to prevent people being poor.

After 1906 the Liberals brought in Social Reforms

1) In 1906 the Liberal Party won a landslide general election victory over the Conservatives.
2) 29 Labour Party MPs were elected — giving them a good position to push for help for the poor.
3) The Minority Report, the success of the Labour Party and pressure from the general public all encouraged the Liberals to bring in laws to deal with poverty.
4) The Liberals had to compete with Labour for the support of working-class voters — this led to the emergence of "New Liberalism" which favoured government intervention to help the poor.
5) The poor physical condition of volunteers for the Boer War had been a shock. If Britain was involved in a major war, it would need a healthy working class to fight as soldiers.
6) David Lloyd George and Winston Churchill* were the MPs who worked hardest to drive the bills through. They wanted to help the poor, but were also keen to make a name for themselves.

David Lloyd George — so good they named him thrice...

We're used to the idea of benefits and pensions being paid by the government but at the time this was a new idea. Scribble down the reasons why the Liberals brought in social reforms after 1906.

* Watch out for Churchill — he was a Liberal until the 1920s, when he became a Conservative.

Laws to Help Children and Old People

The Liberals didn't plan to help everyone — just the people with the worst problems — children from poor families, old people, ill people, and people who were out of work or badly paid. Unfortunately they've left you reams of laws to learn...

Children needed Special Protection

In 1906 the School Meals Act allowed LEAs to supply free school meals paid for out of rates.

LEAs = Local Education Authorities. They were in charge of running state schools. rates = local council tax

In 1907 LEAs started giving children at their schools free medical inspections. Many of them built clinics where they could hold the inspections.

In 1908 Parliament passed the Children and Young Persons' Act (also known as the Children's Charter) to give children some legal protection. The Charter made it illegal for children younger than 16 to buy cigarettes, go into a pub or beg. It also set up special juvenile courts — so young offenders wouldn't be tried in an adult court.

Herbert Samuel from the Home Office tried to help young offenders:

1) He set up special prisons, known as borstals, for young offenders — so they wouldn't have to go to adult prisons.
2) He set up the probation service to try to keep young people from reoffending.

Elderly people got State Pensions

In 1908 David Lloyd George was Chancellor of the Exchequer. He introduced the Old Age Pensions Act. These are the most important bits of the Act:

1) The pension was for people over 70 on low incomes.
2) The scheme was non-contributory — you didn't have to pay money in to get a pension when you retired. The pensions were paid for by money raised through ordinary taxes.
3) In the 1908 budget £1 200 000 of tax money was set aside to pay for pensions.
4) Single people with an income of less than £21 per year got 5 shillings per week. Married couples with an income of less than £21 per year got 7s 6d (7 shillings & 6 pence) per week.
5) Anyone whose income was between £21 and £31 per year got a smaller pension.
6) People with an income of over £31 per year didn't get a pension at all.
7) The first pensions were paid on 1 January 1909.

Although Labour said 5 shillings was too little, the pension was immensely popular. Lloyd George took the credit.

Remember the aim wasn't to help everyone, just the poorest people.

The Old Age Pensions Act — an over-70s free-for-all...

Children got legal protection, school dinners, medical check-ups and borstal.
Old people got pensions. Make sure you know the dates and names of the acts.

Laws Protecting Working People

The Liberals also passed laws to help working people. Get all of these clear in your mind now — you need to know the name and date of each act, and what it did to help people.

The National Insurance Act of 1911

In 1911 Lloyd George introduced the National Insurance Act. Lloyd George got a lot of the ideas for this Act from a similar scheme running in Germany.

The Act came in two parts. Part One's covered here. Part Two's covered on the next page.

Part One helped with Health Insurance

Part One was to help workers pay for health insurance. The insurance was to pay for treatment and provide sick pay when people were too ill to work. The National Insurance Act said the government would top up the money that workers paid into insurance schemes.

1) The Act covered workers earning less than £160 per year.
2) Each week workers paid 4 old pence out of their wages into a central fund. Employers added 3 old pence per week and the government added another 2 old pence per week.
3) Sick pay of up to 10 shillings per week was paid to male workers if they were off work ill for more than four days. This sick pay would be paid for several months. The worker was also entitled to medical attention.

4) Women didn't pay as much in or get as much out, because they didn't earn as much in the first place.
5) Women were paid 7s 6d a week sick pay. They also got a one-off maternity grant of 30 shillings.

6) Names of workers on the National Insurance scheme were put on a special list known as a doctors' 'panel'. Doctors were paid a sum by the government for every patient on the panel.
7) The scheme was organised through organisations approved by the government — friendly societies, trade unions and private insurance companies.
8) The scheme caused controversy — Conservatives said the government had no right to force people to contribute from their wages, and many socialists said there should be higher taxes on rich people to pay for it instead of workers having to contribute. But it was still passed.

friendly society = a kind of voluntary society in which members paid a subscription in exchange for financial and medical help if they became sick.

Workers are getting nine pence for four pence.

David Lloyd George

Ten million workers now had health insurance.

I can't wait to find out what happens in part two...

These laws were to help some of the poorest people in the country. Remember that Britain was a lot more industrial at the time, so there were more accidents and industrial illnesses.

Laws Protecting Working People

Here's Part Two of the National Insurance Act, and a couple of other Liberal laws to help workers.

Part Two set up Unemployment Benefit for a few trades

Part Two of the National Insurance Act provided unemployment benefit for workers in shipbuilding, iron founding and construction. These were industries where workers were quite regularly out of work for several weeks at a time.

It was a contributory scheme. Employers and employees each paid 2½d per week into an unemployment fund and the government paid 1¾d.

In return workers were paid 7 shillings per week for up to 15 weeks in any one year if they were unemployed. Payment started from the second week of unemployment.

The Trade Boards Act of 1909 set a Minimum Wage

Winston Churchill and William Beveridge put together the Trade Boards Act in 1909 to help sweated industry workers.

Sweated industries included tailoring, lace-making and cardboard-box making. The workers were often women or foreign immigrants who worked from home doing long hours for low wages.

1) The Act set up trade boards for each of the 'sweated industries'.
2) Every board was made up of equal numbers of workers and employers, and a neutral chairman.
3) The board's job was to decide a minimum wage for the industry.
4) Employers paying less than their trade board laid down could be fined.
5) Factory inspectors made sure the Act was put into practice.

By 1914 half a million workers were covered by the trade boards and so had the security of a minimum wage.

The Labour Exchanges Act set up Job Centres

Churchill and Beveridge also worked together on the Labour Exchanges Act. This was passed in 1909 too.

1) Labour exchanges were like job centres. Unemployed workers could go there to find out about job vacancies.
2) Within five years there was a network right across Britain.
3) One million jobs a year were filled through the exchanges.

The Labour Exchange Act — perfect for swapping jobs...

There's a lot of nasty fiddly detail here — don't panic if you can't remember it all. The easiest way to learn the important bits is by making a timeline of acts and dates. Then make sure you can scribble down the main point of each act — who it was meant to help, and what they got.

Effects of the Liberal Reforms

The Liberals' reforms wouldn't do much good if they couldn't pay for them. They had to get the money through taxes — one reason why some people didn't welcome them with open arms.

Lloyd George wanted to Raise Taxes to pay for reforms

In 1909 the Liberal Chancellor of the Exchequer Lloyd George decided he'd have to raise taxes to pay for the reforms. He proposed the tax increases in the 1909 budget. It was designed to tax the rich more heavily than the poor — so it became known as the People's Budget.

- Income tax would go up from 5 pence to 6 pence in the pound.
- There'd be a new super tax of 1s. 2d. in the pound on incomes over £3000 per year.
- The inheritance tax — called death duties — would go up.
- Tax on tobacco and spirits would go up.

The Liberals had to call a General Election in 1910

To become law the Budget had to be passed by the House of Commons and the House of Lords.

1) Although the Conservatives were opposed to the Budget, the bill got through the Commons. But it was rejected in the House of Lords where Conservatives held the majority.
2) The Liberals couldn't see any way of getting the bill through Parliament. This was a constitutional crisis — the unelected House of Lords was blocking the will of the elected House of Commons.
3) The Liberals called a general election to make sure they had the British people's support. The only issue of the campaign was the People's Budget.
4) The Liberal Party won the election. They reintroduced the Budget and finally it was passed by the Commons and the Lords.

To prevent such crises the Parliament Act was passed in 1911. The Lords were no longer allowed to reject bills on financial issues. They could reject other bills twice.

The Liberal Reforms left some problems Unsolved...

1) Hardly any of the new schemes were designed to help the whole population.
2) The National Insurance Act Part One didn't cover the worker's family. Part Two only covered a few industries.
3) The reforms didn't replace the old Poor Law. Workhouses weren't abolished until 1930.

...but Changed Attitudes to helping the poor

1) This was the first time that national taxes had been used to help the poor.
2) The state took on responsibility for protecting citizens from extreme hardship in sickness, old age and unemployment for the first time.
3) The schemes were introduced all across the country — they weren't just local affairs.
4) Large numbers of people were covered by some of the schemes — the National Insurance Act Part One covered 10 million workers.
5) The new provisions didn't have the same stigma as the workhouse and because of the new laws fewer people had to rely on the Poor Law system.
6) The number of non-government welfare organisations, e.g. friendly societies, schemes run by churches etc, declined.

"The People" 1 — "Peers of the Realm" 0...

The fact that the Liberals had to call a general election and change the law about the House of Lords shows what a stir they'd caused. The way they changed attitudes is really important too.

Women's Rights in the 1890s

Women in the 1890s were treated differently from men. Most women didn't go to school or university, and instead spent their lives raising children and working to run a house.

Women's legal rights Weren't Equal — but Getting Better

For a long time married women were not protected in law — but several new laws in the 19th century gave them more rights in marriage.

1857 The Matrimonial Clauses Act made it easier for a woman to get a divorce through ordinary law courts. You had to prove your husband had committed adultery and another offence such as cruelty or desertion (leaving you). Before the Act, only Parliament could grant divorces.

1870 The Married Women's Property Act gave women the right to keep their earnings when they got married. Before the Act it all went to the husband automatically. In 1882, a second Married Women's Property Act gave married women the right to keep their property as well.

1886 The Married Women (Maintenance in Case of Desertion) Act said that a husband who left his wife had to keep paying for her maintenance — i.e. her living expenses.
The Guardianship of Children Act allowed women to be their children's legal guardians if the father died or if the marriage broke up. Being the legal guardian meant having responsibility for any property left to the children as well as seeing they were properly looked after.

Some Professions were Open to Women

1) Many working-class women had jobs as well as running the home, e.g. in the textile industry. These jobs tended to be low paid with poor conditions.
2) Middle-class women were less likely to work outside the home. Access to higher education and professional jobs was limited.
3) Queen's College, London was opened to train women teachers in 1848.
4) Florence Nightingale established nursing as a respectable job. She set up a training school where women could train to become nurses.

Florence Nightingale

Women Couldn't Vote in national elections

During the 19th century, several reform acts had given more people in Britain the vote — but only men. Most people thought it was perfectly sensible that women didn't have the vote.

1) They thought the public sphere was for men. Women should look after the home.
2) Many people believed that women weren't very rational and so couldn't make big decisions.
3) Many politicians thought that men needed to be householders to get the vote. Only a very few rich women owned houses or paid the rent, so it would be a bit odd to give them a vote.
4) If only rich women got the vote they'd probably vote Conservative. The Liberals didn't like that idea.

After 1894 married women were allowed to vote for district councils, and to sit on the councils. But they still couldn't vote in national elections for MPs or become MPs themselves.
Campaigners for votes for women argued that:

1) Women's rights and opportunities were improving — being given the vote was a natural step forward.
2) Women were just as capable as men of making sound decisions.
3) Women had gained the vote in some other countries, e.g. in New Zealand in 1893.

You've got to fight for your right — to vote in local elections...

Learn why people thought women shouldn't vote, and the four acts which gave women more legal rights.

The Campaign for the Vote 1900-1914

The campaign for women's votes wasn't brand new in 1900 — but the campaigns from 1900 to 1914 were more energetic than ever. Some campaigns were peaceful, some weren't...

The Suffragists were Moderate in their protests

1) The suffragists' formal name was the NATIONAL UNION OF WOMEN'S SUFFRAGE SOCIETIES (NUWSS).
2) They were founded in 1897. Their leader was Millicent Fawcett.
3) Their main tactics were persuasion, meetings and petitions to Parliament.

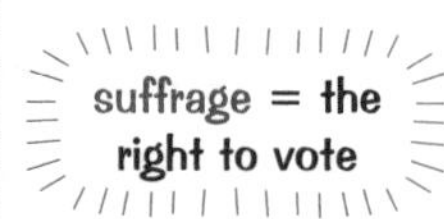

The Suffragettes were more Direct

1) The suffragettes' formal name was the WOMEN'S SOCIAL AND POLITICAL UNION (WSPU).
2) They were founded by Emmeline Pankhurst in 1903, with her daughters Christabel and Sylvia. Emmeline Pankhurst had previously founded the Women's Franchise League (WFL) which campaigned to get women the vote in local elections.
3) The suffragettes thought the suffragists took things too slowly. They wanted results fast.
4) The suffragettes didn't mind getting arrested. It attracted some sympathy and showed they were serious. In 1905 Christabel Pankhurst and Annie Kenney heckled Sir Edward Grey, who was speaking at a meeting in Manchester, and ended up in prison for a week.
5) They hoped the Liberal government after 1906 would be sympathetic. They were encouraged by the 1907 Qualification of Women Act which let women become county and borough councillors, or mayors. However, in 1908, Asquith, a Liberal, became Prime Minister — he was against votes for women.

After 1912 the protests got More Extreme

By 1912 the Liberal government had accepted the idea of some women voting, and tried to put it into their Plural Voting Bill for Parliament to discuss. But the Speaker refused to let them add it. The suffragettes were furious and protests got far more extreme and violent.

1) Suffragettes chained themselves to railings outside Downing Street and Buckingham Palace.
2) They physically assaulted politicians. The Prime Minister, Asquith, was attacked on a golf course. Suffragettes tried to tear off his clothes, and beat him with dog whips.
3) They destroyed paintings in the National Gallery, and smashed shop windows.
4) Suffragettes made arson attacks on post boxes, churches and railway stations. In 1913, they even bombed the house of Lloyd George, who was fairly sympathetic to votes for women.
5) At the 1913 Derby at Epsom, a suffragette called Emily Davison threw herself under the feet of the King's horse. She died of her injuries.

Suffragists thought these tactics held the campaign back. The government didn't want to be seen to be giving in to violence. The violence also put off many moderate supporters.

The Government dealt with the protests Harshly

1) They sent many suffragettes to prison. The suffragettes often went on hunger strike, so the prison authorities force-fed them, but this was dangerous and violent.
2) The so-called "Cat and Mouse" Act was passed in 1913. Under this act the authorities could release hunger strikers then rearrest them when they were fit again.

Women's suffrage — I get the -gist...

Try not to get suffragettes and suffragists mixed up. Watch out for questions on whether protests helped win the vote — you'll need to write about all the types of protest, and what effect they had.

The Start of World War One

For Britain the First World War began with the British Expeditionary Force (BEF) going over to Europe to fight the Germans. British people were keen to join up and fight in the war. Nobody imagined it was going to last four years, or take the lives of 3 million Allied soldiers.

Britain Declared War on Germany on 4 August 1914

1) Britain was allied to France and Russia by an agreement called the Triple Entente.
2) Germany was allied to the Austro-Hungarian Empire and Italy by an agreement called the Triple Alliance.
3) The Austro-Hungarian Archduke Ferdinand was assassinated by Serbs, in the Bosnian capital Sarajevo on 28 June. Austria-Hungary declared war on Serbia. Russia agreed to help Serbia. Germany declared war on Russia, then on Russia's ally France.
4) Germany already had a strategy for invading France — it was called the Schlieffen Plan.
5) The plan was to push down through Belgium and then capture Paris. According to the Schlieffen Plan the Germans should be able to take control of France within weeks.
6) But Belgium was a neutral country — Britain stepped in to help them and declared war on 4 August.

Britain sent the BEF to help France and Belgium

1) The BEF sent 4 divisions of troops to France. The French Army in the field had 70 divisions.
2) The BEF commander was Sir John French.
3) The British and French aim was to stop the Germans from invading or capturing France.
4) The BEF and the French didn't manage to stop the Germans in Belgium, or to stop them invading France.
5) But once the Germans were in France, the BEF and the French fought three major battles at Mons, the river Marne and Ypres (it's pronounced a bit like EEPr), which brought the Germans to a standstill.

The German First Army met British forces at Mons on 23 August 1914. The Germans were flummoxed because they didn't expect to see British soldiers. The small British force beat them back — but it wasn't a lasting victory as the French army retreated and the British had to follow.

The Germans needed to cross the to get to Paris. In September 1914, the French managed to beat them back as far as the river Aisne. They were supported by the BEF. The Germans dug trenches to defend their position. It became clear that the war was going to last longer than a few weeks.

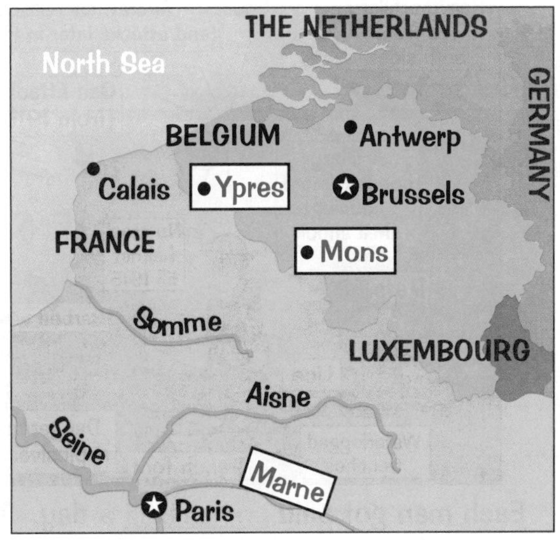

The Germans tried to outflank the Allies by advancing west towards the sea. The Allies tried to block them off — this was known as the 'race to the sea'. The armies met at Ypres — they fought through October and November 1914. There were terrible casualties. Half the BEF were wounded and around 75 000 were killed.

After Ypres the British Army needed More Men

1) Kitchener, the Secretary for War, wanted conscription but Asquith, the Prime Minister, refused.
2) Instead of conscription there was a massive poster campaign, e.g. "Your Country Needs You".
3) By September 1914 there were half a million volunteers. Another half million joined by February 1915.

The ultimate lottery — your country needs you...

Get the order of events in 1914 clear. Remember — the BEF went to help Belgium and France. Write down what happened at Mons, Marne and Ypres from August to November 1914. Learn it.

Trench Warfare

One of the big reasons why the war was so terrible was the development of trench warfare.

Trench Warfare created Deadlock

1) The generals in charge, including Sir John French, weren't used to this type of fighting. They knew more about the type of battles where everyone met up on a big field, then the cavalry charged in, followed by footsoldiers and backed up with artillery.
2) After the Marne and Ypres, neither side could drive the other back. Both armies dug trenches. By the end of 1914 the trenches stretched from the Alps to the North Sea. This line of trenches was called the Western Front.
3) The trenches were easy to defend...

- machine guns mowed down attacks
- heavy guns were behind the trenches
- guards spotted attacks from the other side
- trenches led back from the front line to bring in men and supplies
- trenches were protected by barbed wire

...and difficult to attack.

- artillery was meant to break through the enemy's barbed wire and wear them down to make attacks easier — in practice it just warned the other side an attack was coming
- the land between the trenches was often knee-deep or even waist-deep in mud

4) Even if you made it to the enemy trench in one place, it was hard to hang on to your position because you were surrounded by the enemy's forces in the rest of the trench.

Life in the trenches was Hard and Dangerous

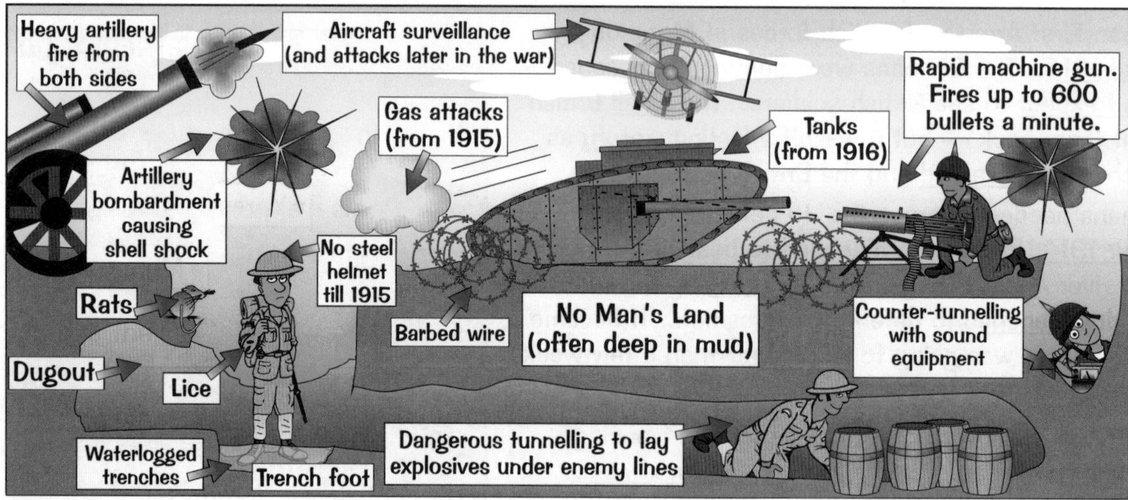

Each man got paid one shilling a day. The main rations were bully beef (also called corned beef), jam and tea.

Thousands of lives were lost for Small Gains

1) Both sides had plenty of men and plenty of money for ammunition and weapons, so the generals kept sending more and more men 'over the top' — even though it didn't achieve any obvious success.
2) The major battles in 1915 were Neuve Chapelle, Loos and the 2nd Battle of Ypres. Thousands of lives were lost but neither side gained much from the battles — the front line hardly moved at all.
3) Sir John French was replaced as commander by Sir Douglas Haig.

Trench warfare — wearing the other side down...

You definitely need to know what the trenches were like. The picture will help you.
You also need to learn the lists of points about attacking and defending the trenches.

New Weapons

New weapons were used in the First World War. Not surprisingly they made a massive difference to the way wars were fought. That's what you've got to learn about.

Aircraft were Developed throughout the war

1) On the Western Front both sides used planes and balloons to find enemy weak points to attack.
2) The Germans used airships called Zeppelins to carry out bombing raids like the May 1915 one on London.
3) In 1915 new planes carried synchronised machine guns which wouldn't shoot the propeller. One man could fly and handle the gun — where before they'd needed two people. Fighter planes escorted bombers on raids, attacked enemy bombers, and fought each other, especially on the Western Front.
4) Both sides developed planes for long-distance bombing raids. The first serious raid on Britain was in May 1917 — 71 people were killed at Folkestone. Britain sent bombers into Germany too.

Tanks made it easier to attack on the Ground

The tracks on tanks meant they could go over very rough ground, and plough through barbed wire without problems. The heavily armoured body of the tanks meant ordinary gunfire couldn't stop them. Tanks should have allowed the British army to break the deadlock on the trenches, but it took a while to develop effective tactics, and the early tanks often broke down.

1) The first time tanks were used was at the Battle of the Somme in July 1916. Sir Douglas Haig sent in 49 tanks. He could have waited for more, but he decided it was more important to surprise the Germans, and went ahead anyway. The tank division captured 2 km of German-held territory but couldn't hold on to it.
2) At Cambrai on the Western Front in November 1917, tanks were used more successfully. Nearly 500 tanks advanced about 6 km into German territory, but again couldn't hold on to their gains.

Poison Gas was a deadly weapon

1) The Germans were the first to use chlorine gas — in the Second Battle of Ypres, April-May 1915. It caused terror, and killed many. The British tried it at the Battle of Loos (September 1915) but the wind blew some of it back on them. Chlorine has the military disadvantage of being highly visible.
2) In December 1915 the Germans tried phosgene, which is invisible and deadly but slow-acting. At the battle of Riga, in September 1917, they introduced mustard gas, which causes horrible blisters and internal bleeding.
3) Gas became a standard weapon used by both sides, not a war-winning weapon. Countermeasures like masks, pads and gas helmets meant few British battle losses were due to gas.

The Creeping Barrage became a standard tactic in 1916

1) First used on a large scale by the British at the Battle of the Somme (July-November 1916), the creeping barrage was an advancing curtain of artillery fire preceding the advancing infantry.
2) It was a difficult and dangerous tactic because it depended upon precise timing. When the barrage outpaced the infantry, the gap between them allowed the Germans to re-emerge from shelter and man their positions. But when the infantry moved too fast, they ran into their own shellfire.

New technology — it changed warfare for ever...

The development of aeroplanes and tanks as weapons is one of the most important long-term effects of the First World War. Draw a timeline for each weapon, giving dates for the main events.

The Western Front

The Battle of the Somme was a major attack by the British army against the German line. It led to a staggering loss of life — and had a long-term effect on how the war was remembered.

The Battle of the Somme killed 1 million men

In February 1916, the Germans began an attack on Allied forces around Verdun. If they captured Verdun, Paris would be open to attack. By July, 700 000 men were dead. In order to relieve the pressure on Verdun, Haig decided on a major attack.

1) This was the Battle of the Somme. It began on 1 July 1916.
2) After a massive artillery bombardment, the soldiers were sent 'over the top' to charge the German trenches.
3) British soldiers were under orders to advance slowly, not run.
4) This gave the Germans time to get ready. The slow-moving British soldiers were an easy target.
5) 57 000 Britons were killed or wounded on the first day alone. 21 000 died in 1 hour.
6) The battle dragged on to November. By then over one million soldiers had died.

The Battle of the Somme had Mixed Results

1) Despite months of fighting and all the deaths, very little ground was gained. In some places the Allied forces advanced about 6 kilometres, in others it was only a few hundred metres.
2) The Germans weren't beaten at the Somme, but they took a severe battering. The battle probably helped to wear them down. This was what Haig wanted — a "war of attrition".
3) Many men in the army were appalled at how many lives were lost. They felt the generals' tactics were wrong — and some started to lose confidence in the officers commanding the war.
4) There was less confidence in the artillery too. They were supposed to destroy the German barbed wire before the attack and didn't manage to do it.

People still Disagree on whether the Tactics were right

Many people nowadays feel that the tactics used at the Somme and in other battles were wrong. Their picture of the First World War comes from TV, books and films — which often see Haig as a "Butcher". But in fact, it's much more complicated than that. Here are some of the main opinions on both sides:

AGAINST

- Hundreds of thousands of men were killed under Haig's command.
- Haig could have waited for more tanks, which might have saved many lives.
- Once he saw the first day's slaughter he could have changed his tactics.

FOR

- Haig's overall strategy was to wear the Germans down, whatever the cost. It's every general's job to win wars, not to save lives.
- Haig couldn't wait for more tanks — he had to relieve the pressure on Verdun, or the whole war might be lost. He used the tanks he had.
- By 1918, Haig had learnt to adapt these attacking tactics so that they became highly successful.

The Somme — be sure to give both sides of the story...

The Somme was a disaster — but some people argue it was necessary. If you're going to write about it, you have to give both sides of the argument. Don't miss out the actual facts though.

The War at Home

When the First World War broke out the government had to be sure Britain was ready to cope. They gave themselves special powers by...surprise... getting Parliament to pass a law.

Parliament passed the Defence of the Realm Act

The Defence of the Realm Act (DORA) was passed in August 1914, right at the start of the war. There were two basic things the government was trying to do:

1) Make sure the country had enough resources to fight the war.
2) Make sure British people were in a fit state to fight and support the war effort.

The law allowed the government to...

- take control of vital industries like coal mining
- take over 2.5 million acres of land and buildings
- bring in British Summer Time for more daylight (working) hours
- control drinking hours and the strength of alcohol

- introduce conscription

- stop people talking about the war or spreading rumours
- censor newspapers
- enforce rationing

Thousands Volunteered to fight — but it Wasn't Enough

When war broke out, thousands of men rushed to volunteer for the fighting. They believed the war would be over quickly — 'by Christmas'. They thought it was going to be an adventure, and wanted to be part of it. The enthusiasm didn't last.

By 1915 the number of casualties was going up — and the number of volunteers was slowing down. On the Western Front so many men were being killed and wounded that there weren't enough volunteers to replace them.

There was also a growing feeling in Britain that it wasn't fair that some men were avoiding military duty.

The Government introduced Conscription in 1916

1) All single men aged between 18 and 40 had to fight.
2) When there still weren't enough soldiers married men had to join up too.
3) People who didn't believe in fighting were called conscientious objectors. They were treated as criminals and sent to prison. They were seen as traitors because they refused to fight. Some were members of groups like the Quakers, who had religious objections to fighting. Many agreed to carry out non-violent war work, such as driving ambulances.

Women started doing "men's jobs"

Many of the original volunteers came from heavy industries like coal mining. There was a shortage of workers in these industries and without them Britain couldn't supply the army. When conscription started there were even fewer men available to do the vital jobs. Women started taking their places in the pits and factories.

Surviving at home — major changes were needed...

You've got to know all about the Defence of the Realm Act, and conscription — scribble and learn.

Food Shortages

Britain had problems keeping food supplies going in the war. Something needed to be done to make sure nobody starved. The important thing is to learn all three of Lloyd George's tactics.

German U-boats made it hard to Import Food

1) In 1914 Britain was used to importing quite a lot of food from the United States and countries that were part of the Empire.
2) Germany used U-boats (submarines) to attack shipping all round Britain and made it impossible to import all the food Britain needed to survive.
3) By April 1917 Britain only had six weeks' supply of wheat. The Prime Minister, David Lloyd George, took three big steps to solve the food crisis:

1) Navy Convoys protected Merchant Ships

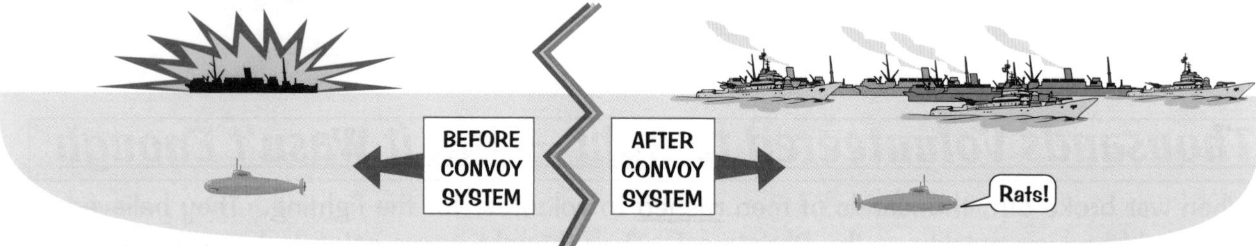

Ships travelling alone were easy targets for the U-boats. 25% of merchant ships coming into Britain were being sunk.

The Navy began a convoy system. Merchant ships travelled in groups with an escort of Royal Navy ships to protect them.

U-boats couldn't attack as easily. With the convoy system less than 1% of ships were sunk.

2) Compulsory Rationing started in 1918

When food rationing started in 1917 it was voluntary. In 1918 shortages were still a problem and rationing was made compulsory for beer, butter, sugar and meat.

1) Everyone got rationing coupons. They had to hand them over when they bought beer, butter, sugar and meat. When the week's coupons for, say, sugar, ran out, they couldn't buy any more that week.
2) Some people hoarded food, partly because they were afraid it would run out, and partly because of increasing prices. They would sell it on later, creating a 'black market' in food.
3) There were shortages of some kinds of food but no-one starved.
4) The government had never been this involved in organising people's daily lives before.

3) Britain Grew more food

1) Farmers were encouraged to use more of their land so they could grow more food.
2) The Women's Land Army was set up in 1917. Women from the Land Army were a big new labour force available to work on the farms.

Food supply — crucial to avoiding a crisis...

How Lloyd George avoided a food supply crisis isn't the most exciting topic in this section — but you've definitely got to know about the three steps he took: convoys, rationing and production.

Attitudes to the War in Britain

There's a dramatic difference between people's cheerful attitude at the beginning of the war and their horror at the waste of life by the end. Make sure you know why attitudes changed so much.

At the Start the war looked like an Adventure

In 1914 there was huge enthusiasm for the war. It seems strange now, but nobody at the time knew what it was going to be like. These are some of the things people felt about the war:

Fighting in the war would be an adventure.

It was right to fight for your country when it went to war.

The war would be "over by Christmas". Britain would win easily.

Obviously not everybody thought exactly like this — but a fair few did.

At first people Didn't Really Know what was going on

The government deliberately kept people ignorant of what was going on:

1) Letters from soldiers were censored.
2) Reporters weren't allowed to see battles very often.
3) Newspapers were censored from 1914.
4) No photographs could be taken which showed dead soldiers.
5) Casualty figures weren't available from the government.

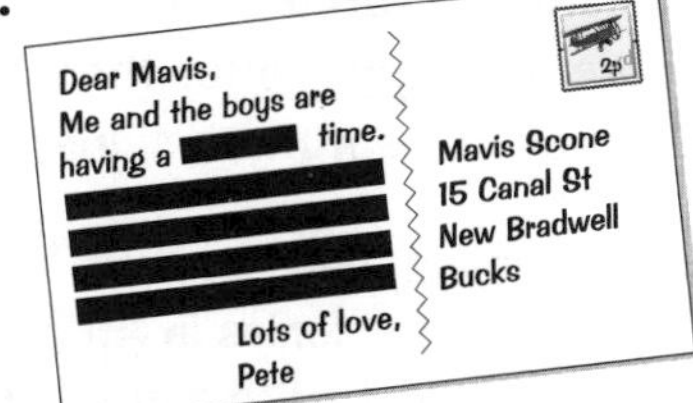

Britain had never before been involved in a war where most of the fighting was done in trenches, or one in which so many people were killed. People away from the front couldn't imagine how terrible the war was.

During the war ordinary people's Attitudes Changed

The government couldn't keep the facts about the war secret for ever.
As the war carried on people couldn't help finding out more, and attitudes began to change.

1) During the war 1500 civilians were killed in bombing raids. This was a new and terrible danger.
2) There were no obvious successes on the Western Front up until 1918.
3) The government could hide the overall casualty figures, but they couldn't hide crippled and blinded veterans who returned to Britain, or keep deaths secret from the families of soldiers.
4) Rationing was difficult, and richer people felt it was a hardship. Taxes had increased to pay for the war. By 1917 most people in Britain were sick of the war, and wanted to see it end.

Britain used Propaganda to encourage people to fight

1) Propaganda posters were used to encourage men to sign up — such as the famous poster of Lord Kitchener with the caption "Your Country Needs You".
2) Some propaganda was aimed abroad — in particular to encourage US military involvement.
3) In September 1914 the newly formed War Propaganda Bureau asked 25 of Britain's leading writers to aid the war effort. They produced pamphlets such as the Report on Alleged German Outrages (1915), which included shocking accusations of German crimes.
4) The Ministry of Information produced propaganda films, but it's not clear how much public support they generated. The propaganda film The Battle of the Somme (1916), made by The British Topical Committee, was so realistic, it could have been seen as anti-war.
5) In June 1917, the government set up a National War Aims Committee to issue propaganda literature and sponsor speeches to improve morale.

Have a propaganda at this...

This page is about people's opinions and attitudes about what happened, as well as the basic facts. Scribble a list of the main reasons why attitudes to the war changed between 1914 and 1917.

The End of the War

The war changed everybody's lives, whether they'd been away fighting or stayed at home. It wasn't easy to get used to normal life again — especially for the soldiers.

The war Finally Ended in November 1918

1) The USA joined the Allies in April 1917 — but at first only sent one division.
2) More Americans were sent during 1918. The German commander Ludendorff decided to try one more big attack before there were so many Allied troops that a German victory would be impossible.
3) The Ludendorff Offensive nearly worked, thanks to new tactics in trench warfare — attacking several points along the line at the same time, with a constant artillery bombardment of the enemy as support.
4) The Allies counter-attacked from different sides. Haig began an attack on the German line near Amiens in France on 8 August 1918. Hundreds of tanks were sent in and the Germans were pushed back through France towards Germany. The Allied forces could have pushed right through into Germany, but before that happened an armistice (a sort of ceasefire) was signed.
5) The trench warfare had worn Germany down. Mutinies, food shortages and revolution in Germany made it impossible for them to carry on. They asked for the armistice and it was signed on 11 Nov.
6) The peace treaty was signed at Versailles in June 1919.

- Germany had to return land taken from France, Belgium, Poland and others.
- German colonies in Africa were shared between France and Britain.
- Germany had to pay reparations of £6600 million to compensate the Allies for the cost of the war.

7) The main negotiators at Versailles were Lloyd George, Clemenceau the French Prime Minister, and Woodrow Wilson the US President. The French thought the peace treaty should punish Germany. Lloyd George thought it was important to punish Germany, but not to make them bitter. The US President favoured a more lenient approach — America hadn't been as badly affected by the war.
8) The Versailles Treaty embittered and nearly bankrupted Germany. It would be remembered in the future.

The war was known as "the war to end all wars"

People in Britain thought there could never be another war as bad as the First World War. The mood in Britain immediately after the war was pretty bleak.

1) The government had tried to control information during the war. Even so, people had found out some real facts about the war. Many now felt that politicians and authority figures couldn't always be trusted.
2) Many people came to believe that the generals had been incompetent, and that they didn't care how many lives were lost. This gave people even more reason to stop trusting people in powerful positions.
3) The public school officers in the trenches turned out to be no more competent than the working class soldiers. Some people began to question the way the upper classes dominated society.
4) Soldiers who'd been through the war were even more disillusioned when they returned home. There was unemployment and poverty. They wondered what they had been fighting for.
5) No war in European history had produced so many casualties. It felt as though the loss of huge numbers of young men had changed the balance of society.
6) Many people in Britain were very angry with Germany — they wanted revenge. Because of this many British people supported the harshness of the Versailles Treaty.

There were some positive outcomes of the war too. Even though people had many reasons to be disappointed there was a sense of satisfaction that Britain had won. Attitudes towards women and the poorer members of society generally improved, as the war showed everyone could do something useful if they were given the opportunity. Lloyd George got re-elected as Prime Minister in December 1918.

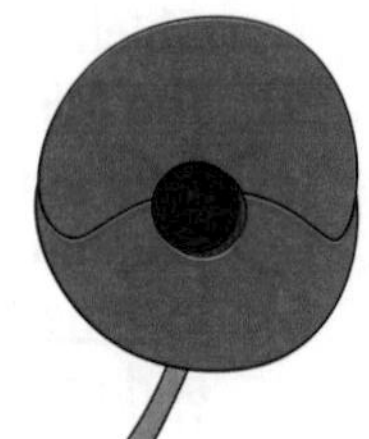

The Versailles Treaty — the roots of another war...

Don't forget the final facts about 1918 and the Versailles Treaty, as well as the effects of the war.

Women and the Vote 1914-1928

After the First World War there was a different attitude to the suffrage movement. Partly, the war had made the suffragette violence of 1913 and 1914 seem a bit less serious (p.126). But there were other reasons too — especially the work women had done for the war effort.

During the war Women did "Men's Jobs"

1) So many men were away fighting in the war that there weren't enough to do vital jobs. The jobs were opened up to women — women were happy to take them, and they proved that they could do them just as well as men.
2) Women worked as: bus conductors, drivers, postal workers, farm labourers and coal deliverers. All these vital jobs kept the country going.
3) They also worked in the munitions factories, and engineering workshops. This work was technical, and directly related to the war effort.
4) Women joined women's branches of the armed forces, and worked as nurses in military hospitals.

By doing work that helped Britain win the war, women proved they were important to public life as well as home life. There was also gratitude towards women for their contribution.

The Other Reasons for giving women the vote were...

1. A shake-up of the voting system was already happening. There was a rule that a man could only vote after living at the same address for 1 year. This needed to be changed to allow soldiers who had been away fighting to vote. If the voting system was going to be changed anyway, it was a chance to include women.
2. People's attitudes to women had changed — and not just because of the war. A lot of people remembered the suffragettes' protests and felt it was unfair that women had been denied full political rights.
3. The suffragettes had called off their campaign at the beginning of the war. Nobody wanted them starting it up again.

Women 30+ got the vote in 1918

1) The Representation of the People Act became law in 1918.
2) Not all women got the vote. The ones who did had to be:

   over 30 and a householder OR married to a householder

   The same act gave all men over 21 the right to vote.
3) Women were also able to become MPs. Constance Markiewicz, a Sinn Fein candidate, was elected in 1918 but didn't take up her seat. The first woman to actually become an MP was Nancy Astor who got elected in 1919.
4) The vote didn't go to all women over 21 until 1928, when women finally got equal voting rights.

Voles for women! — sorry, I think I misread that...

The 1918 Representation of the People Act is a big landmark — make sure you know exactly which women got the vote. But just as important, scribble a list of the main reasons why they got it.

Build-up to the General Strike 1918-1926

As women were gaining influence, so were the trade unions — especially after the First World War. They became much more active in trying to get better pay and conditions by holding strikes.

Unions were in a Strong Position after the war

During the First World War (1914–1918), the unions cooperated with the government. Between 1914 and 1918, there were hardly any strikes. Wages in industry were good. Membership of many unions went up. High wages and membership strengthened the unions. After the war there was less pressure to avoid strikes — and disputes over pay began again.

1) The police and railway workers held successful strikes in 1918 and 1919.
2) Total union membership in 1920 was 8.3 million.
3) Two new unions were founded — the Amalgamated Engineering Union in 1920, and the Transport and General Workers' Union in 1921. Both became extremely large and powerful.

There was trouble in the Coal Industry...

During the 1920s there were constant disputes between the coal miners and mine owners, over pay and the length of the working day. These disputes eventually led to the General Strike.

1) During the First World War the coal industry was nationalised — the government took over ownership and control of the mines.
2) In 1919 a Royal Commission was appointed to decide whether to return the mines to private ownership. The Commission recommended that the government should keep the mines. Lloyd George's coalition government wasn't keen and privatised them in 1921.
3) People were beginning to use gas, oil and electricity more than coal. Also mines in Germany and Poland were using efficient modern machinery, which produced more coal more quickly and cheaply. Customers couldn't afford British coal, and the mines became less and less profitable.

...which led to a Strike in the Coal Industry

1) The new private mine owners announced a cut in wages and longer working hours for the miners. The miners refused to accept this and went on strike. Neither side was willing to negotiate.
2) The miners' union was in a triple alliance with the transport workers and railwaymen. When they went on strike they asked for support from these allies. The transport workers and railwaymen thought the miners should have tried harder to negotiate, and refused to join in with the strike on 15th April 1921. This day became known as 'Black Friday'.
3) The strike was a failure — eventually they had to go back to work and accept worse conditions.
4) In 1925 coal sales dropped off. Mine owners announced more wage cuts and longer hours.
5) The miners began negotiations, backed by the Trades Union Congress — a federation of all the unions.
6) On 'Red Friday' in July 1925, the government agreed to pay a subsidy to keep miners' wages at the same level. The subsidy would be paid for nine months.
7) At the same time a Royal Commission — the Samuel Commission — looked into what could be done to sort out the dispute. The Samuel Commission reported in March 1926.

The minors' strike — toddlers on the rampage...

There's a lot here for you to digest — you'll definitely need to know why the coal industry was doing badly and what year the Samuel Commission was appointed.

The General Strike 1926

The General Strike was one of the biggest showdowns between the people and the government in 20th century Britain.

The Samuel Report was Fair but Nobody Liked It

The Samuel Commission said mine owners should reorganise their businesses and introduce modern machinery. That way the mines would be more efficient and profitable. There would be no need to cut wages and increase hours. This suited the miners but not the mine owners.

The Commission also said the subsidy should stop. Miners would have to take a temporary pay cut until the owners had reorganised the mines. The miners weren't pleased with this.

The General Strike began when the Subsidy Ended

1) Neither side accepted the Samuel Report. The mine owners said they would cut wages on 30 April. The miners said they'd strike on 1 May. The owners locked out the workers on 30 April — starting a strike.
2) The Trades Union Congress (TUC) felt that if the miners' wages were reduced, then those of other workers would soon follow. They threatened a strike of all key workers — a general strike — starting on 3 May.
3) Negotiations between the TUC and the government began on 2 May.
4) But the Prime Minister, Stanley Baldwin, pulled out of the negotiations.

The strikers Couldn't Close the Country Down

Thousands of workers joined in with the strike. There were workers from mining, transport, the railways, construction, shipbuilding, printing, electricity and the steel industry.

1) The printers' strike closed down ordinary newspapers, but the TUC and the government each produced their own. The government paper was called the British Gazette, edited by Winston Churchill. It described the strike as violent, disorganised and an attack on the British constitution. The TUC's paper, the British Worker, emphasised the solidarity of the strike, and said the strike was an industrial issue, not an attack on the government. It also attacked Churchill.
2) 100 000 people volunteered for the Organisation for the Maintenance of Supplies. They were mainly students and middle-class men. They kept the buses, trains and London Underground moving.
3) Food supplies were transported in armoured convoys escorted by special constables. In London, Hyde Park was used as a centre for distributing milk. There were no shortages because of the strike.
4) Although the government expected violence, it wasn't that bad. Some buses were attacked in London, and there was minor crowd trouble in Nottingham, Leeds, Edinburgh, Glasgow and Aberdeen.

The government refused to negotiate, but offered a peace plan drawn up by Sir Herbert Samuel. The TUC called off the strike on 12 May, and everyone except the miners gave up. The Prime Minister, Stanley Baldwin, said the end of the strike was "a victory for common sense".

1926 — a striking year in history...

Don't forget that the Russian Revolution was less than a decade old at the time — so talk of a general strike made a lot of people worried there might be a revolution.

Effects of the General Strike

The General Strike is a bit of an odd event — observers from Russia hoped there would be a communist revolution, but couldn't believe how peaceful it was. But it had major effects long-term.

The General Strike Didn't Last Long

The General Strike lasted just nine days before the TUC gave in.
There were several reasons:

9 days later...

1) The government refused to negotiate. They saw the strike as a test of their strength. The TUC realised that the government was never going to back down, so there was no point in carrying on.
2) The government's reaction was so strong that there was a danger of violence if the strike continued — amongst others, Churchill had said "we are at war", and called for armoured cars to protect food convoys.
3) The TUC wasn't keen on the idea of a strike, and weren't well enough organised.
4) The National Sailors' Union and the Firemen's Union didn't want to strike. They went to the High Court to prove they didn't have to. The court said the strike was illegal.
5) Some unions didn't have enough cash to fund their members for long, and the banks wouldn't give them overdrafts. The TUC had already spent £4m out of their strike fund of £12.5m.
6) The TUC thought it would be better to have a definite end to the strike than for it to fizzle out.
7) There were rumours that the government was going to arrest the leaders of the TUC.
8) The Labour Party didn't support the strike — its leader worried it would lose them votes.

The Strike's failure was a Blow to the Unions

1) The miners stayed out on strike for another six months. When they finally gave in and went back to work they had to accept lower wages and longer hours. The strike hadn't really improved anything.
2) The Trades Disputes and Trade Union Act was passed in 1927. The Act made it illegal for a union to join a general strike or a sympathy strike (one where you go on strike to support workers from a different union).
3) The strike cost the TUC about £4 million. Without funds they weren't in a position to threaten new strikes. Membership dropped to about 3.25 million by 1933, so the unions had less income.
4) There was also a general blow to morale. The unions lost confidence and there were very few strikes in the 1930s.
5) But many workers began to realise that the Labour Party was their best hope of changing the system — and in 1929 Labour won the general election.

Learn it in general — and then in detail...

The 1926 General Strike is dead important. Scribble a quick date list for these two pages to check you've got all the events straight, then learn the effects of the strike on the unions and Labour.

Revision Summary

Britain in 1928 was a very different place to the Britain of 1890. So many big changes, including a massive, terrible war. Such a big period in British history deserves a big load of practice questions...

1) What was the name of the institutions run to give the very poor somewhere to live and work?
2) What are the names of the two men who published reports on poverty in 1889 and 1901?
3) Which government set up a Royal Commission to look at the Poor Law? What year was it?
4) How many reports did they write? What were they called?
5) Who won the general election in 1906?
6) Name three things children under 16 weren't allowed to do after the Children's Charter in 1908.
7) What two new ideas did Herbert Samuel come up with to help young offenders?
8) What was Part One of the National Insurance Act about?
9) How many people got a minimum wage by 1914?
10) What was the popular name for Lloyd George's 1909 budget?
11) Who stopped the 1909 budget from becoming law at the first attempt?
12) Give two reasons why the Liberal reforms changed attitudes to helping the poor.
13) Give two possible jobs that a young woman could do in the 1890s.
14) Give four reasons why some people believed women shouldn't have the vote in the 1890s.
15) Who were the suffragists? Who was their leader?
16) Who were the suffragettes? In what ways were they different from the suffragists?
17) What happened in 1907 to encourage the suffragettes?
18) What happened in 1912 to make the suffragettes' campaign turn more extreme?
19) Give four examples of extreme tactics used by the suffragettes.
20) Who were Britain's allies at the start of the First World War?
21) What was the Schlieffen Plan? How was it supposed to work?
22) Give two reasons why trenches were easy to defend, and two reasons why trenches were hard to attack.
23) Who replaced Sir John French as the British commander in 1915?
24) Give two things aircraft were used for during the war.
25) What was the reason for the British attack on the Somme?
26) Give two reasons why some people say Haig's tactics at the Somme were wrong.
27) Give two reasons why some people say Haig's tactics at the Somme were right.
28) Give four things the government was allowed to do by the Defence of the Realm Act 1914.
29) When was conscription introduced?
30) What three steps did Lloyd George take to avoid a food supply crisis?
31) Give three reasons why people's attitudes to the war changed between 1914 and 1918.
32) Give two of the main points from the Versailles Treaty of 1919.
33) Give four reasons why some women got the vote after the First World War.
34) What categories of women got the right to vote in the Representation of the People Act, 1918?
35) When did women finally get equal voting rights to men? What age did they have to be?
36) What does "nationalisation" mean?
37) Name the two big new unions set up in 1920 and 1921.
38) What did the Royal Commission say the government should do with the coal mines in 1919?
39) Why did British mines have trouble selling their coal during the 1920s? Give three reasons.
40) Give three possible reasons why the General Strike didn't last very long.
41) What sort of strikes were made illegal in the Trades Disputes Act of 1927?

How to Study History

You've learnt the facts — now you need to learn how to use them effectively. There are four key ideas that'll help you use your facts — the four 'C's: Cause, Consequence, Change and Continuity.

You'll get questions about Causes and Consequences

1) Cause means the reason something happened — e.g. the causes of the First World War. Any time you have an event in History, think about what caused it and why it happened. There are always reasons why an event takes place and it's your job to work them out.
2) Consequence means what happened because of an action — it's the result of an event, e.g. a consequence of the Second World War was that the USA and USSR became superpowers because the big powers in Europe were then too weak.

> 1) Some questions will ask you to give an opinion about causes and consequences — e.g. 'The Great Depression was the main cause of the failure of the League of Nations — do you agree?' or 'Which was a more important factor in ending communism in the USSR — glasnost or perestroika?'.
> 2) It's up to you what opinion you give — but you've got to be able to back it up with reasons and facts.
> 3) With this type of question, it's good to look at the different causes / consequences — and then explain which you think was the most important and why.

You also need to think about Change and Continuity

1) Change is when something happens to make things different — there can be quick changes, e.g. the assassination of Archduke Franz Ferdinand contributed to the outbreak of the First World War. Or there can be slow changes, e.g. the tensions between Britain and Germany in the early 1900s were a long-term factor leading to the start of the First World War.
2) Continuity is the opposite of change — it means when things stay the same, e.g. the Romanov dynasty ruled Russia for 300 years.
3) These ideas are opposites — think of continuity as a flat line going along until there is a sudden change and the line becomes a zigzag:

> Use the four 'C's in your answers — link facts together and tell the examiners why something happened and what the results were. Explain if there was a change and if so, what things changed from and what they changed to.

Time for some exam tips...

Obviously, you're going to need to learn all the info for your topics. But to get high marks, you need to do more than just trot out the facts. You need to be able to discuss topics in a thoughtful way, showing good understanding. The four 'C's are really useful for this.

Handling Sources

There are few certainties in life — but you will get source questions in your exam...

There are Two main kinds of Sources

1) Primary sources — this is evidence from the period you're studying, e.g. a newspaper report on the First World War from 4th September 1914.
2) Secondary sources — this is evidence about a historical period, e.g. a 1989 book entitled 'Origins of the First World War'.

Sources may be visual extracts, e.g. photographs and maps, or written extracts, e.g. diaries, newspapers etc.

If you want to Do Well look at sources Carefully

1) You've got to find evidence from the source which is relevant to the question.
2) Show you understand the source, and use the facts you already know about the period to explain what the source is saying, and how it says it.
3) Say how reliable and useful you think the source is. Think about whether the source gives enough information about the topic or if there are gaps or inconsistencies. Say if you think the source is biased (one-sided in its opinions) — and if so, why.

Don't confuse facts and opinions — always think about who is writing, why they are writing and what they are trying to say.

Top Tips for answering source questions

Do

1) Use the source material to help answer the question — not just what you know already.
2) Read the question carefully. E.g. if it says to use the three sources A, B and C, you must use all three.
3) Check what the source tells you — look out for what a source says, who wrote it and when they wrote it.
4) If you're asked to look at more than one source, then compare them.
5) Use the facts you already know about the period to help you understand the source and judge how useful it is.

Don't

1) Don't get carried away writing down everything you know about the topic — focus on the source(s) given.
2) Don't jump to conclusions — e.g. don't assume that every eyewitness account is accurate.
3) Don't always take sources at face value. E.g. a history book about the Russian Revolution that was written in Stalin's USSR might exaggerate his role and leave out people like Trotsky.

Historians love ketchup — they're obsessed with sources...

Evaluating sources is an important skill for historians — and one you have to demonstrate in the exam. So if you want decent grades, put the effort into learning this page right now.

Exam Essay Skills

You've also got to be able to tackle essay answers...

Planning Your Exam Time

1) On the exam paper, it'll say next to each question how many marks it's worth.
2) Look out for which questions have most marks — make sure you spend most time on these.
3) There'll be at least one or two questions which require essay-length answers.

> Learn the rule — the more marks a question is worth, the longer your answer should be. Don't get carried away writing loads for a question that's only worth 4 marks — you need to leave time for the higher mark questions.

Remember these Three Tips for writing good Essays

1) Plan your Essay

Sort out what you want to say before you start writing — think about how to answer the question, and what the key words are. Scribble a quick plan of your main points — cross through this neatly at the end, so it's obvious it shouldn't be marked.

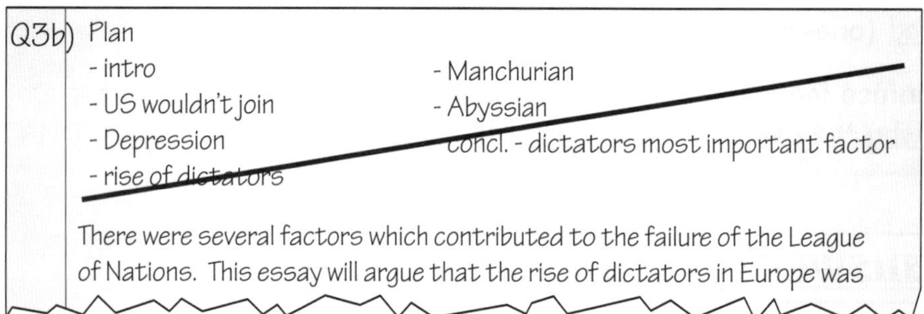

Q3b) Plan
- intro
- US wouldn't join
- Depression
- rise of dictators
- Manchurian
- Abyssian
- concl. - dictators most important factor

There were several factors which contributed to the failure of the League of Nations. This essay will argue that the rise of dictators in Europe was

2) Stay Focused on the Question

Make sure that you directly answer the question. Back up your points with relevant facts. Don't just chuck in everything you know. You've got to be relevant and accurate — e.g. if you're writing about the rise of the Nazi Party, don't include stories about a London camel called George who moved rubble during the Blitz.

3) Use a Clear Writing Style

Your essay should start with a brief introduction and end with a conclusion. Remember to start a new paragraph for each new point you want to discuss. Try to use clear handwriting — and pay attention to spelling, grammar and punctuation (see p.143-146).

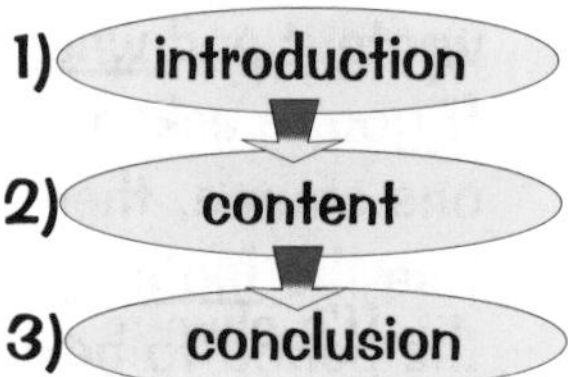

There's no need to panic in the exam...

Even if you've revised properly, remembered a spare pen and arrived early for your exam, there's a chance you'll suffer from 'mind blank syndrome' when you open the paper. But don't panic, just stay calm, read the questions carefully, and use the advice you've learnt here.

Spelling, Punctuation and Grammar

You get marks in your exams for having good SPaG (spelling, punctuation and grammar). This stuff might not be particularly thrilling but if you can get it right, it's easy marks.

Remember to Check what you've Written

1) Leave 5 minutes at the end of the exam to check your work.
2) 5 minutes isn't long, so there won't be time to check everything thoroughly. Look for the most obvious spelling, punctuation and grammar mistakes.
3) Start by checking your answers to the questions which award SPaG marks. There'll be instructions on the exam paper telling you which these are. Only check the rest of your answers if you've got time.

Check for common Spelling Mistakes

Check for missing words as well as misspelt words.

When you're writing under pressure, it's easy to let spelling mistakes creep in, but there are a few things you can watch out for:

1) Look out for words which sound the same but mean different things and are spelt differently. Make sure you've used the correct one. For example, 'their', 'they're' and 'there':

   Woodrow Wilson thought colonies should have a say in their own future.

   East Germany and West Germany were divided for 45 years, but now they're one country again.

   During World War One, there were food shortages, demonstrations and strikes in Russia.

2) Don't use text speak, and always write words out in full. For example, use 'and' instead of '&' or '+'. Don't use 'etc.' when you could give more examples or a better explanation.
3) Make sure you've used the appropriate technical terms (like 'collectivisation', or 'détente'). If they're spelt correctly, it'll really impress the examiner.

Make sure your Grammar and Punctuation are Correct

1) Check you've used capital letters, full stops and question marks correctly (see p.146).
2) Make sure your writing isn't too chatty and doesn't use slang words. It should be formal.
3) Watch out for sentences where your writing switches between different tenses. You should usually stick to one tense throughout your answer (don't worry if you quote from a source that's in a different tense).
4) Check that you've started a new paragraph every time you make a new point. It's important that your answer isn't just one long block of text (see p.146).
5) Watch out for tricksy little grammar mistakes:
   - Remember — 'it's' (with an apostrophe) is short for 'it is' or 'it has'. 'Its' (without an apostrophe) means 'belonging to it'.
   - It's always 'should have', not 'should of' (and also 'could have' and 'would have' too).

   If you know that you often confuse two words, like 'it's' and 'its', watch out for them when you're checking your work in the exam.

Check, check, check, goose, check, check, check...

It's really useful to practise all this stuff before the exam if you can. That way it'll become second nature — you'll do it all automatically and make fewer errors in the first place. Hurrah.

Spelling, Punctuation and Grammar

Making a mistake in your exam is not the end of the world, so don't panic if you find one. If you just cross it out neatly and correct the mistake, you won't lose any marks at all.

Make your corrections Neatly

1) If the mistake is just one word or a short phrase, cross it out neatly and write the correct word above it.

> Communist party members loyal to Stalin ~~recieved~~ received privileges such as holidays.

2) If you've forgotten to start a new paragraph, use a double strike (like this '//') to show where the new paragraph should begin:

See p.146 for more on paragraphs.

> Collectivisation helped peasants work together and provided large-scale organisation for food production. // However, the new system was not very successful at first. Many people died of starvation after a serious famine caused by a bad harvest. This was made worse by the kulaks, who had started to destroy crops and animals in protest.

Use an Asterisk to add Extra Information

1) If you've missed something out, decide if you have space to write the missing bit above the line you've already written. If you can, use a '^' to show exactly where it should go.

> Civil rights issues became a particular focus in 1955, with the Montgomery bus boycott. Rosa Parks was arrested for refusing to give up her bus seat for a white man. Martin Luther King reacted by organising a ^bus boycott with other black ministers. The success of their peaceful protest was inspirational to everyone who opposed segregation.

2) If the bit you've missed out won't fit above the line, use an asterisk (like this '*') to show the examiner where the missing bit should go.
3) Write the missing words at the end of your answer with another asterisk next to them.

> The Treaty of Versailles was very harsh on Germany. A lot of land* was confiscated and Germany was forced by Article 231 to accept the blame for the war.
>
> *including Alsace and Lorraine

Cross Out anything you Don't want to be Marked

1) If you've written something that you don't want the examiner to mark, cross it out neatly.
2) Cross out any notes. If you don't finish your answer in time, don't cross out your plan — the examiner might look at it to see what you were going to write.
3) Don't scribble things out without thinking — it'll make your answers look messy.

When making corrections, neatness is the name of ^the game

Examiners love it if your answer is neat and tidy — it makes it super easy for them to read. This means they can spend more time giving you lots of marks for the great stuff you've written.

Spelling, Punctuation and Grammar

Some words are darn tricky to spell. There's no way around it — you need to learn them off by heart. This page has some of the most common ones you'll need for your history exams.

Learn these Useful Words

The underlined words are useful in a lot of answers, so you need to know how to spell them.

There are convincing arguments for and against Haig's tactics in World War One.

The Nazis were successful at controlling people through fear and propaganda.

Chamberlain signed the Munich Agreement because he believed Hitler would keep his promises.

Fidel Castro attempted to overthrow Batista.

American banks were encouraged to lend money to lots of businesses in the 1920s.

The Wall Street Crash affected companies across the world.

There are many differences between the New Economic Policy and War Communism.

Spell Technical Words Correctly

There are a lot of technical words in History. You need to be able to spell them correctly. Learn these examples to start you off. The coloured letters are the tricky bits to watch out for.

agriculture	constitution	evidence	parliament
alliance	defence	fascism	rebellion
biased	democracy	foreign	reliability
conflict	diplomacy	league	resistance
controversial	effective	military	source

You'll also have to learn how to spell the names and technical terms from the options you're studying. So for Germany you'll need to be comfortable with names like 'Stresemann' and terms such as 'the Luftwaffe'. Go back through the option you've studied and make a list of tricky names and words — then learn them.

Learn this page and make spelling errors history...

Mnemonics can help you remember how to spell tricky words. For example, you can remember 'biased' with the phrase 'Bleary Insomniacs Avoid Sleep Every Day'. Or something similar...

Spelling, Punctuation and Grammar

You need to Punctuate Properly...

1) Always use a capital letter at the start of a sentence.
Use capital letters for names of particular people, places and things. For example:

All sentences start with capital letters. → In 1933 Hitler was made Chancellor of Germany.

The name of a person. A title. The name of a country.

2) Full stops go at the end of sentences, e.g. 'Franz Ferdinand was killed in June 1914.'
Question marks go at the end of questions, e.g. 'How successful was the New Deal?'

3) Use commas when you use more than one adjective, or to separate items in a list:

Hitler envisioned a highly militarised, racially superior German nation.

Lenin's April Theses promised peace, bread, land and freedom.

4) Commas can join two points into one sentence with a joining word (e.g. 'and', 'so' or 'but'):

Old communist leaders opposed change, so they decided to get rid of Gorbachev.

Hoover tried to help big business, but he didn't do enough to help ordinary people.

5) Commas can also be used to separate extra information in a sentence:

Malcolm X, who was an African-American Muslim, rejected non-violence and integration.

David Lloyd George, the leader of the Liberal Party, pushed for social reforms to help the poor.

When you use commas like this, the sentence should still make sense when the extra bit is taken out.

...and use Grammar Correctly

1) Don't change tenses in your writing by mistake:

Some business people were angry that the New Deal allowed trade unions into the workplace.

Both verbs are in the past tense — which is correct. Writing 'allows' instead of 'allowed' would be wrong.

2) Don't use double negatives. You should only use a negative once in a sentence:

It was called the Cold War because there wasn't any direct fighting. Don't put 'no' here.

3) Write longer answers in paragraphs. A paragraph is a group of sentences which talk about the same thing or follow on from each other. Start a new paragraph when you make a new point. Show a new paragraph by starting a new line and leaving a gap before you start writing:

This gap shows a new paragraph. →

From 1933 Hitler started a programme of public works, such as the building of huge new motorways. This gave jobs to thousands of people.

Even though there was increased employment, the Nazis altered the statistics so that things looked better than they were. Wages were also poor.

Remember that you should start a new paragraph for each of your main points.

Phew, now you're fully SPaG-ed and ready to go...

You should now be feeling fighting fit and ready to tackle any History essay that comes your way.

Index

A

Aaland Islands 11
Abyssinia 16
Affirmative Action 113
Afghanistan 34, 36, 42
African Americans 73, 110-113
Agadir Crisis 2
Agent Orange 105
Albany Movement 117
Algeciras Conference 2
alphabet agencies 79
Al-Qaeda 42-44
American Indian Movement (AIM) 115
Anschluss 21
Anti-Comintern Pact 16
anti-semitism 55, 61, 63
Anti-War Protests 43, 107, 108, 117
appeasement 22, 23
April Theses 86
Arafat, Yasser 42
arms race 2, 26, 29, 35, 36
Asquith, H.H. 126, 127
asterisks 144
atom bombs 26
Austria-Hungary 1, 3, 4, 9, 127

B

Balkans 3
Berlin Wall 28, 37
Beveridge, William 123
bin Laden, Osama 42
Black Hand 4
Black Panther Party 113
Black Power 113
Black Thursday 76
Bolsheviks 85-90
Bonus Army 78
borstals 121
Brest-Litovsk, Treaty of 52, 89
Brezhnev Doctrine 29, 36
Brezhnev, Leonid 29, 34
British Expeditionary Force (BEF) 2, 46, 127
Brüning, Heinrich 58
Brusilov Offensive 52
Bulgaria 3, 9, 11, 26

C

Cambodian Campaign 108
Capone, Al 74
Castro, Fidel 31
"Cat and Mouse" Act 126
censorship 61, 84, 131, 133
Chamberlain, Neville 22
Chavez, Cesar 114
Children's Charter 121
Christmas bombing 109
Churchill, Winston 25-27, 50, 120, 123, 137, 138
Civil Rights 110-115, 117
Clemenceau, Georges 6, 134
Cold War 26-31, 34-38, 101
Collectivisation 97, 98
commas 146
communism 19, 22, 25-32, 34-37, 54, 55, 58-61, 63, 65, 66, 73, 86, 88-99, 101-103, 108
Communist Control Act 102
concentration camps 61, 65, 66
Confessing Church 61, 65
Convoy System 51, 132
Corfu 12
Cuban Missile Crisis 31, 34
Czechoslovakia 9, 22, 23, 26, 29, 38

D

Dardanelles 50
Davison, Emily 126
Dawes Plan 12, 13, 56
Depression 14, 15, 17, 19, 20, 58, 77, 78, 82
détente 34, 35
Detroit riot 113
disarmament 13, 19, 20, 36
Dreadnought 2, 51
Dual Alliance 1
Duma 84

E

Eastern Front 49, 52, 85, 90
economic aid 13, 101
Edelweiss Pirates 64
Entente Cordiale 1

F

Fall of Saigon 109
Fawcett, Millicent 126
'February' Revolution 85, 86
Ferdinand, Archduke Franz 4, 127
Final Solution 66
Five-Year Plan 96
Fourteen Points 6, 11, 69
Four-Year Plan 62, 67
Franco-Russian Alliance 1
Freedom Rides 112, 117
Freedom Summer 112
Freikorps 54, 55
Friedan, Betty 116
Fulbright hearings 107
full stops 146

G

Gallipoli 50
General Strike 136-138
Geneva Protocol 13
German economy 55, 57, 62, 67
Gestapo 61, 64, 66
ghettos 66
Glasnost 36
Goebbels, Joseph 60, 61, 66
Goering, Hermann 62, 67
Good Friday Agreement 41
Gorbachev, Mikhail 36, 37
grammar 143, 146
guerrilla war 31, 104
Gulf War 39, 43

H

Haig, Sir Douglas 47, 48, 128-130, 134
Harding, Warren G. 70
health insurance 122
'hearts and minds' 105
Helsinki Agreement 34
Himmler, Heinrich 60, 61, 66
Hindenburg, Paul von 58-60
Hispanic Americans 114
Hitler, Adolf 14-17, 20-23, 57-65, 96
Hitler Youth 63, 64
Ho Chi Minh Trail 32, 104, 108
Hollywood Ten 102
Hoover, Herbert 77, 78, 82
Hoover, J. Edgar 102
House Un-American Activities Committee (HUAC) 102
Hungarian Rising 28
Hussein, Saddam 39, 43, 44
Hyde Amendment 116
hyperinflation 55

I

immigration 70, 73, 114
Iraq 38, 39, 43, 44
Irish Republican Army (IRA) 41, 42
Iron Curtain 26
isolationism 12, 19, 69, 70

J

Japan 15-17, 26, 104
Johnson, Lyndon B. 32, 103, 106, 109, 112, 113
Jutland, Battle of 51

K

Kapp Putsch 55
Kellogg-Briand Pact 13, 56
Kennedy, John F. 28, 30, 31, 34, 103, 112, 116
Kent State Massacre 107
Kerry, John F. 107
Khrushchev, Nikita 28, 29, 31
King, Martin Luther 111-113
Korean War 30, 101
Kosovo crisis 38, 39
Kreisau Circle 64
Kronstadt 91
Ku Klux Klan 73, 110
Kulaks 84, 87, 97, 98

L

LA Games 34
Labour Exchange Act 123
Laos Campaign 108
Lausanne, Treaty of 9
League of Nations 6, 7, 11-17, 20, 21, 23, 25, 56, 69
League of United Latin American Citizens 114
Lenin, Vladimir 86-92
Lloyd George, David 6, 51, 120-122, 124, 126, 132, 134, 136
Locarno Treaties 13, 19, 21, 56

M

MacArthur, General 30, 101
Majority Report 120
Manchurian Crisis 15, 17
Mao Tse-Tung 30, 101
Marne, Battle of 46 127, 128
Marshall Plan 27, 101
McCarthyism 102
Mein Kampf 57
Mensheviks 86
Ministry of Enlightenment and Propaganda 61
Ministry of Information 133
Minority Report 120
mir 84
Monkey Trial 73
Mons, Battle of 46, 127
Montgomery Bus Boycott 111
Moscow Olympics 34
Munich Agreement 22
Munich Putsch 57
Mussolini, Benito 12, 15-17, 21, 22
My Lai Massacre 32, 105, 106

Index

N

Nagy, Ferenc 28
napalm 105
National Association for the Advancement of Coloured People (NAACP) 111
National Broadcasting Company (NBC) 75
National Insurance Act 122-124
National Labour Service 62
National Organisation for Women (NOW) 116
National Origins Act 73
Native Americans 115
Nazis 14, 20-23, 38, 39, 57-67, 96
Nazi-Soviet Pact 23
New Deal 78-82
New Economic Policy 91, 92
Ngo Dinh Diem 103
Nicholas II, Tsar 1, 52, 84, 85, 90
Night of the Long Knives 60
Nixon, Richard 32, 34, 107-109, 113
Non-Violent Protest 111-113
North Atlantic Treaty Organization (NATO) 27, 101
Northern Ireland 38, 41
November Criminals 55

O

Old Age Pensions Act 121
Operation Rolling Thunder 105
Oslo Accords 42
overproduction 14, 72, 76

P

Pact of Steel 16, 23
Palestinian Liberation Organisation (PLO) 42
Pankhurst, Emmeline, Christabel & Sylvia 126
Papen, Franz von 59
paragraphs 143, 144, 146
Paris Peace Conference 109
Parks, Rosa 111
Passchendaele, Battle of 52
Perestroika 36
Permanent International Court of Justice 11
Petrograd Soviet 87
'Plan 17' 2, 46
Poland 9, 11, 23, 25, 26, 35, 37, 38
Politburo 92, 93, 95
Potsdam Conference 25
Prague Spring 29
probation service 121
Prohibition 74
propaganda 61, 63, 65-67, 98, 133
punctuation 143, 146
purge 92, 94, 95

R

Rákosi 28
Rasputin 85
rationing 67, 131, 132
Reagan, Ronald 35
Red Army 26, 89-91, 93
Red Guards 87, 88
Red Scare 73, 101, 102
Reichsleiters 60
Reichstag 54, 58, 59
reparations 7, 55, 56, 78, 134
Representation of the People Act 135
Rhineland 7, 21
Roe v Wade (1973) 116
Röhm, Ernst 60
Rome-Berlin Axis 16
Roosevelt, Eleanor 116
Roosevelt, Franklin D. 25, 78, 79, 81
Rosenberg, Julius and Ethel 102
Rowntree, Seebohm 119
Royal Commission looking at the Poor Law 120
Ruhr 12, 55, 56, 67

S

SA 57, 59, 60
Saar, the 21
Sacco and Vanzetti 73
Saigon 32, 109
SALT '1' and '2' 34
Samuel Commission 136, 137
Schlieffen Plan 2, 46, 49, 127
School Meals Act 121
'search and destroy' 105
Second New Deal 80
segregation 73, 110-112, 114
Serbia 3, 4, 38, 39, 85, 127
Social Security Act 80
Solidarity 35, 37
Somme, Battle of 47, 48, 129, 130
sources 141
Southern Christian Leadership Conference 111
Space Race 29
Spartacist Revolt 55
spelling mistakes 143
SS 61, 66
St Germain, Treaty of 9
stalemate 47, 49, 85, 96, 106
Stalin, Joseph 25-28, 93-97
Star Wars 35
Stauffenberg Bomb Plot 64
stock market 14, 71, 76, 79
Stop the Draft Week 117
Strategic Arms Limitation Talks Agreement 34
Strategic Defense Initiative 35
Stresemann, Gustav 56
Student Nonviolent Coordinating Committee (SNCC) 111-113, 117
student protests 107, 112, 117
Students for a Democratic Society (SDS) 117
suffragettes 126
Summer of love 117
Swinging Sixties 117

T

Taliban 42
tariffs 70, 76, 78
technical words 145
Tennessee Valley Authority (TVA) 79, 80
Terrorism 41, 42
Tet Offensive 32, 103, 106, 108
Trail of Broken Treaties 115
trenches 46-48, 127, 128, 134
Trianon, Treaty of 9
Triple Alliance 1, 4, 127
Triple Entente 1, 3, 127
Trotsky, Leon 87-91, 93, 94
the Troubles 41
Truman Doctrine 27, 50, 101
Turkish Empire 3, 50

U

U-2 Spy Planes 29, 31
U-Boat 51, 52, 132
Ulster Volunteer Force 41
unemployment benefit 70, 80, 82, 123
United Nations 25, 30, 38, 39, 43, 101
Upper Silesia 11
useful words 145

V

Verdun, Battle of 47, 48, 130
Versailles, Treaty of 7-9, 13, 20, 21, 54, 55, 69, 134
Viet Minh 103, 104
Vietcong 32, 103-106, 108
Vietnam Veterans Against the War (VVAW) 107
Vietnam War 30, 32, 34, 103-109, 113, 117,
Vietnamisation 108
Volkswagen 62
Voting Rights Act 112

W

Wagner Act 80
Walesa, Lech 35
Wall Street Crash 14, 56, 76, 77
War Communism 90-92
War-Guilt Clause 7
Warsaw Pact 27-29, 37, 38
Washington Conference 13
WASPs 70
Weimar Republic 54, 56, 57
White forces 90
White Rose 64
Wilhelm II, Kaiser 1, 52, 54
Wilson, Woodrow 6, 12, 69, 134
Women's Land Army 132
Women's Rights 116, 125
Woodstock Music Festival 117
workhouses 119, 120, 124
World Trade Center 42
Wounded Knee 115

X

X, Malcolm 113

Y

Yalta Conference 25, 26
Yeltsin, Boris 37
Young Plan 13, 56
Ypres, Battle of 46, 47, 52, 127-129
Yugoslavia 9, 26, 38